Tactical Readings

Tactical Readings

Feminist Postmodernism
in the Novels of Kathy Acker
and Angela Carter

Nicola Pitchford

Lewisburg
Bucknell University Press
London: Associated University Presses

©2002 by Rosemont Publishing & Printing Corp.

All rights reserved. Authorization to photocopy items for internal or personal use, or the internal or personal use of specific clients, is granted by the copyright owner, provided that a base fee of $10.00, plus eight cents per page, per copy is paid directly to the Copyright Clearance Center, 222 Rosewood Drive, Danvers, Massachusetts 01923. [0-8387-5487-2/01 $10.00 + 8¢ pp, pc.]

Associated University Presses
440 Forsgate Drive
Cranbury, NJ 08512

Associated University Presses
16 Barter Street
London WC1A 2AH, England

Associated University Presses
P.O. Box 338, Port Credit
Mississauga, Ontario
Canada L5G 4L8

The paper used in this publication meets the requirements of the American National Standard for Permanence of Paper for Printed Library Materials Z39.48-1984.

Library of Congress Cataloging-in-Publication Data

Pitchford, Nicola.
  Tactical readings : feminist postmodernism in the novels of Kathy Acker and Angela Carter / Nicola Pitchford
    p. cm.
  Includes bibliographical references and index.
  ISBN 0-8387-5487-2 (alk. paper)
  1. Acker, Kathy, 1948—Criticism and interpretation. 2. Women and literature—United States—History—20th century. 3. Women and literature—England—History—20th century. 4. Carter, Angela, 1940—Criticism and interpretation. 5. Feminist fiction, American—History and criticism. 6. Feminist fiction, English—History and criticism. 7. Postmodernism (Literature)—England I. Title.

PS3551.C44 Z8 2002
813'.54099287—dc21
                                                                          2001035797

PRINTED IN THE UNITED STATES OF AMERICA

Contents

Acknowledgments	7
Introduction	11
1. A Politicized Postmodernism: Feminist Reading Tactics	20
2. Kathy Acker's Unreasonable Texts	59
3. Angela Carter's War of Real Dreams	105
4. Reading Feminism's Pornography Conflict	151
Epilogue: Readers, Disciplinarity, and Social Practices	181
Notes	188
Works Cited	207
Index	218

Acknowledgments

My first, huge thanks must go to Dale M. Bauer for her perfect suggestions and sustained encouragement. Jill Dolan, Jacques Lezra, Tom Schaub, and Jonathan Veitch read portions of this project and provided valuable guidance, as did Tom Foster and the anonymous readers for *Genders*. Early drafts benefited greatly (as did I) from the advice of the Wisconsin writing group: Kari Kalve, Susan Koenig, Tracy McCabe, Michael Peterson, and Stacy Wolf. And I am deeply grateful to all my supportive colleagues at Fordham, especially Phil Sicker.

My mother, Ann Roberts, first introduced me to Angela Carter's work, which is probably only the least of all the things for which I owe her thanks—along with all my family.

This book is for Wilson Neate, with thanks and love.

◊◊◊◊◊◊◊◊◊

Portions of chapter 4 appeared in slightly different form as "Reading Feminism's Pornography Conflict: Implications for Postmodernist Reading Strategies," *Genders* 25 (1997). Copyright © 1997, New York University. Reproduced by permission of publisher.

Grateful acknowledgment is made to the following for permission to reprint:
    Kathy Acker, from *Don Quixote: Which Was a Dream, Empire of the Senseless,* and *My Life My Death by Pier Paolo Pasolini*. Copyright © 1986, 1988, 1984, Kathy Acker. Reproduced by permission of Grove/Atlantic, Inc. and the Estate of Kathy Acker.

Angela Carter, from *The Infernal Desire Machines of Doctor Hoffman*. Copyright © 1972, Angela Carter. Reproduced by permission of the Estate of Angela Carter, c/o Rogers, Coleridge & White Ltd., 20 Powis Mews, London W11 1JN.

David Harvey, from *The Condition of Postmodernity: An Enquiry into the Origins of Cultural Change*. Copyright © 1989, David Harvey. Reproduced by permission of Basil Blackwell Ltd.

Fredric Jameson, from *Postmodernism, or, The Cultural Logic of Late Capitalism*. Copyright © 1991, Duke University Press. Reproduced by permission of publisher.

Tactical Readings

Introduction

This study concerns the potential of feminist politics in the work of postmodernist women writers. More broadly, it addresses ongoing attempts in the past several decades to theorize what political and social role literature might play in the rapidly changing, capitalist-secular societies of the wealthier portion of the world. My intention, in part, is to revisit debates over the value of postmodernism as a cultural and political phenomenon, debates that—like so many previous discussions in cultural theory—have been conducted with very little reference to the work of women. I find this omission significant not because of the slight to women writers and other artists (although I would be pleased if refining the conceptual framework "feminist postmodernism" made more accessible a body of fascinating work), but because it misses the especially rich opportunity offered by this work for theorizing the political implications of various rhetorical and interpretive strategies. The question of how aesthetic texts act politically on their readers forms the core of the postmodernism debates, as it did of arguments for and against modernism.

I also want to shift the terms of that question, however, by looking centrally at how readers act (politically) on texts. I am particularly interested in postmodernist feminist writing because it foregrounds this issue. Its rereadings of existing imagery suggest the varied uses to which specific groups of readers can put literature in the early twenty-first century; such writing presumes that literature still performs crucial "cultural work," in Jane Tompkins's sense of "articulating and proposing solutions for the problems that shape a particular historical moment."[1] The central thesis of my project derives from the explicitly political work of artists such as Kathy Acker (1947–97) and Angela Carter (1940–92), whose novels are the primary object of my study. I argue that analyzing these texts *as* a form of postmodernism offers one possible answer to the vexed question of how cultural products play a role in both producing and changing relations of power.

Taking into account the sort of feminist fiction I discuss here would mean putting reading and *use* at the center of a redefined postmodernist practice. Doing so might offer a more hopeful vision of the transformative potential of contemporary culture than most current formulations of the postmodern afford.

It is my sense that critical discussion of postmodernism as an aesthetic has come, of late, to seem rather tired; maybe cultural pundits have begun looking around for the next big thing.[2] Even in 1990, Susan Rubin Suleiman suggested that all the major critics engaged in debating postmodernism had come to see the significance of the concept in its status "as an object 'to be read,' an intervention in the sense of an action or a statement requiring a response, rather than as an object of descriptive poetics."[3] The question has increasingly become how to "read" postmodernism most usefully, and how reading the larger world through a concept of the postmodern might affect how we live in it. In fact, the growing emphasis in the newest analyses of contemporary culture on more narrowly defined objects of study—temporally, nationally, or locally specific contexts of production and reception—reflects less a search for the "next big thing" than an increased attentiveness to the importance of *small* things, small practices.

This study also tends in that direction. But I think it important, nevertheless, not to jettison the large-scale concept, "postmodernism," completely; there is so much of value in the term's ability to link a particular (still very much current) moment in history with a set of cultural strategies prevalent during this moment. Employing postmodernism as a periodizing term (but not a homogenizing one) is the only way to make clear why *reading* has become a central, defining practice (if not *the* defining practice) in contemporary political life. So if the main thesis of this project is that discussions of contemporary culture have much to gain from a more thorough look at the practices modeled by feminist work, a secondary thesis is that feminists and other politicized cultural critics can yet benefit from coming to terms—however ambivalent those terms may be—with the categories postmodernism and postmodernity.

Postmodernism is a useful term for feminists precisely because it signals a particular relation between cultural production and material conditions. In its more materialist forms, postmodernist theory provides an apparatus for describing the multiplicity of specific circumstances in which gender takes meaning in contemporary society. Thinking postmodern-ly can prevent the pitfalls of a universalizing feminism that would simply invert essentialized gender categories and deny the significant differences among women, the effects of race, class, sexuality, and nationality. When insistently historicized, feminism and postmodernism can together produce a theory of reading as a historically attuned political action. The introductory chapter of my study argues for such a complementary relation, exploring the general lack of a sufficiently local and specific consideration of *use* in even the most materialist (such as Fredric Jameson's) of the dominant theories of postmodernism.

One of the stumbling blocks facing any attempt to construct feminism and postmodernism as mutually beneficial is the theoretical problem of how feminist ethical claims can coexist with the apparently antiethical or postethical formation of postmodernism. Postmodernism's radical antifoundationalism and its emphasis on the fictive character of all categories—such as "women"—have been taken by many feminists and postmodernists alike to remove the basis for any ethical position but an implicitly conservative relativism. So how can I justify this study's feminist-materialist perspective, within the terms of postmodernism? How can I assume the desirability of developing a fuller understanding of the role contemporary literature can play in producing political change, in making the world a somewhat more just place? And as I ask this, I am forced also to ask the more relativist question, "justice" according to whom?

My particular biases and goals cannot be objectively justified, but it is also impossible to operate *without* such a limited viewpoint. Postmodernist theory situates all perspectives as partial, in both senses of the word: biased and incomplete. Any critical position can only be evaluated on practical grounds. So while I recognize that my agenda is neither universal nor objective, I would argue its *utility*, under some current circumstances and for specific people. The category "woman" may be artificially bounded—a fiction—but it is nevertheless an *operative* fiction. It carries real consequences in terms of how I and others are viewed, treated, and how we conceive of ourselves and the world. When I invoke "women" or similar identity categories, it is therefore with the assumption that to do so is both rhetorically effective and informative. Throughout this study, I will return repeatedly to the importance of recognizing the rhetorical and material effects of such fictions. These effects, which in combination with one another define specific histories, provide the basis for taking an ethical stand within the terms of postmodernism.

Barbara Herrnstein Smith has offered a clear articulation of the bases for such a postmodern ethics in her book *Contingencies of Value*, emphasizing that we can only undertake "various continuously developing analyses that account for, in the sense of *making sense of and implying ways of changing*, particular current states of affairs that we, *given and in relation to our identities and consequent perspectives*, see as undesirable" (italics in original).[4] My strategy, nevertheless, is to argue that a historicized, feminist reading of postmodernism can produce desirable results for as many people as possible: multiculturalists, queer theorists, postcolonialists, Marxist and post-Marxist campaigners for economic justice, readers who want to believe that literature still has an effect on the world, and various combinations thereof. So I will draw frequently on a vocabulary of utility and effectiveness.

I know I am far from the first critic to argue for a politicized postmodernism. Nearly two decades ago, Hal Foster posited in his introduction to the influential collection *The Anti-Aesthetic* the existence of such a "postmodernism of resistance."[5] In the same volume, which also included an early version of Fredric Jameson's powerfully gloomy definition of postmodernism as the cultural logic of late capitalism and Jean Baudrillard's euphoric (though equally unhopeful) theory of the reign of simulacra, Craig Owens located this resistant postmodernism in the project of feminist artists. Owens wondered at "[t]he absence of discussions of sexual difference in writings about postmodernism."[6] Since that time, a significant body of writing about gender and postmodernism has appeared; I would cite, among others, the work of Judith Butler, Donna Haraway, Bell Hooks, Biddy Martin, Gayatri Chakravorty Spivak, Susan Rubin Suleiman, Trinh T. Minh-ha, and the contributors to Linda Nicholson's collection, *Feminism/Postmodernism*.[7] The existence of this theoretical work on feminism and postmodernism makes my study possible and provides its foundation.

However, despite the growth in the years since Foster's volume of feminist-postmodernist studies and of an audience for overtly political postmodernist art, the interested parties to whom I direct my study have remained "special-interest groups" (to borrow a magically marginalizing term from mainstream politics) when it comes to defining the contested territory of postmodernism. Postmodernism's true center is assumed to be elsewhere, in some space of ethical and political indifference. It is still entirely possible to ask: Can a feminist really be a postmodernist (and why would she)? Can a postcolonial writer also be a postmodernist (and what would the benefit be)? The two types of category can seem mutually exclusive, the one a set of fixed, positive beliefs while the other is characterized primarily by slippages, absences, and denials, by what it is *not*: not totalizing, not teleological, not utopian.[8]

I believe the lingering uncertainty is due in part to the inherent difficulty of envisioning a theory (feminist-postmodernist) that doesn't pretend to universality but instead attends to a variety of divergent circumstances. Feminist postmodernism will look different depending on where one encounters it; its theorists describe it as an "explicitly historical [approach], attuned to the cultural specificity of different societies and periods and to that of different groups within societies and periods . . . , using multiple categories when appropriate."[9] It is composed of what Michel de Certeau calls "tactics." A *tactic*, as opposed to a fully orchestrated (top-down) *strategy*, is contingent, reactive, and resistant; it has no stable base or ground of its own, but rather "is always on the watch for opportunities that must be seized 'on the wing.' Whatever it wins, it does not keep."[10]

That elusiveness is why I see a real need for extended studies of feminist-postmodernist texts, of the novels and poems and visual artworks and performances that produce and embody the combination of feminist politics with postmodern approaches to reading. Not wanting to draw on a false hierarchy between theory and practice, I would characterize these cultural products as performing feminist-postmodernist theory in relation to various specific contexts. For this reason I devote the majority of this study to detailed analyses of selected novels by Acker and Carter. I know of very few studies such as this that give extended space to readings of novels under the rubric of feminist postmodernism. While both Acker's works and, especially, Carter's have become more widely read and discussed in recent years (both authors' tragically early deaths playing a role in the increased attention), there is a sense in which these novels remain hard to categorize and are often seen as simply idiosyncratic or unique. Reading them together with a feminist-postmodernist theory may help to see how central their textual modes are to a contemporary practice of rereading culture. And conversely, without the novels and their vivid specificity, the theorizing can seem prohibitively vague and slippery.

Another obstacle facing attempts to outline an actively political kind of postmodernism may be, simply, the long history of Anglo-American academic resistance to suggestions that literature inevitably serves particular political interests or social groups. But more significantly, the influential modern theories of literature's political effect that *are* available generally rest on the assumption that art's value depends on its "autonomy"—that is, its fundamental separation from both commercialized mass culture and any concrete, specific involvement in politics. Such an attitude toward mass culture makes it hard to theorize postmodernist writing; such a suspicion of politics works to the detriment of feminist writing. As Andreas Huyssen and others have argued, during the modernist period women artists suffered particular marginalization as a result of such tenets; and these autonomy theories continue to persist anachronistically in many attempts to establish a postmodernist canon.[11]

An autonomous space for art may no longer exist. My first chapter's historical analysis suggests that the most significant change between the circumstances of modernism and those shaping the meanings available to art in the overdeveloped world today is the rapid rate at which any image or discourse can now be absorbed into the mass media and the marketplace. The resulting loss of any oppositional space outside hegemonic culture means that resistant modes of representation must now involve employing the same rhetoric and images as the "mainstream," but employing them in *different contexts of reception,* in order to offer readers alternate images of their political role and identity.

The following chapters develop this historicized concept of feminist postmodernist practice through readings of Acker and Carter, both of whom draw on existing texts and discourses to an unusual extent, opening hegemonic rhetorics to new uses and new readings. I have chosen an author from the United States and one from Britain (although each spent time living in the other country) not in order to suggest that feminist postmodernism is the same everywhere, but to highlight both its continuities across the two contexts and its variation. For similar reasons, I have focused on three of Acker's novels from the 1980s and three of Carter's from the 1970s. (Carter began publishing somewhat earlier than Acker.) While bracketing each author's work by decade in that manner felt rather arbitrary, it allowed me to focus on their textual strategies of resistance during a quite specific period. Acker, writing in the Reagan eighties, focuses primarily on breaking apart the apparently stable subject constructed by the rational, paternal rhetoric of conservatism. Carter's work dates from the years of political turmoil that ended with the ascension of the Thatcher regime, investigating both the internal inconsistencies of 1960s' utopian visions and the lingering allure of such visions in the chaos of the following decade.

In the chapter on Kathy Acker, I focus on the ways in which her novels *My Death My Life by Pier Paolo Pasolini*, *Don Quixote*, and *Empire of the Senseless* reuse fragments of a multitude of previous texts, literary, historical, and popular. Comparing the political meaning those textual scraps might have had in their original context to the new valence they take on from Acker's recontextualization of them in her narrative collage, I find in her tactics a theory of the agency of readers or users of language. Acker's work recognizes that in the text-saturated environment of postmodernity, the resistant subject can only ever repeat the language and the stories that have served to perpetuate oppression. But it also points out that these existing texts have different meanings in different reading contexts, and that they will in fact contradict one another when read beyond the boundaries of their intended context. Acker and her characters exploit this potential for contradiction among the utterances of authority. This irrational pastiche serves primarily to challenge rationalism, the reigning logic of capitalism, but I also note changes in Acker's strategy from one novel to another as the multinational capitalism of the Reagan years proves as able to digest the discourse of irrationality as any other.

In my discussion of Angela Carter, I develop further this general theory of the contingent, local nature of political meaning in postmodern reading by addressing in more detail the contemporary political discourses with which Carter's novels engage. In reading Carter's *The Infernal Desire Machines of Doctor Hoffman*, *The Passion of New Eve*, and *Love*, I not only trace the material effects of the texts on which she draws, but suggest how her own intense aestheticism functions as a political commentary in the context of 1970s Britain. Like Acker, Carter constantly invokes previous texts, but in Carter's case this immersion both provides narrative structure and results in an intensely "literary" language quite unlike Acker's blunt irreverence. Critics have damned this elaborate style as an aestheticization of violence, assuming that an aesthetic treatment of oppression is incompatible with a politicized one. But her work needs to be set against the background of a turbulent decade of economic and governmental crisis, marked by a widespread loss of faith in all the existing political visions and images—what Paul Gilroy calls Britain's "crisis of representation," or, to borrow a Carter title, "The War of Dreams."[12] Carter's reproduction of the language of high literature, coupled with her novels' exploration of the dire consequences of utopian visions, suggests how representation itself plays a key role in shaping Britain's political regime.

These two writers are particularly exemplary of feminist-postmodernist practice because of the extent to which their rhetoric occupies the position Linda Hutcheon has described as "complicitous critique."[13] More than most, their work recognizes the lack of separation in postmodern culture between politics and representation. It recognizes both the complete mediation of political life through images and the absence of an outside space from which to launch an aesthetic critique. Both writers have at times been denounced by Left and feminist critics as well as by more conservative readers, on the assumption that they merely reproduce existing culture, regardless of context. I take these attacks to demonstrate the need for a feminist-postmodernist reading of their work that highlights the different uses to which they put the largely patriarchal, ruling-class texts around which they build their own novels. For otherwise, if we can only duplicate the stories we've grown up on, how is agency possible?

In my final chapter I draw on some of these feminist critiques of Acker's and Carter's work—critiques, specifically, of both writers' use of explicit representations of sexuality and sexual violence, which have earned them the label "pornographic"—to demonstrate the potential for a feminist-postmodernist theory of reading to help avoid any replay of the divisive debates over representations of sexuality that developed among feminists during the 1980s. These "sex wars" are themselves responses to a combination of particular historical circumstances: on the one hand, the achievement of a certain level of success by the women's movement in the 1970s, which allowed internal differences of race and sexuality among women to emerge, posing, for some women, a threat to the movement's unity; and, on the other, attempts by ever-voracious capitalism to expand and diversify its marketing of erotic commodities by co-opting feminist demands for sexual self-realization. The tendency of antipornography feminists to assert that explicit representations of female sexuality operate regardless of who is reading them also leads them to believe that porn is always oppressive to women. Reading these debates through Acker's and Carter's recontextualizations of obscene images suggests again the varied political ends to which representations can be employed, as well as the necessity of theorizing sexual images in relation to specific groups of readers.

I spend this final chapter analyzing "sex" because it is one site at which both an indiscriminate postmodernism and an un-postmodern feminist theory tend to break down. The former, without feminism's insistence that representation is always political, cannot account for the very real violence produced by the fictive categories of gender difference. The latter may find in postmodernism's rejection of universal explanations a tool for theorizing the fluid and multiple relations possible between a given representation and political meanings. In this way, the study begins as broadly as possible, making an argument about the dynamics of art and politics in the late twentieth century, and concludes by suggesting the usefulness of this rhetorical analysis to a specific, concrete instance of representational struggle in heated debates that continue into the twenty-first.

1
A Politicized Postmodernism: Feminist Reading Tactics

I want to begin this study, which argues for the existence and the significance of feminist postmodernism, by making explicit two assumptions central to my argument. First, what one makes of cultural objects or texts—one's sense of their meaning and of their implications—depends to a great extent on the conceptual framework through which one approaches them. Current debates over how to frame literary postmodernism are therefore as much about determining what postmodernism can *do* as about pinning down what it *is*.[1] Second, what is all too frequently left out of those debates is any theory of what readers might do *with* it.

If there is no true or authentic postmodernism to be divined among the multiple competing constructions critics offer of it, this does not necessarily mean (to summon the dread phrase) that "anything goes." If models of postmodernism are "mere" rhetoric, it becomes crucial to conceive of rhetoric as *invested* speech and to evaluate the rhetorical effects of each model. The utility of any definition of postmodernism depends on the extent to which it provides a framework that enables readers to incorporate texts into their postmodern lives, to meet their varied needs and desires. The kind of framework I am interested in arguing for is a conception of postmodernism that would highlight the ways in which variously positioned readers might manipulate texts to make meanings that further their ability to affect the political and social conditions of postmodernity. I hope that what emerges here, for readers who share my investment in locating the possibility of agency in contemporary culture, will be a set of tactics for reading the postmodern. Feminist postmodernism, I propose, offers just such a tactical model.

1 / A POLITICIZED POSTMODERNISM

When I use the term postmodernism, as I will do frequently despite its inevitable ambiguity, it will be to invoke a way of reading that takes into account the circumstances of contemporary readers and the place reading occupies in their overall sense of contemporary reality. By this I mean to assert that reading is different now than it has ever been before; the act itself has a different social meaning because texts (i.e., cultural texts in general) play an unprecedented role in the contemporary formation of postindustrial society. This role is characterized by the diffusion of the formerly more-or-less discrete realm of cultural consumption across the entire fabric of society, so that all experience has become a text to be read, lacking a meaning until interpreted and manipulated. This shift, although it manifests itself in part in psychic structures, is not existential but historical. In order for a model of postmodernism to highlight its political potential, that model must recognize this contemporary cultural situation.

Postmodernism therefore functions in my formulation to describe a practice, manifest in both theory and specific cultural products, that attempts to account for the experience of living in *postmodernity*. The *postmodernist novel* designates, somewhat tautologically, the novel that can be read as having a significant relation to this contemporary context.

Does this mean that, for instance, Gertrude Stein's *The Autobiography of Alice B. Toklas* (1933) or *Ida* (1941), if read in a postmodern way, could now be recognized as postmodern novels before their time? Critics do perform such readings; during the 1990s, book-length studies appeared on the "postmodernism" not only of Stein, but of Virginia Woolf, Marcel Proust, W. B. Yeats, and even Plato. These studies often capitalize on the polyvocal plurality of postmodernist theory in order to produce richer readings of the authors in question than might previously have been possible. In the case of such a misunderstood innovator as Stein, being able to separate her work from a narrow, canonical construction of apolitical, "autonomous" modernism has also enabled critics to argue for the feminist implications of her experimental practice.[2] However, reclassifying historical works in this way does not, I believe, serve the goal I have articulated above: to elucidate the relation between postmodern culture and postmodern political change. Rather, it raises two problems: such ahistorical treatment obscures both the nature of the political uses to which readers in their own day were able to employ those texts and the specifics of the interventions available to writers and readers of literary texts today. For my purposes, postmodernism cannot merely be treated as a (transhistorical) style, divorced from its context of reception.

Defining postmodernism historically, as a literary period, opens up all contemporary texts to consideration as postmodernist, rather than reserving that term for a limited group of stylistically innovative works that are often taken to reproduce and reaffirm "the contemporary condition." This broader application of the term allows critical attention to seek out texts different from those commonly considered exemplars of postmodernism, to focus—again, as a strategic move—on texts, and on readings of texts, that seem to offer most hope for agency, and to see this too as a possibility offered by postmodernism. I will argue for focusing on texts such as Kathy Acker's and Angela Carter's novels in developing a model of what postmodernism might enable readers to *do* with their historical location. My agenda, my interest in reframing postmodernism such that it emerges as a site where (various) politics are actively manufactured, is primarily feminist.

I think feminism can shift how postmodernism conceives of itself, from a practice of theorizing postmodern conditions to a practice of engagement with those conditions. Answers to the companion question of what postmodernist ways of thinking can offer to feminism (and to other "special interest" theories seeking to connect literary practice and the politics of everyday life) should emerge more thoroughly later, through my readings of Acker's and Carter's novels and, most explicitly, in chapter four's discussion of the strategies that feminist-postmodernist readings of these novels suggest for negotiating debates within feminism.

Toward a flexible feminism

Claiming a feminist agenda begs the question, *which* feminist agenda? It is worth repeating that no consensus on *the* feminist agenda exists, even among feminists writing (about) postmodernism. In order to delineate what position I am advocating for feminism, and what political needs I see feminism most suited to address, let me briefly map out this chapter's argument about postmodernism and postmodernity.

Much of this chapter is devoted to establishing what feminism might offer to (a politicized) postmodernism. The answer, I believe, is a theory of agency. This agency is located in the practice of rereading available representations. I will begin my argument by establishing that feminism and postmodernism do have some shared interests; both focus critically on the construction of otherness, as a system of opposed identity positions. Drawing on both feminism and postmodernism, I will propose this otherness as the source of agency—if one sees it as both a division within each subject (as postmodernism proposes) and a politically charged division between groups (as feminism insists). Then, in order to establish that otherness is produced in postmodern subjects primarily through reading—and that reading is therefore the site where existing constructions of identity might be changed—I will survey Marxist periodizing models of the economic, social, and cultural conditions that comprise postmodernity; these models suggest that the experience of postmodern subjects is mediated by texts to an extent unprecedented in history. However, the rhetoric of such periodizing models creates an implied reader who merely reproduces existing ideology; in order to counter this pessimistic tendency and theorize a reader with agency, I will pursue in the chapter's final section a rhetorical analysis of two feminist-postmodernist texts. Both of these—one a novel by Acker, the other an autobiographical essay by Minnie Bruce Pratt—posit readers who are constructed as "other" by existing texts, but who are also able to find a source of politicized agency in the tendency of texts to produce different forms of otherness in different contexts.

This argument necessitates a kind of feminism that can conceive of otherness as a multiple system of oppressions—not simply a binary division between a monolithic male norm and an equally monolithic female Other—yet will also, depending on the tactics a particular struggle requires, sometimes insist on the primacy of the difference between genders. A postmodernist feminism recognizes the existence of many images of "woman," with quite divergent social meanings, but also recognizes that none of these images ever means the same as any image of "man."

However, the form of feminism I am advocating raises worries for many feminists, which I believe need to be addressed. Some feminists fear that postmodernism's focus on the fictional or textual nature of all identities removes the basis for the category "women," a category without which feminist analyses of inequity become impossible.[3] Their positions range from Linda Hutcheon's rather reluctant admission, "Feminisms are not really either compatible with or even an example of postmodern thought" because "their political agendas would be endangered, . . . their historical particularities and relative positionalities would risk being subsumed," to Nancy Hartsock's more pessimistic assertion that "postmodernism represents a dangerous approach for any marginalized group to adopt."[4] While those dangers are real, I want to suggest that they are not insurmountable.

Female Others, Postmodern Others

Feminism and postmodernism share, in all their guises, a general and central tendency toward antiuniversalism. The existence of this common impulse suggests it is possible to approach the two schools of thought as having more in common than not. Emphasizing their commonality means seeing most of their differences as simply the different ways in which each pursues its antiuniversalism. Such an emphasis serves my attempt to sketch a postmodernism that functions as a political critique; it enables me to draw on both the pervasiveness of postmodernism's challenge to universalism and the political-historical specificity of feminism's similar challenge.

Indeed, these different tendencies are the main point of divergence between feminist and postmodernist antiuniversalisms. Whereas feminism, since its earliest manifestations, has challenged the centrality and neutrality of the masculine subject as a basis for epistemology, various postmodern theorists have raised similar (although frequently not gendered) challenges to *any* representations depending on a single-centered, comprehensive, and objective world view. Both focus on subjects marked by otherness; by "otherness," each tendency means something slightly different, yet for both it implies the existence of subjects who are *other* than the centered, knowing subject assumed by science and by common sense until very recently. Many feminists, following the work of Simone de Beauvoir, have conceived of otherness as a binary framework of subject formation, in which women are constructed as only the shadow, opposite, or Other of men. This same binary framework has also been invoked by various theorists to account for the otherness of people of color, who are constructed by hegemonic ideology in opposition to an assumed norm of whiteness. Postmodernists tend to frame otherness as a more diffuse and multiple condition common to all subjects—including white males—who are necessarily fragmented and "other" to themselves. A final commonality is that many (but not all) feminisms and most (if not all) postmodernisms extend their critique of the centered subject to offer fundamental challenges to formerly dominant teleological accounts of historical and individual development—among them Christian-salvational, Marxist, and Freudian accounts—Jean-François Lyotard's *"grands récits"* or "metanarratives," which are also, in Craig Owens's deliberately gendered term, "master narratives."[5]

However, the key difference between the two antiuniversalist tendencies—constructing otherness either as an external condition specific to particular disempowered groups, or as a generalized internal phenomenon—comes to seem far more significant than their common ground to those theorists who find the similar historical timing of the two highly suspicious. More than one critic has pointed out that the first statements of postmodernist theories of the death of the subject emerged at about the time when concrete and specific challenges to the dominance of the white, male subject were being posed by the second wave of feminism, the emerging peace, ecology, and gay rights movements, and the surge of nationalism among colonized, internally segregated, and "Third World" peoples (what Owens calls "the voices of the conquered").[6] Thus some have seen the new willingness of white, male critics to theorize away their own identity as a sleight-of-hand trick aimed at diffusing these challenges by declaring both the object of their attack (the hegemonic subject) and the initiating subjects (oppositional identities) nonexistent, illusory. This is the implication of Nancy Hartsock's question, "Why is it that just at the moment when so many of us who have been silenced demand the right to name ourselves, to act as subjects rather than objects of history, that just then the concept of subjecthood becomes problematic?" and of Bell Hooks's sympathy with "black folks" who comment ironically, "'Yeah, it's easy to give up identity, when you got one.'"[7] So this particular account of postmodern otherness's origins can lead (as it does for Hartsock, although not for Owens and Hooks) to a condemnation and dismissal of postmodernism as an intellectual fad, parasitical on the claims of marginalized Others, that subsequently ignores them and undercuts their positions. As Sara Ahmed puts it, "[t]he West calls the other to speak, but hears the speech as a sign of a crisis that already belongs to the West."[8]

I agree with these critics' suggestion that the significant impact of the international and internal "new democratic struggles" on shaping both postmodernist thought and postmodernity has too frequently been suppressed or overlooked.[9] Nevertheless, I propose that rather than seeing postmodernist theories of otherness as a response to the critiques originating in the new social movements, *both* can be seen as symptoms of something larger called postmodernity. I will argue at more length later that postmodernity, seen as a stage in the development of capitalist society, both produces a historically new form of otherness internal to every subject and continues to produce differentiations between groups of Others. The conditions of postmodernity variously undermine the notion of identity and, in other contexts, reassert it.

Therefore I want to argue that feminist and postmodernist models of otherness are entirely compatible, when seen in historical context. I think it important to adopt both approaches to the concept because, from their combination, a theory of agency can arise.

Why are both concepts of otherness necessary to a theory of agency that could be employed toward progressive ends? First, the version of otherness arising from feminism and other politically committed thinking functions to make sure that an otherness understood as *everywhere* is not assumed to be *everywhere the same*. The danger many skeptical feminist critics have pointed out is that the postmodern *ubiquity* of otherness can too easily be construed as the *uniformity* of otherness, as, for instance, in Robert Siegle's assumption that in the world of postmodernist fiction, "we are all 'women' submitting to the paternal state."[10] Tania Modleski, in her book *Feminism without Women,* takes a number of critics to task for similar appropriations of the historical experience of exclusion specific to marginalized groups as a trope of "the" general subject. She cites, for instance, various (mis)applications of "the by now clichéd view of a certain strain of deconstructionism that writing can be seen as feminine";[11] in the most extreme examples of such generalized notions of otherness, all men come to occupy the metaphorical position of femininity in relation to a hegemonic system from which they feel themselves to be "other." Such an egregiously vague use of the concept of otherness results, as Biddy Martin succinctly charges in relation to some uses of Foucauldian theory, in "reproduc[ing] the androcentric and fundamentally humanist universalizing 'I,' this time in the apparent form of the 'Not-I.'"[12] Positing all subjects as disempowered, this version of otherness denies the legitimacy of any effort at political change based on the claim that major power inequities exist.

However, agency should also not be theorized as deriving from an otherness that belongs exclusively to the marginalized. As Hooks has noted from a black feminist perspective, reessentializing the identity of less-powerful groups, as the basis for an epistemology rather than as a useful *temporary* tactic, only reinforces the constructions of their unchanging "nature" offered by dominant ideologies.[13] It also results in the necessary reintroduction of a theory of false consciousness to explain why not all marginalized subjects oppose existing configurations of power. Such a theory produces the same power dynamic of center and margin, simply shifting the mapping of those spaces onto the vanguard (as subject-of-knowledge) and the deluded masses. Reading otherness as a property of all subjects in a postmodern analysis can actually aid struggles for a more egalitarian society by preventing the reintroduction of a privileged viewpoint. As long as the justifications for the existence of a (any) privileged position are widely accepted, they are most likely to serve the purposes of those who already occupy it.

I aim to develop my account of agency throughout this study, particularly in my readings of Acker and Carter; here I will only outline it, with an eye to establishing its dependence on both understandings of otherness. First, a postmodern account of agency must cover the fragmentation or non-self-identity of all subjects, including the most hegemonic ones. The inability of any one discourse to finally define and fix the subject depends on this internal difference. The fragmented, internally "other" subject is comprised of—or in Althusserian terms, interpellated by—a number of hegemonic discourses, each of which is an attempt to define him or her. S/he may be "hailed" by discourses of national citizenship, of class, of age, of race and sex, and many others—and aspects of these various definitions are inevitably at odds. For instance, that discourse of Americanness that attempts to secure a subject's loyalty to government and law by creating an identity based on concepts of self-determination and egalitarianism is often fundamentally at odds with the discourse of (American) female identity that defines femininity as deferral to men's superior judgment. But each identity-category such as American or woman is also itself composed of multiple discourses that may also contradict one another; thus "woman" may mean passionless moral angel in one version, unrestrained animal in another. Agency becomes possible at the points where these various partial accounts of the subject (and his/her role in contemporary society) overlap and their inconsistency with one another becomes pressing. At that point—the point where choice or selection must take place—one discourse wins out.

This is the point at which the other (feminist) account of otherness enters in, insisting on the role of power and context in determining which version of the subject will prevail at each of these crisis moments. If power accrues differently to different discursive identities, agency exists at the moment when the subject recognizes which one is most advantageous and therefore adopts it. I am not, let me immediately emphasize, suggesting this recognition needs to be conscious or deliberate; I am not distinguishing between aware subjects who have agency and unaware subjects who do not. All people have agency, and having to make these choices is inevitable. But turning that agency to progressive ends—or any specific goal—depends on a certain conscious analysis. Feminism provides one such analysis of the power implications of adopting each "fiction" of who one is in a specific context.

This concept of agency and otherness considers all identities as fictions, evocative stories of the self rather than exhaustive descriptions. Feminists skeptical of postmodernism often resist such positions, which they see as manifesting a "nominalist" theory of identity that evacuates its truth value, collapsing into an anything-goes relativism. They worry that if "the category 'woman' is a fiction," it necessarily follows that "feminist efforts must be directed toward dismantling this fiction."[14] These critics recognize, importantly, that "women"—like "feminism," for all its internal contestations—remains a signifier with enormous strategic value, too important to relinquish. But a postmodernist-feminist approach suggests that a term need not have essential or absolute value to have practical value. For instance, I have suggested that the term "postmodernism" is most useful for its ability to evoke a historically specific relation between contemporary cultural objects and their social-political moment; but it does so not by bringing into view an objectively existing situation, but by creating a frame within which disparate features become organized into a (somewhat) coherent image. Such framing functions as a political maneuver, by emphasizing some connections and downplaying others.

"Feminism" can function, similarly, to frame a group of subjects in such a way that they perceive a need for political unity and can make claims premised upon it. It yokes together a wide variety of beliefs and practices by drawing them into the frame of what they have in common: a commitment to achieving social justice for women—

whether that amorphous justice is to be attained through legislative measures aimed at institutionalizing equality, through cultural interventions, through the establishment of a separate/ist sphere that encourages women's difference (from men), through materialist revolution, or through a combination of these and other practices. This yoking-together can be and has often been counterproductive, especially for those women who have been made aware of their distance from feminist spokespeople on the grounds of race, class, ethnicity, sexuality, and/or national origin. But such a dangerous elision of differences can be minimized by employing the term "feminism" as a *fiction* of unity, which can allow alliances among women to function "under erasure," basing their legitimacy not on any essential likeness but on a contingent and shifting commonality of interests.[15] I am not suggesting women can effortlessly pick up and discard various identities, but that recognizing the various circumstances under which different identities are forced on specific groups of women can illuminate the range of possible responses to oppression.

In this conception of a tactical postmodernist feminism, as throughout this study, I assume that while fictions or "stories" may not be able to appeal to truth, they are nevertheless operative in shaping attitudes and actions. Thus, recognizing "woman" as a fiction does not imply therefore working against it in the name of some more accurate, objective truth. One can reject the usual value-loaded opposition between fiction and truth by recognizing that fictions have the power to *create* subject-positions and alliances—to become true—through the operation of framing. As I will argue later, that ability is stronger in postmodernity than ever before. The assertion that fictions offer images of identity and identifications provides the basis for continuing to study such apparently outmoded cultural forms as novels. The fictions on which this study will focus are emblematic of the process by which political identity is created and recreated in postmodernity.

My approach draws significantly on that of Michel de Certeau. In *The Practice of Everyday Life*, Certeau turns to "everyday practices" or "ways of operating" as the often overlooked site in which consumers actively make something of the texts, products, and arrangements of space imposed upon them. Without minimizing the extensive control exercised by top-down systems of social and cultural power (whose constant expansion "no longer leaves 'consumers' any place in which they can indicate what they *make* or *do* with the products of these systems"), he seeks to emphasize the dispersed, elusive, and contingent ways in which everyday consumption itself becomes an act of production—of (mis)using, remaking, and "making do."[16] The purposes toward which dominated people put the texts and public spaces available to them are always more or less tangential to any originally intended uses or meanings. Certeau likens the relation between the "dominant cultural economy" and the behaviors of its users to that between a language (Saussure's *langue*)—which exists fully only in the abstract—and the particular acts of enunciation (*parole*) through which that language is brought into actual existence.[17]

This framework leads Certeau to share the poststructuralist view of acts of language (or "stories") as themselves a significant *practice*, not merely a secondary means of describing an object that exists outside of language. As he puts it, "in the art of telling about ways of operating, the latter is already at work."[18] Even the act of naming organizes (frames) its object according to the namer's interests. This view opposes the common-sense view derived from the scientific discourse of the Enlightenment, which supposes that language should simply reflect observed facts.[19] Certeau's concern with language as one of the practices by means of which people reshape the world around them leads him to affirm, as I do here, the vital and contemporary "theoretical value of the novel, which has become the zoo of everyday practices since the establishment of modern science."[20] The appealing analogy suggests that perhaps analysis of the practices contained in novels can aid in their reintegration into their natural habitat, the larger world of common discourse—not so that they might be tamed and domesticated, but in order for a bit more wild diversity to be available.

There is one other aspect of Certeau's approach that I want to outline briefly now, because of its relevance to the idea of a feminism based on operative fictions. Certeau makes a central distinction between the extensive *strategies* of established power and the localized *tactics* of users/consumers. Strategies operate from a stable and discrete social location, an institutional home; they are enacted *from* somewhere and *upon* a clearly distinguished elsewhere. They simultaneously presume and reproduce a division between self and Other. Tactics, on the other hand, are unsystematic. They are opportunistic—appearing, responding, shifting, adapting, and disappearing, in fleeting forms. Certeau says of the tactic, "Whatever it wins, it does not keep. It must constantly manipulate events in order to turn them into 'opportunities.' The weak must continually turn to their own ends forces alien to them." Tactics involve scavenging, *bricolage*. And "[m]any everyday practices (talking, reading, moving about, shopping, cooking, etc.) are tactical in character."[21]

Tactics imply both kinds of otherness that I have described above. They are, on the one hand, brief flashes that highlight the presence in society of power's Others: those who are not originators but consumers, not the strong but the weak. But tactics also operate *within* the given culture and upon its products, which cannot be integrated into daily life *without* the operation of tactics upon them; everywhere the strategic culture is, tactics are. In terms of spatial metaphors, tactics "cannot count on a 'proper' (a spatial or institutional localization), nor thus on a borderline distinguishing the other as a visible totality. The place of a tactic belongs to the other. A tactic insinuates itself into the other's place, fragmentarily, without taking it over in its entirety, without being able to keep it at a distance."[22] Tactics disrupt the binary construction of otherness by underlining its necessary presence throughout the social fabric, in every act of consumption.

In fact, there is not such a binary division between strategies and tactics as Certeau's own analysis sometimes implies.[23] His work is primarily concerned with the practices of subcultural groups—"groups which, since they lack their own space, have to get along in a network of already established forces and representations." So while emphasizing the fact that consumption is always an act of (tactical) production, he does not address the possibility that the official producers of culture—the "subject[s] of will and power"—are themselves engaged in acts of consumption and reuse.[24] In terms of my concerns, women writers and readers certainly fit the description of subcultural operators who "have to get along" in a patriarchal textual economy designed neither for nor by them *as women;* but it also seems important to acknowledge that women sometimes occupy positions of relative power—especially in relation to other, less-privileged women—because of their race, class, national origin, or similar centralizing categories. And in some, limited contexts, feminism itself has a claim to its own, "proper" institutional space. Within this strategic space, various tactics operate.

Nevertheless, I shall treat feminism as, on the whole, a *tactical* fiction. This provisional status means that the notion women have more to gain from working together than from pursuing divergent agendas must be continually reexamined, and adopted or temporarily dropped depending on its usefulness to the various groups of women concerned in a particular context.[25] Gender may take precedence over other axes of identity (and mobilization)—or it may yield precedence to them. Feminism may itself assume various shapes and forms depending on the moment's needs, appearing as materialist feminism, as liberal feminism, or as a temporary essentialism. A postmodernist feminism can incorporate other feminisms without subsuming them. The fact that such a happy intrafeminist pluralism is not easily achieved, but is a matter of much negotiation among women based on a continual contextual analysis of stakes, I will address in more depth in my final chapter's discussion of the "sex wars" within feminism.

Seen in this way as a contingent practice, feminism provides a useful model of postmodern political work. But it remains to explain why I am privileging feminism over other forms of political work as the viewpoint from which to develop a model of postmodern political change. Most existing critical work on the politics of postmodernism that attempts to take into account the multiple axes of identity along which power operates has been influenced by feminist thinking. But I would not want to privilege feminism as "*the* political conscience of postmodernism," to borrow Laura Kipnis's ironic phrase, to the exclusion of important political work on postmodernism being done from the position of nonfeminist people of color or white lesbians (whose analysis, in Laura Doan's edited collection on *The Lesbian Postmodern,* overlaps with feminism but is not coextensive with it).[26]

However, I have a specific, disciplinary reason for making gender the primary category shaping my approach: in studies of literary postmodernism, feminism is frequently absent. As a version of postmodernism has grown canonical in U.S. literary institutions (academic English departments, publishing, etc.), contemporary "significant" literature, especially U.S. fiction, is frequently divided into two entirely separate categories: postmodernism, and "multicultural/multiethnic" writing or, more narrowly, "writing by women of color." Postmodernism, in this construction, is implicitly white and male. The literary category postmodernism has thus tended to function as a means of *bracketing* the issue of otherness, of keeping what I have called the two types of otherness rigidly separate.

For example, Ihab Hassan's influential gesture "toward a postmodern literature" (the subtitle of *The Dismemberment of Orpheus*) lists nine white men as the postmodernist writers working in the United

States in the 1980s: Walter Abish, David Antin, John Ashbery, John Barth, Donald Barthelme, William S. Burroughs, Thomas Pynchon, Sam Shepard, and Robert Wilson.[27] Barth, in his roughly contemporary definitional essay, "The Literature of Replenishment," provides a slightly different list of eight white men who are the "American fictionists most commonly included in the [postmodernist] canon."[28] He notes that, "for better or worse," most U.S. women writers remain too hung up on "the eloquent issuance of what the critic Richard Locke has called 'secular news reports'" to catch up with the stylistic innovations of the twentieth century.[29] Barth's matrimonial rhetoric here may betray his vision of the appropriate relation of women to male writers.

My point is not to argue that some women ought to be added to this nebulous list of postmodernists (which exists only in specific forms such as particular class syllabi). And I am certainly not begrudging the attention being paid on another front, at long last, to writing by African-American, Asian-American, Native-American, and Latino/a men and women. Rather, I am struck that the exclusion of work by white women functions as perhaps a *constitutive exclusion* on which the prevalent separation of contemporary U.S. fiction into two categories depends. For white women are apparently neither postmodernists nor women writers of color. Their absence allows a clean boundary to be constructed between white men, as racial-sexual norm, and those who are both racially *and* sexually other (a boundary that also implicitly feminizes men of color). This is a case where a critique that strategically emphasizes gender, by insisting on the presence of women within whiteness, may be one way of dismantling the clean separation that allows some critics to act as if white men had neither gender nor race.

Admittedly, approaching the work of women of color (for instance) through a specific, appropriate rubric is crucial for theorizing certain political and stylistic implications of their work and for making visible a previously ignored audience. However, maintaining a rigid boundary may also function to devalue and contain the production of women of color. Refusing the term postmodernism to women of color keeps them from the "higher" cultural ground of innovation and experimentation that it signifies. Postmodernism holds an implied place at the center of contemporary high-cultural production; its very name marks it as modernism's heir, inheritor of the position formerly occupied by the dominant literary-artistic movement of the first half of the twentieth century.

This implicit centrality is evident even in attempts to write more progressive and inclusive literary histories, such as the 1991 *Columbia History of the American Novel* (called by Brian McHale, at the time, "the most politically correct American literary history to date").[30] In the *Columbia History*, which includes chapters on postcolonial, Caribbean, and Canadian literature in its contemporary section, women of color are relegated to a separate space that remains, somehow, marginal. Toni Morrison and Maxine Hong Kingston are mentioned not in the chapter on U.S. postmodernism (which does add two white women—Acker and Joanna Russ—and two black men—Ishmael Reed and Samuel R. Delaney—to the usual list of eight white men), but in a chapter on magic realism, which they share with influential Latin Americans and other writers of "pan-American narratives": "women and men of color, Jews, gays and lesbians, and so on."[31] While creating a space for the formerly excluded is crucial, doing it this way reinforces the sense that Morrison and Kingston and other marginalized U.S. writers have more in common with "foreigners" than with the mainstream of literature in this country. And while (presumably straight, non-Jewish) white women indeed have less difficulty entering the inner rooms of power than many Others, this separation also consigns their work to a depoliticized position.[32]

A different division between domestic postmodernism and the "foreign" occurs in the more recent, two-volume *Encyclopedia of the Novel* from Fitzroy Dearborn—but again it hinges on the separate treatment of U.S. women novelists. While the range of writers, national novel traditions, and works covered in the encyclopedia is truly global and inclusive, Elizabeth Deeds Ermarth's essay on postmodernism again cites only a few white men as its exemplars in the United States, alongside a cluster of Latin-American and continental European writers (no Britons). Ermarth comments that "with a few notable exceptions, the most original postmodern writing" has not been in English. From this, she concludes that the "postmodern critique of culture and knowledge is least understood and most resisted in Anglo-American cultures because they are so thoroughly invested in empiricism and in the representational politics and capitalist economies that seem to accompany empiricism."[33] Here again, despite a meaningful attempt to decenter English-language literature in global terms, both the definition of postmodernism and the resulting, gloomy evaluation of the status of literary innovation and political resistance in the United States and United Kingdom depend on overlooking the work of women writers (and men of color) entirely.

As my discussion in this chapter aims to establish, such separations are damaging for theorizing both the extent to which postmodernism can be the location of political action and the roles of race and gender in contemporary representation. "Neutral" postmodernism and the work of those writers on the *Columbia History*'s list of outcasts must be considered in interaction with one another if the goal is to produce a way of reading the politics of representation in contemporary culture. Thus this study's feminist focus to articulating a politicized postmodernism, and my readings of the work of white women writers, are not intended as an *alternative* to race-based analyses. Rather, they attempt to break up whiteness, as one step in a larger, ongoing rethinking of the possible politics of contemporary writing. This new postmodernist project entails a multiple-variable analysis of subject-positions including (but not limited to) race *and* gender.

The separation of postmodernism from the writing of "special interests" in discussions of contemporary fiction suggests that many influential U.S. literary critics have yet to connect the otherness of the disoriented white male subject, as found in the novels of Barth or Pynchon or DeLillo, with the specifically racial and gendered experience of otherness evoked by writers such as Morrison. Even as postmodernism may be in the process of being consigned to the past (along with the twentieth century), that separation has not been sufficiently questioned.[34] No wonder agency and postmodernism are still also generally considered incompatible. Considered in this way as the evocation of a general psychic condition, "postmodernism" designates an object rather than an approach; diagnosing it is often a matter only of locating certain stylistic practices: narrative fragmentation, decentering of character, pastiche, self-referentiality, irony, or a number of similar traits. (Hassan's early taxonomy of postmodernist features, in *Paracriticisms,* is the prototype of such analyses; it served the important function of establishing the term as a marker of a significant shift from modernism.)[35] Critics then read these textual practices either as the hallmarks of a new mimesis, means of representing the current phase of the human condition, or as symptoms of a generalized failure of representation.[36] Read in any of these ways, postmodernism does, as feminist skeptics have charged, become guilty of evacuating the political content from otherness.

Here I return to the need to conceive of postmodernism as a historical, periodizing category rather than the ahistorical description of a stylistic tendency. Only by reconceiving the category on such broad terms can texts by Others be understood as an alternative reading of the crisis of the subject that white, male postmodernists address. Then the more hopeful account of politicized action that can be read in these texts can be seen not only as a strategy of the marginalized—although this is, in itself, important—but as a model of the political uses of texts and reading in a postmodern world. A periodizing account of postmodernism can also explain why reading is emblematic of all political activity under postmodern conditions.

Periodizing models: otherness in historical context

One impact of linking postmodernism with postmodernity, as a periodizing concept, is that it positions the new ubiquity of otherness not as a co-optation of historically marginalized people but as a ground for alliances. As Bell Hooks steps back and considers postmodernism—a term she uses broadly to describe the general conditions of postmodernity, not just cultural production—she suggests:

> The overall impact of postmodernism is that many other groups now share with black folks a sense of deep alienation, despair, uncertainty, loss of a sense of grounding even if it is not informed by shared circumstances. Radical postmodernism [that is, cultural production] calls attention to those shared sensibilities which cross the boundaries of class, gender, race, etc., that could be fertile ground for the construction of empathy—ties that would promote recognition of common commitments, and serve as a base for solidarity and coalition.[37]

Work such as Hooks's reads the subtle contexts that give meaning to various postmodernist texts, suggesting when such "empathy," built on a *common* experience of otherness, can be deployed toward progressive ends and when the lack of "shared circumstances"—which determine the *specific* forms of otherness—must be highlighted in order to prevent the elision of one group's needs. Considering the historical context of postmodernism can also suggest the means by which such empathy might be evoked or created; for understanding postmodernism as a periodizing concept means, above all, coming to terms with the increased role of images and fictional representations of "identity" in shaping political life.

The remainder of this chapter describes how the context-sensitive impulse of postmodernist feminism can be read together with broader periodizing accounts of postmodernism, creating sites for agency by providing a theory of localized reception that recognizes the different significance of images for different audiences. Influential accounts of postmodernity provide a sketch of the unprecedented conditions under which politics happen in contemporary industrialized societies: increasingly, the realm of representation, and of reading, is the location of politics. The danger of such periodizing readings, however, is that they tend to minimize synchronic variations—the cases in which the circumstances of postmodernity, including the experience of otherness, are not shared equally by all. To address this oversight, I will offer my own "meta-"reading of the reading tactics applied to exemplary postmodern texts by Fredric Jameson and David Harvey, whose primary aim is to sketch the "condition of postmodernity"; I will try to tease out their implications for feminist attempts to theorize resistance. Finally, I will propose that recent feminist-postmodernist work (such as the novels of Acker and Carter) brings to Marxist theories of postmodernism such as Jameson's and Harvey's the ability to theorize agency and change by offering models of active and contextual readership.

Let me begin by connecting this discussion of periodizing accounts of postmodernism back to the criticism of contemporary fiction in the United States. I suggested earlier that the categorization of only a certain kind of recent literature as postmodernist makes it much more difficult to theorize the potential importance of other writing—or, the writing of Others. Drawing the category on historical, rather than formal, grounds removes the occasion for that definitional anxiety that restricts postmodernism only to those works most distinct from canonical modernism. This allows *all* contemporary writing to be considered centrally connected to or representative of its age. For, as Jameson writes, "even if all the constitutive features of postmodernism were identical with and coterminous to those of an older modernism . . . the two phenomena would still remain utterly distinct in their meaning and social function, owing to the very different positioning of postmodernism in the economic system of late capital and, beyond that, to the transformation of the very sphere of culture in contemporary society."[38] To claim that all contemporary cultural products belong in the same category because of their position in a political and economic system is not to say that they are all equally useful to an analysis of ways to intervene in that system. However, beginning with a sense of the current location of culture in relation to overall political and economic conditions allows the critic to identify which textual practices do carry the most potential for agency.

Granted, feminist literary critics have problematized the whole project of periodization on two levels. First, the archival work of recovering and rereading previously devalued texts by women has resulted in challenges to the narrow basis on which the dominant aesthetics of a period have until now been defined.[39] I see this not as an argument against periodization, but as an argument for the advantage of historicist definitions of a period rather than formalist ones. As Susan Rubin Suleiman argues in relation to modernism and postmodernism, any attempt "to try and establish clearcut formal differences" between the literature of the two periods "invariably involve[s] oversimplification and flattening out of both categories."[40] But in contrast, historicist definitions can ideally be inclusive, able to extend to the heterogeneous ways in which various art works functioned (or function) in their particular historical context and to analyze the dynamics by which some styles and practices carried (or carry) more power and cachet than others.

If part of the problem with periodization so far has been its limited synchronic depth, feminists have also challenged the boundaries of periodization more fundamentally on a diachronic basis.[41] They have pointed out that the changes seen as epoch-defining shifts by men have often been experienced quite differently by women and other economically subordinated, culturally unrepresented people. Certainly, when Jameson refers to the Vietnam war as the first postmodern war, I find myself wondering how many Vietnamese experienced it as qualitatively different from previous warfare, despite the high-tech means by which it was pursued.[42] Nevertheless, it was not only Americans whose understanding of the war was shaped by the unprecedented mediation of photographic representations, by their instantaneity and by the feeling of detachment that resulted from the almost unreadable incongruity of such images of carnage beamed into the presumedly safe American domestic space. One of the characteristics of postmodernity that Jameson and others recognize is the greatly increased internationalization of cause and effect under the regime of multinational capitalism. What Americans experience postmodernly in their living rooms—and how they subsequently act or fail to act as a result of this experience—all too often has profound effects not only on the Vietnamese, but on Iraqis,

Kosovars, and the inhabitants of the internal "Third World" of the American inner cities.

I am suggesting that to a certain extent, the legitimacy of attempts to periodize postmodernity comes from its unprecedented nature as an international, multinational phenomenon. This is not at all to say that experiences of postmodernity across nation, race, class, gender, or other axes will be homogeneous. Donna Haraway's analysis of the changing role of women in Southeast Asia in the "integrated circuit" of high-tech industry offers an example of both the ways in which multinational production directly affects people outside the power corridors of the industrialized West, and the ways in which these effects are not the same as those elsewhere.[43] But my point here is to defend the periodizing project from the charge that it *necessarily* homogenizes. Rather, it can yield an understanding of the role of cultural production at this particular moment not only in hegemonic segments of society but also for marginalized groups who must, to varying extents, negotiate with postmodernity in their own particular contexts.

The accounts of the shift in the configuration of society, from the postwar years through today, that I summarize here focus primarily on the United States and Britain, although echoes and repercussions of the changes in those nations have been felt across the globe. My primary aim in this overview is to establish the radically increased role of culture (i.e., images and fictions) in the contemporary social, political, and economic formation. Jameson identifies as perhaps the most telling feature of postmodernity "an immense dilation of [the cultural] sphere (the sphere of commodities), an immense and historically original acculturation of the Real, a quantum leap in what [Walter] Benjamin still called the 'aestheticization' of reality."[44] While Jameson generally sees this trend pessimistically, as marking the end of any chance for resistant actions whose meanings need not pass through the marketplace, my study attempts to read it more ambiguously. The "signifierization" of everything may even create room to move within the marketplace in such a way that the capitalist marketplace might itself provide a breeding ground for desires fundamentally incompatible with capitalism. As the marketplace of representations expands, attempting to increase its contact with diverse groups of consumers whose identities had formerly been largely unrepresented, those new consumers will not only be subject to more extensive co-optation than previously; they will also be able to articulate new desires and demands that exceed current power relations.

What evidence is there to argue the existence of such a historical shift? David Harvey's wide-ranging study *The Condition of Postmodernity* draws on sources from economic theory and statistics, architecture and urban planning, anthropology, sociology, art history, literary theory, film criticism, advertising, geography, and cartography, to forge an overall argument that the industrialized world is experiencing a shift from the Fordist system that had previously defined both the *"regime of accumulation"* and the accompanying *"mode of social and political regulation"*—terms that correspond roughly to the older "base" and "superstructure." Postmodernism is the mode of regulation corresponding to the new phase, "what might be called a 'flexible' regime of accumulation."[45]

Harvey marks the date of the establishment of this new phase at approximately 1972, when the long postwar period of economic growth collapsed in the industrialized West. If the oil crisis was the immediate trigger of this collapse, signs of both the economic breakdown and the changing function of culture had been increasingly prominent for some years beforehand. I am inclined to follow Andreas Huyssen in identifying a significant emergent postmodern cultural practice in the 1960s, of which Pynchon's early novels and pop art are only two of many examples.[46] But dating a fully fledged postmodernism from the early seventies seems useful since, by that point, the utopian aspirations of the sixties had dimmed considerably, and the conditions that were established then are more or less those that pertain today.

Flexible accumulation, the new guise of capitalism, was a departure from Fordism in its emphasis on the adaptability and mutability of production processes, labor organization patterns, and financial resources; but it also represents a fulfillment of Fordism's internal logic.[47] By the mid-1960s, the success of Fordist modernization in the United States, Western Europe, and Japan had resulted in both the saturation of internal markets and their constriction by the rising domestic unemployment caused by more efficient manufacturing technologies.[48] This produced three results: an increase in corporate multinationalization, in terms of a search for markets in less-developed nations combined with a cost-cutting relocation of manufacturing plants overseas; a growing emphasis on market research and more sophisticated advertising, aimed at exploiting every nook and cranny of the domestic consumer base; and intensified development of planned obsolescence, of methods for accelerating the consumption of commodities domestically.

The latter two of these features are the most significant for the rising importance of the image, simulacrum (Baudrillard), or spectacle (Debord). (This ascendancy also, paradoxically, triggered the much-touted "crisis of representation," for once the image took over the realm formerly known as reality, it lost the distinction between object and image on which the very notion of representation depends.) The unprecedented rate of commodity turnover made durable, material objects less attractive to capital than more ephemeral commodities. "The half-life of a typical Fordist product was, for example, from five to seven years, but flexible accumulation has more than cut that in half in certain sectors (such as textile and clothing industries), while in others—such as the so-called 'thoughtware' industries (e.g., video games and computer software programmes)—the half-life is down to less than eighteen months."[49] The most ephemeral products are those, like video games, geared toward offering the consumer an experience. Ideally, as is the case for many segments of the rapidly expanding service industry, such an experience could be repeated again and again with little or no variation. But whereas the Western consumer's need for, say, a vacuum cleaner or a car has come to seem relatively self-evident, the need or desire for less-tangible experiences must be instilled, implanted. Thus the immense growth of the advertising industry.

Images have become a (if not *the*) primary commodity form, both in and through advertising. The expansion of the mass electronic media may represent a reaction to capital's efforts to reach more and more consumers, or a precondition for those efforts; either way, what is significant is the sheer extent to which mass media permeate virtually every nation. If images have always been the primary tool of advertising, this is especially so in postmodernity because companies can offer improvements on the *image* of a competitor's product (or their own) far faster than they can develop products with improved performance.

But images are also a significant *object* of advertising now, and culture itself is a commodity to be advertised. The aesthetic object, and the experience it offers, is an ideal postmodern commodity precisely because it is not quantifiable; since the experience of each book, painting, CD recording, web site, or live performance is unique, one can consume a presumably infinite number of such objects. While most consumers won't buy more than one vacuum cleaner, or for that matter more than one copy of a particular book, the same consumer may be induced to buy any number of books based on their presumed similarity to the first book. Popular fiction genres (romance or crime series) have capitalized on this dynamic for many years; as I write, the current more "serious" literary examples of immensely successful series marketing are the late Patrick O'Brian's seafaring novels and J. K. Rowling's "Harry Potter" books for children. (But both of these depend, unlike "pulp" genres, on the identity of single authors.)

One example of this increased commodification of aesthetic objects (as one form of what I am calling, broadly, the image) is the explosion of the art market, especially in New York in the 1980s. During that decade, more than forty new galleries opened in the city.[50] Compared to the "handful of galleries" available to artists in New York City in 1945, by the mid-eighties local artists were exhibiting their work in 680 locations.[51] This commodification also meant that art became a major investment tool during that decade's corporate boom, a boom that was itself a prime example of the reign of the image, based as it was on largely fictional capital.

The importance of the image in the postmodern political sphere is almost self-evident, its classic examples ranging from the Nixon-Kennedy debate to the irrelevance of economic facts (such as a major recession) in the successful images of both Ronald Reagan and Margaret Thatcher during the 1980s. "Spin doctors" and "handlers" may have been political fixtures in various guises for some time, but the challenge posed by political practice to the distinction between ideology and facts has been growing. This tendency of fact and representation to blur has been greatly magnified by the all-pervasive presence of the media, and the way in which personal experience (of, say, unemployment) has come to feel unreal or, precisely, unrepresentative in the face of cheery televisual representations of national boom. In this sense, individual or group experience of political conditions has been usurped by mediating images and fictions.

Harvey speaks of postmodernism's basis in "the aestheticizing of politics," and both he and Jameson diagnose, to their concern, an accompanying depoliticization of aesthetics.[52] For Jameson, this depoliticization takes the form, famously, of a postmodern aesthetic marked by depthlessness, a loss of historicity, and the "waning of affect."[53] These characteristics are a function of the changed position of the artwork as commodity in the accelerated world of postmodern capitalism; in Jameson's view, postmodern artworks also reproduce and reinforce that world by accustoming the postmodern reader to the disorientation she or he inevitably experiences when versions of reality are too numerous and fragmented to provide any sense of stability. In the modernist era, an artwork could survive for a long time (sometimes for a depressingly long time) outside the market, frequently occupying an oppositional space by virtue of its shocking, unsettling aesthetics. The time-lag between the production of, say, D. H. Lawrence's *Lady Chatterley's Lover* and its almost-universal acceptance as a classic could be marked in decades; under postmodern capital's demand for constant innovation, the time-lag for a similar postmodern work might be measured in weeks. The material reality formerly legible in a work, in the form of the circumstances of its production and its intended, discrete audience, has been evacuated in a world where new images are immediately snatched from their initial context to be circulated in the depersonalized systems of advertising and the market. A producer's name may circulate with the work, but it generally functions not to point back to materiality but as another image, more like a brand label by which the image can be distinguished from other images and grouped with some similar images.

The bottom line of all these changes is that in postmodernity, there can be no such thing as an oppositional image. To be more specific, the linkage of image with context that formerly determined the oppositionality of an image's meaning is ruptured by postmodern market pressures, such that an image may now appear in any number of contexts and can thus have any number of meanings. The postmodern image goes everywhere, flashing from the museum to the Internet to T-shirts and back. Andy Warhol's Campbell's soup cans might be a paradigmatic early example, although in 1962 they might still have been read in the light of the historical avant-gardes as a parodic critique of the museum's complicity with commerce. Perhaps they would become fully postmodern if Warhol had, at some point during the corporate art-buying frenzy of the 1980s, sold them to the Campbell's company for display in their corporate headquarters.

If the image occupies a central location in contemporary society, what does this mean for a postmodern-feminist way of reading? And for the potential of contemporary fiction to intervene in the political conditions of postmodernity?

There is an aspect of this impressive periodizing paradigm that neither Harvey nor Jameson explores in any detail: the reader.[54] In the creation of meaning at the intersection of an image and its historical-political moment, the reader is a third term to be considered. For a text, be it a billboard or a novel, does not exist in any social sense until it is read. So if the image is central to postmodernity, so is the activity of readers. Without himself diagnosing the specific conditions that have led to this situation, Certeau calls reading the "focus of contemporary culture." He continues, "From TV to newspapers, from advertising to all sorts of mercantile epiphanies, our society is characterized by a cancerous growth of vision, measuring everything by its ability to show or be shown and transmuting communication into a visual journey. . . . The economy itself, transformed into a 'semeiocracy,' encourages a hypertrophic development of reading." Ultimately, "the text is society itself."[55]

And reading is a location of difference—both of its strategic creation and reinforcement, and of its tactical redeployment. (I am not concerned here with how readers differ from one another as *individuals*, but rather in their distinct social locations.) It can be argued that in the postmodern context, readers are themselves produced by the texts they've read, their identities shaped by the intersection of an assortment of received, subject-forming discourses. But those discourses nevertheless appear in different combinations marked by differences of power; otherness is not everywhere the same. Capitalism continues to produce subjects marked by discourses of race, gender, class, and the like—not only because the texts that comprise postmodernity are all inherited and recycled from previous moments, but because capitalism (even postmodern capitalism) *depends* on power differentiations in order to function. This is the strategic function of reading; but there are also multiple tactical productions of difference possible in how we "make ourselves" out of texts. Bearing both in mind, the postmodern aestheticization of politics can also mean a renewed politicization of aesthetics.

In order to think agency in the interaction between the great text of postmodernity and its readers, a localized and specific theory of reception must be added to the periodizing framework. In the following reading of Jameson's postmodern reading praxis, I will compare his systematic or "top-down" interpretations of the postmodern text (which he shares with Harvey) to a more contingent, tactical, "bottom-up" reading. While the latter cannot exist without a sense of the context of postmodernity that the larger, periodizing systems offer, it is a supplement necessary for the production of a theory of agency. For if reading is the paradigmatic activity for the formation of postmodern subjects, politically committed criticism cannot

Postmodern Cities as Postmodern Texts

Architecture has been, as many critics have noted, one of the most significant sites of theorizing about postmodernism. The architecture of the contemporary city provides an ideal object of analysis to materially oriented theorists of the postmodern, for in the city one finds both a spatialized image—a representation—and the determining presence of the material practices of commerce and domesticity. The city is both imaginary and real. In tracing the particular characteristics of the postmodern city, one can also chart the imaginary distance traveled since modernism, for so many of the modern era's dreams and fears—from Rimbaud's hallucinatory *villes* to the "Unreal City" of *The Waste Land*—were embodied in the newly grown, great urban centers.

Not surprisingly, both Jameson and Harvey direct a lot of attention to reading postmodern urban archi-texts. But so do a number of contemporary feminist writers whose approach I would deem feminist-postmodernist; for instance, images of the city figure prominently in the novels of both Acker and Carter. These various theorists' readings of the city provide a very telling point of comparison.

Jameson's reading of John Portman's Westin Bonaventure Hotel in downtown Los Angeles is central to his theory of postmodernism; it remained a fixture of his "cultural logic" essay through each version since its 1984 appearance in *New Left Review*.[56] Jameson himself is careful to warn that none of the texts he chooses to read should be taken as fully exemplary of postmodernism, but a certain air of the typical nevertheless manages to attach itself to the Bonaventure. Its special importance comes from its ability to offer "some very striking lessons about the originality of postmodernist space"—for "we are here in the presence of something like a mutation of built space itself."[57] This aspect of his reading of the hotel—his contentions about the changed experience of space and embodiedness—interests me most. While all the features of the object itself may not be generalizable, Jameson's *way of reading* the Bonaventure does offer insight into the implications of his particular approach.

I will begin by quoting at some length from Jameson's guided tour of the hotel:

> Now consider the escalators and elevators. Given their very real pleasures in Portman, particularly the latter, which the artist has termed 'gigantic kinetic sculptures' and which certainly account for much of the excitement and spectacle of the hotel interior . . . , I believe one has to see such "people movers" (Portman's own term, adapted from Disney) as somewhat more significant than mere functions and engineering components. We know in any case that recent architectural theory has begun to borrow from narrative analysis in other fields and to attempt to see our physical trajectories through such buildings as virtual narratives or stories, as dynamic paths and narrative paradigms which we as visitors are asked to fulfill and to complete with our own bodies and movements. In the Bonaventure, however, we find a dialectical heightening of this process: it seems to me that the escalators and elevators henceforth replace movement but also, and above all, designate themselves as new reflexive signs and emblems of movement proper (something which will become more evident when we come to the question of what remains of older forms of movement in this building, most notably walking itself). Here the narrative stroll has been underscored, symbolized, reified, and replaced by a transportation machine which becomes the allegorical signifier of that older promenade we are no longer allowed to conduct on our own.[58]

In this reading of the postmodern space, Jameson proposes that the former, bodily reality of walking has been displaced by signification and simulation, and the "very real pleasures" of art (the "'gigantic kinetic sculptures'") undergo Disneyfication so that they serve only to divert the viewer from his or her loss of freedom in the total orchestration of postmodernist space-as-control.

One of the striking and impressive aspects of Jameson's entire analysis of the Bonaventure is its sense of materiality, of bodily experience. This has, however, its problematic side. His readers are walked around the hotel, taken from one site to the next, and at each we pause while the guide delivers his analysis. He directs and controls our gaze: "Now consider the escalators and elevators." In this context, the "we" that Jameson customarily uses in place of an authorial "I" (as in "We know in any case that recent architectural theory . . .") also incorporates the reader-tourist, the pronoun itself functioning as a "people mover" in which the reader stands passively and is carried along. Admittedly, such a tour-guide dynamic may be an unavoidable component of any textual exegesis. The critic must always choose some kind of order in which to approach the object's various parts, just as I am doing now. Yet there is something illustrative in the level to which this dynamic becomes explicit in Jameson's language.

Who is the "we" here? (The "we" that, a page later, becomes the more emphatically interpellating "you" of "You are in this hyperspace up to your eyes and your body.")[59] Who are the implied owners of the passage's "our own bodies"? Jameson's reading of this hotel as marking "the disjunction point between the body and the built environment" calls to mind Adrienne Rich's reminder that no such thing as "the body" exists; there are only *bodies,* specific bodies differentiated by the markings of power.[60]

The body for whom this reading is conducted is, I would suggest, the hegemonic body of the straight, white, economically comfortable male. Who else was formerly "allowed to conduct on [*his*] own" "that older promenade" through the urban fabric this building has replaced? Women have certainly never been able to wander alone through city spaces without a tacit awareness always of which places were off-limits, dangerous, liable to subject them to loss of bodily autonomy. Ditto for the particular internalized map of gay men, since their emergence as a visible urban identity group. And one glance outside the Bonaventure at the apparently extratextual reality of Los Angeles—the city where, supposedly, nobody walks, and where the lack of an extensive public transit system might make poorer residents *glad* of a chance to be transported passively from A to B— makes it clear that postmodern architecture is not responsible for the city's brutal division between poverty-ravaged areas where the streets are filled with people of color and other pristine neighborhoods where the "Private Security" signs remind those same people that walking here will most likely subject them to the twitching of drapes in front windows and an impromptu interview with the forces of law and order.[61] Admittedly, well-off white men have never *really* been safe to walk through the city as they wish either; but the ideology of what has come to be called the Enlightenment subject allowed them to feel *entitled* to that right.

As Thomas Foster has suggested, and as Hartsock's, Hooks's, and Miller's suspicions of the timing of the "death of the subject" imply, postmodernism may simply mean that formerly privileged men are now experiencing a similar loss of self—and of their sense of bodily autonomy—to that which had previously been all other peoples' condition.[62] Certeau, too, proposes that because of the hugely increased emphasis on the "silent" and anonymous act of consumption, "[m]arginality is today no longer limited to minority groups, but is rather massive and pervasive. . . . Marginality is becoming universal." However, he also adds, "That does not mean the [marginal] group is homogeneous."[63] As the city reminds us, the postmodern loss of self still gets played out in very different ways among the privileged versus economic, racial, and/or sexual Others.

This same holds true for the freedom to travel through narrative, to which Jameson explicitly and insightfully connects "our physical trajectories." Literary critics have pointed out that the implied reader of most classic texts is not universal but raced (white) and gendered (male). Actual readers who have not shared this implied reader's subject-positions have had to choose between a smooth passage through the narrative predicated on a kind of erasure of self (a masquerade) or repeatedly bumping up against their unwelcomeness in the narrative, in the form of painful representations of their "peers" or their painful absence. What has been lost in postmodernism, in the loss of a unified narrative, is again something that was never a universal possession.

However, "when we come to the question of what remains of older forms of movement in this building, most notably walking," the tour group finds not that walking has become impossible—as Jameson's reading of the elevators as a compensation for the loss of walking might lead "us" to expect—but that it has become *multiple*. While there is no one privileged narrative route through the building (architects call this the *marche*), there are several entrances and exits, several (admittedly almost indistinguishable) towers to explore. This explains the connection between the building and postmodern written texts. For if the only example of narrative movement in the Bonaventure were the invariable trajectory of the elevators and escalators, what would it have in common with postmodernist writing, whose features (in Jameson's own description) are pastiche and schizophrenic fragmentation? (An elevator ride sounds like one of the more reductive descriptions of classic realism.) What bothers Jameson is only in small part the forced movement; his larger objection is to the loss of the sense of autonomy provided by one clear narrative path. He confuses this loss with the "breakdown of *all* previous narrative paradigms"; this latter phrase is his description of a literary text that he equates to the Bonaventure, Michael Herr's *Dispatches*, in which the narrative is fractured and unable to account conclusively for the characters' experiences.[64] But Herr's text still uses narrative, to compelling effect. And when Lyotard, for instance, attacks the grand or metanarratives, he also emphasizes the importance of

1 / A POLITICIZED POSTMODERNISM   49

retaining existing narrative modes of knowledge in a newly pluralistic arrangement. Postmodernism, whether in the Bonaventure or in an Acker novel, does not mean the loss of *all* narratives but the rejection of one, privileged narrative.

Jameson's method of reading postmodernism, as it emerges in this case study, ends up producing the very object it criticizes, a generalized and indiscriminate condition of otherness. "We" the readers are carried along helplessly, offered only his narrative and denied the use of our own (various) bodies. As Suleiman has pointed out, Jameson discusses meaning as though it inhered in the text itself, so naturally he finds only the meaning he was looking for.[65] This is the problem of all systematizing or text-based models, and why they need to be supplemented by variously situated, reader-based microanalyses. To be fair, Jameson himself seems to admit this necessity at one point, rejecting the "explanatory choice between the alternatives of agency and system."[66] System analysis, which Jameson's often seems solely to be, can only be performed from one point of view, whether it be that of the Enlightenment subject or that, in a patriarchy-based model, of the white middle-class female. Like Certeau's evocation of looking down on the sprawling fabric of New York from the World Trade Center, a historical-theoretical overview "transforms the bewitching world by which one was 'possessed' into a text that lies before one's eyes. It allows one to read it, to be a solar Eye, looking down like a god."[67] One can forget the specificity of embodiedness—the body through which one can be "possessed"—in this specular project. The theorist looks down on the crowded lobby-space of postmodernism from the glass elevator, perhaps protesting the passivity to which that location restricts him; still, he prefers the pleasure of mastery it affords to the confusing milling-about going on down there on the floor.

Harvey, for his part, pauses in his analysis of the economics of postmodern architectural development in real cities to offer extended readings of two films, *Blade Runner* and *Wings of Desire*, that attempt to represent postmodern cities from alternating bird's-eye and street-level perspectives. Both films also explore the boundaries and pleasures of embodiment. Harvey finds little political merit in either, little basis on which to develop a theoretical approach that could address the power dynamics of both locations (strategic and tactical). Yet in Harvey's own analysis, the problems caused by the lack of such an approach become apparent. One example is an endnote concluding his overview chapter, "Postmodernism." The essay has been accompanied by a number of plates, reproductions of a series of female nudes, ranging from classical art to a Citizen watch ad featuring snippets of text superimposed on a rearview photograph of a woman naked but for her timepiece. Here is the bulk of that note:

> The illustrations used in this chapter have been criticized by some feminists of a postmodern persuasion. They were deliberately chosen because they allowed comparison across the supposed pre-modern, modern and postmodern divides. The classical Titian nude is actively reworked in Manet's modernist Olympia. Rauschenberg simply reproduces through postmodernist collage, David Salle superimposes different worlds, and the Citizen's Watch advertisement . . . is a slick use of the same postmodern technique for purely commercial purposes. All the illustrations make use of a woman's body to inscribe their particular message. The additional point I sought to make is that the subordination of women, one of the many 'troublesome contradictions' in bourgeois Enlightenment practices (see p. 14 above and p. 252 below), can expect no particular relief by appeal to postmodernism. I thought the illustrations made the point so well that no further elaboration was necessary. But, in some circles at least, these particular pictures were not worth their usual thousand words. Nor, it seems, should I have relied on postmodernists appreciating their own technique of telling a slightly different story by way of the illustrations as compared to the text.[68]

Superimposing my own feminist reading, with its specific agenda, on Harvey's reading of the plates, I would argue that this note suggests a frustration (almost a nostalgia) similar to Jameson's, in response to the loss of a single thread of meaning that is *the* correct reading. His quick, one-phrase summaries of what each picture means (repeated from the body of the essay) assume that such things are clear, self-evident, should "ma[k]e the point" without "further elaboration."

The problem is not that the pictures did not speak volumes, but that they "were not worth their *usual* thousand words" because of the interference of some clearly *un*usual readers. Harvey marginalizes these readers by identifying them as "some feminists of a postmodern persuasion"—unnamed critics, adopting their theoretical viewpoint not with a serious conviction but with a questionable, vague "persuasion." Harvey has already made it clear that this persuasion is not to be taken seriously; he nowhere engages with it in any depth, but rather notes that, "[c]uriously, most movements of this sort [the new democratic struggles] . . . pay scant attention to postmodernist arguments, and some feminists (e.g., Hartsock, 1987) are hostile."[69] Their objections therefore represent only the failure of "certain circles" (again, a term evoking not a rigorous theoretical position but a clique or coterie) to hear what the pictures *actually* say.

What is exemplary in Harvey's rather pained response is his failure to imagine how Others might read, and the accompanying assumption that readings can be controlled by the author. He expects these female nudes to convey, on the one hand, the centrality of indiscriminate appropriation to postmodernism—and, on the other, a message to women that postmodernism will not save them. His authorial intention, in "deliberately" using the images toward critical ends, should surely (he presumed) have exempted him from being considered like those other men who "make use of a woman's body to inscribe their particular message." But this particular appropriation seems to have failed because of its limited sense of what context means. Here, context means only the context of production: what the author intended. Harvey wants to claim the multiplicity of postmodern textual meaning—the possibility that the illustrations might be "telling a slightly different story" from the one on which his essay focuses—but also to maintain control over it, so the two stories will be sure to work in concert with one another, not produce potential ruptures. But the context of production must also extend to the subsequent production of the text by various readers. Reading is not passive reception but productive activity.

"Some" feminist readers apparently took the materials at hand and came up with a different possible meaning. This reading focused on a male critic whose engagement with feminism seemed less than impressive: the discussion on "p. 14 above and p. 252 below" amounts to one phrase in each location. These readers then saw images of female nudes being used to *flesh out* a discussion of something other than gender, and reached their own conclusions about the message being sent.

Again, bodies are part of the narrative movement here, but their difference (from other bodies) is not accounted for. In looking at how bodies use textual spaces, I might emphasize that I am not reading bodies as essences, as the grounding-points of experience that determine how one reads. Rather, bodies are themselves one of the texts that comprise each subject; they too take on varied meanings across space and time and inflect the meanings of other experiences. (I will develop the implications of this reading of specific postmodern bodies in my discussion of Kathy Acker.) There is certainly no simple opposition between male, nonfeminist critics—who like to map the world from the disembodied vantage of the skyscraper—and female, feminist critics who think through their earthbound bodies. The postmodernist feminists whose work I now turn to read both cities and bodies as texts that confine readers but whose meanings are also subject to active production by readers (who are themselves, bodies and all, newly produced in the process).

WALKING THE STREETS: WOMEN IN THE CITY

As I noted in first raising the trope, thinking of a city as the image of a postmodernist text is useful in part for maintaining an awareness of both terms' insistent materiality. Various people may live in a city in any number of ways, but there are basic facts and structures that cannot be wished away. The structures of money and power are built into the city's fabric, as into the fabric of texts. One inevitably negotiates these structures in moving about the city and in reading a text, but the postmodern textualization of reality means that one also inevitably negotiates these structures internalized in one's own body and consciousness. There is no space for forming oppositional identities outside of these structures. Jameson's and Harvey's maps of postmodernity emphasize the determining power of this material infrastructure.

But the trope of the city suggests to postmodernist feminism (at least) three things: first, the impossibility of avoiding existing power structures and their materiality, as they determine where various bodies may walk and how they are treated in the city's various quarters; but also the irreducible difference between, and diversity of, the experiences and trajectories of various people in the city (what philosopher Iris Marion Young refers to as the inevitable acknowledgment of "unassimilated otherness" that comes from the overlapping of city neighborhoods); and the possibility of pursuing new paths *within* and *among* the city's existing material confines.[70]

Certeau suggests, "Rather than remaining within the field of a discourse that upholds its privilege by inverting its content (speaking of catastrophe and no longer of progress), one can try another path: . . . one can analyze the microbe-like, singular and plural practices which an urbanistic system was supposed to administer or suppress, but which have outlived its decay."[71] He adds a note to historical descriptions of the postmodern city that qualifies the pessimism of Jameson's and Harvey's visions, suggesting that the decline of the great urban centers of the modern era has allowed neglected, no-longer-useful parts of the city to nurture more than weeds. The city-as-concept (rather than accident or organic growth) arose as a means of *strategic* planning, aimed at containing troublesome elements. (This was the case, for instance, with Hausmann's counterrevolutionary restructuring of the Paris streets after the uprisings of 1848.)[72] But now, according to Certeau, "if in discourse the city serves as a totalizing and almost mythical landmark for socioeconomic and political strategies, urban life increasingly permits the re-emergence of the element that the urbanistic project excluded."[73] It is a space where—within certain very operative limits—public and private spaces are constantly redeployed by different factions, diverted from their intended uses. It is a text constantly being rewritten.

The same fragmentation is taking place in texts informed by a postmodernist theory of reading. The immense postmodern commodification of discourses and texts puts all language in circulation at once, rendering it available for both commercial development and subversive redeployment. Texts read as feminist-postmodernist themselves perform such a redeployment, moving among the material structures of the discourses of power by taking back-routes and shortcuts that create new narrative trajectories. Like Certeau's "figures of pedestrian rhetoric," these texts each represent a reading of the map of postmodernity.[74]

In closing, I want to read segments of two texts that I would consider postmodernist-feminist—Pratt's essay and Acker's novel—and suggest how their visions of the city supplement the bird's-eye view and open up the possibility of agency. The two authors represent cities both as examples of the material conditions of postmodernity and as texts to be read/produced—in fact, as the unavoidable intersection of these two vectors.

Pratt's autobiographical essay explicitly juxtaposes the view from above with the practices of below. As a child, Pratt was taken by her father to the top of the courthouse in her small southern American town, to see "a view that had been his father's, and his, and would be mine."[75] In this viewpoint from the position of the Law, the town is orderly and literally subject-centered. The institutions of hegemonic power are visible: school, church, jail, county offices. The outlying homes of blacks and poor whites are not visible.

Pratt learns, however, that the literal oversights and absences of this centered account render it a misrepresentation—not only of the social fabric but of the subject herself. Bit by bit, she rejects both such composed texts and the unitary language that composes them. She learns, in part, by unknowingly deviating from the narrative trajectory this text asks her to fulfill with her body; as a lesbian, she finds herself cast out from her family place of economic privilege specifically because she has altered or misread the meaning of the female body. She also hears gaps in the language of this narrative: when an African-American waiter interrupts the guests at an all-white luncheon (at which Pratt is present) to contradict their claims that there was never slave-trading in their town's history, this awakens in her an awareness of the forced silences that enable the production of a single coherent narrative of a space (21).

This cohesive view is contrasted with Pratt's life now in the city: "I live in a part of Washington, D.C. that white suburbanites called 'the jungle' during the uprising of the '60s—perhaps still do, for all I know. When I walk the two-and-a-half blocks to H St., NE, to stop in at the bank, to leave my boots off at the shoe-repair-and-lock shop, I am most usually the only white person in sight. I've seen two other whites, women, in the year I've lived here. (This does not count white folks in cars, passing through. In official language, H St., NE, is known as 'The H Street Corridor,' as in something to be passed through quickly, going from your place, on the way to elsewhere)" (11). This is not the radially organized space of "the courthouse square with me at the middle" (17); trajectories across, into, and through it are divergent, shaped by material needs (the bank, shoes, getting "elsewhere") and material circumstances (car or foot). With this fragmenting of space goes a fragmenting of identity and language. Identity is not only divided into black and white; whites are divided, too, into "white suburbanites," "whites, women," and "white folks in cars." Each group has its own language that produces divergent meanings for the same physical space: where "I live," "the jungle," the "Corridor."

But Pratt suggests room for intervention in this thoroughly fragmented, urban, postmodern condition. She uses her daily (and economically necessary) walks through her non-neighborhood to analyze the institutionalized power imbalances that affect language and make political alliances difficult and necessarily temporary. Pratt develops a practice she calls "speaking-to," noticing her own and others' decisions to communicate or not to communicate as they pass on the street. The person to whom she says "hey" may be a young urban African-American man, an older African-American raised in the segregated south, an elderly disabled white woman, or an African-American woman Pratt's own age. She acknowledges that these "speakings-to" are inflected by the histories of oppression that have passed between the groups (racial, sexual, economic) to which these individuals belong (12).

But momentary microalliances also develop through the specificities of Pratt's urban walks; each occasion subtly reconfigures the city neighborhood, depending on not only the intersection of group histories but also the changing physical conditions. Thus Pratt may feel (and act) alienated by class differences from "the young professional white woman" on her way to work; but meeting her in the dark, Pratt speaks, in order to form a momentary alliance, a bond and agreement, needing her "for physical safety" (13). Here, gender and race take precedence. Similar microalliances generate between Pratt and the southern-raised, older black men, who talk about "home" together when regional identity and homesickness push a history of racism temporarily aside; and between Pratt and the black women who act friendly to her and her white lover because they are women enjoying each other's company. Pratt suspects that the women choose to emphasize this sisterhood rather than her lesbianism, but fears that such an alliance might be fractured if they realized her lover was not only white but Jewish (12–13).

Yes, these are small and seemingly insignificant moments of solidarity; they are only tactics, which means they do not make the *space* their own, but rather have only fleeting moments of *time*.[76] But even they can suggest how both space and language are not fixed from above, and can be—to a certain extent—reconfigured through localized practices and complex notions of identity. Such a reconceptualization of politics can be of great utility to feminists negotiating postmodernity. This model, this way of reading the city-text, allows for movement and exploration within the given architecture of political structures including language. It enables resistant movement within these structures without relying on the homogenizing and reductive positing of a pure, oppositional subject-space that elides differences among women (and) Others.

The basis of Pratt's alliances in language—in the interpellating moments when, by speaking, she offers or invokes a temporary image of identity based in shared interests—has implications for the feminist postmodern novel. Acker's 1986 novel *Don Quixote*, which I discuss at more length in the following chapter, explores the dangers and potentialities of the positioning of different subjects in the textualized space of postmodernity. Acker's text, too, locates the city in language as well as in literal geography. But more than Pratt, who rejects the overview offered her as a child, Acker retains a sense of both the big-picture context of postmodernity and the local movements that can alter and reconfigure it.

Don Quixote takes place primarily in a shifting urban landscape that is sometimes 1980s London, sometimes a vaguely postapocalyptic New York, and sometimes St. Petersburg/Leningrad in the years surrounding the Russian Revolution. The protagonist is a female knight who tries to claim an identity by naming herself Don Quixote.[77] But in putting on the name, she finds she has also assumed an obligation to fulfill Quixote's narrative; she finds that existing structures of language act materially on the living. However, the contemporary context and the reader's specific location in it unavoidably alter the pretext, and this new knight's crusade is against the "evil enchanters" who have rendered romantic love impossible for the heterosexual woman in postmodernity: the forces of capitalism and patriarchy.

This knight's journey is dislocated not only by her sudden, unexplained movement from city to city (perhaps because the evil enchanters operate multinationally) but also by the narrative's tendency to peter out and to take excursions through numerous fragments of previously existing texts. Characters from the various texts appear, exit, or blur with Quixote or with other characters, so that the idea of consistent subjectivity is undermined by the inherited and composite nature of consciousness in a fully textualized society.

The juxtaposition of textual fragments connects spatial displacement (Don Quixote's dispossessed position as a poor person in the city) with the linguistic homelessness of postmodern subjects. Quixote recalls, "I ran away to the city because I didn't feel normal in a normal household and, wanting to be me, I wanted to express me" (115). What she finds, however, is that she cannot "express" herself because language cannot be purely oppositional: "I wanted to find a meaning or myth or language that was mine, rather than those which try to control me; but language is communal and here is no community" (194–95). Acker is quite clear, however, that this condition is not an indiscriminate postmodern condition, but is also complicated by gender, for women have been constructed by this existing communal language as silent objects of desire. Quixote was unhappy in the nuclear home because she was raped by her father; and when she leaves that old narrative, "Don Quixote could no longer speak. Being born into and part of a male world, she had no speech of her own. All she could do was read male texts which weren't hers" (39). The male-authored texts Acker chooses to pass through emphasize the ideology of female inferiority and its material consequences for women.

Histories of domination are likewise inscribed in the structure of Acker's cities; as language attempts to determine the possible paths the speaker's thought might follow, so the city's architecture prescribes the lives lived within it. As in Certeau's model, the historical architecture of cities, like language, seeks to contain subversion:

> Walking the streets.
> Tatlin designed a city. Tatlin took unhandlable passion and molded it. . . . When Biely described this passion, he constructed language as if it was a building. If architecture isn't cool cold, people can't live in it. (46)

Being a streetwalker has, of course, a different meaning for women than for men; this is not a factor that Certeau's "figures of pedestrian rhetoric" explicitly consider. "Walking the streets" can mean occupying a designated space (the red-light district) where potentially disruptive desires can be contained within the semiofficial map of the city's commercial transactions—but it also seems the only alternative to the passive, asexual femininity that existing representations offer the knight. For she is dependent on the structures of city and language: "It is you, city. Market of the world, that is, of all representations. Since you're the only home I've ever known, without your representation or misrepresentation of me I don't exist" (197).

But if escape is impossible because no outside of the postmodern city-of-representations exists, subversive movement *within* existing spaces remains possible. The single, prescribed narrative trajectory (*marche*) is not the only option. *Don Quixote* first disrupts that *marche* by its textual wanderings, questioning the desirability of the journey's expected end and frustrating the usual desire-driven movement through plot with an aimless accretion of fragments. For instance, a "girls'-school" sex scene lifted from the Marquis de Sade's *Juliette* is disrupted by the repetition of each line of dialogue from two to four times (166–71). This repetition intervenes in the smooth progression of arousal and satisfaction that would normally characterize the implied reader's *marche* through pornography.

In its overall pastiche structure, Acker's novel offers a model—like Jameson's reading of the Bonaventure—of one way of reading postmodernly (and reading postmodernity). It enacts the theoretical notion that readers change texts even as they are themselves shaped by them. Both "classic" texts like *Macbeth* and "lowbrow" monster movies take on surprising (and sometimes funny) meanings when read from the position of the space they create for women and/or the poor. But more importantly, they take on surprising meanings when read against one another, as one appropriated textual fragment becomes part of the context in which the next can be read. Such a strategy again highlights the fragmentation, the incommensurability of the postmodern subject constructed by texts and images. While Acker's Quixote is constrained and physically hurt by those structures that every text seems to reproduce—constructions of women, for instance, as object and victim—she also identifies the network of alleys that cuts across them: the racial, economic, and other differences of location that make these images, these structures of subjectivity, read differently.

This feminist-postmodernist strategy of reading suggests another possibility to Jameson's and Harvey's characteristic readings of postmodernist structures as offering only fictive consolations for the real dislocations of the time. Both Acker's and Pratt's texts point out the activity of readers in producing the meanings that the overall map of postmodernity assumes in various contexts, meanings whose multiplicity allows agency through the tactical deployment of different fragmentary fictions of the self (as raced, sexed, economically identified, etc.). When read from a feminist-postmodernist perspective, these texts are able to turn the generalized postmodern condition of textually induced otherness toward specific, resistant uses. The production of embodiment through cultural spaces need not only be, as Jameson documents, a disorienting experience that induces passivity. Through fictions, readers' bodies also become differently configured; different meanings of those bodies come into play. What emerges at each reading is not only a new text, but a new reader.

2
Kathy Acker's Unreasonable Texts

The question that runs throughout Kathy Acker's work is how people outside the mainstream of power—primarily women, but also men of color, gay men, and the poor—can claim agency when in fact they are very much "insiders," their identities defined within existing systems of language and power. In Acker's novels, society is a series of texts written by the powerful; its unfortunate characters must exploit the subtle differences among the multiple discourses of dominant culture if they are to rewrite themselves.

The question of agency is a troubling one for postmodernism, but any feminist work depends on the assumption that some agency remains possible despite the power of oppressive structures. While my treatment of the issue in this chapter engages with a major debate in contemporary theory, I suggest Acker's model of identity—a model based on acts of rereading—as only one possible answer. It presumes that the texts constructing "the subject" never wholly *determine* that subject, to draw on Judith Butler's distinction.[1] No single text defines anyone, nor tells the whole story of our identifications and allegiances. The plagiaristic, pastiche technique of Kathy Acker's writing—the way she builds her novels out of scraps from various literary and popular traditions—breaks up the homogeneity of culture, exposing the numerous and varied discourses that at any moment influence and shape each of us. Contradictions arise among these discourses, allowing for new deployments and combinations.[2]

Stuart Hall has suggested that the success of any emergent political force rests on its ability to exploit the contradictions among various accepted versions of "the truth about the world" and to recombine parts of existing stories to offer new identifications, new stories that appeal to already formed subjects.[3] Acker's work begins to suggest how feminism might do this, by offering its characters and readers the possibility of variations within the repetition of existing language and narratives. Acker finds, in the discrepancies among various (undeniably oppressive) narratives of identity, subversive pleasure, humor, and agency.

However, there is always a second impulse in Acker's work, alongside this largely poststructuralist insistence on identity as received and textual. This is a more angry, oppositional model of both identity and text, which draws on Marxism, on feminist identity politics, and even on a certain, more old-fashioned faith in the inherent revolutionary potential of the genuine artistic act.[4] The two are by no means always in harmony. But to read Acker as feminist-postmodernist necessarily means pursuing aspects of both these apparently contradictory approaches. Rather than canceling one another out, the two models of textual politics lead Acker's novels to a fruitfully complex vision of the ambivalent relation of marginal readers to received texts. Recognizing, on the one hand, that history is composed only of texts and, on the other, that texts are always mired in history (and thus, *material* in their impact) produces a practice of reading that moves beyond either mere relativism or binary opposition to create an identity patched together from local, tactical acts of reuse.

In this chapter, I want to focus on how the tension between poststructuralist and oppositional approaches plays out in Acker's attacks on one central aspect of postmodern capitalism: the logic of rationalism and its accompanying economic activity, rationalization. I follow this issue through three of her novels from the 1980s, *My Death My Life by Pier Paolo Pasolini* (1984), *Don Quixote* (1986), and *Empire of the Senseless* (1988). These texts respond to the period of full-grown Reaganism in the United States—a time marked by deindustrialization and the ascendancy of charismatic politics; Acker's postmodernist strategies seem particularly suited to such a conjuncture. My discussion of these novels seeks to trace a historical development from novel to novel, not so much to create a narrative of Acker's own career but, rather, in order to see how shifting rhetorical tactics can respond to the unfolding logic of postmodern capitalism, especially its growing ability to co-opt and rationalize even direct opposition.

Rationality and monstrosity

I want to set up this chapter's readings of Acker's work by looking at one emblematic scene from *Don Quixote* that offers a vivid image of the contingent, half-inside/half-outside self produced by her rereadings of existing texts.

Throughout her work, and perhaps particularly in the three novels under discussion here, Acker proceeds largely by collaging together portions of other texts within a loose narrative framework. The constant acts of reading in which Acker and her characters engage (for scenes of reading are also frequently featured *within* the novels) exemplify the tactics available to postmodern subjects, who must build a self out of existing images and stories. People who seek a resistant politics, a resistant identity, have available to them only the language already in circulation and already infused with oppressive power relations. They cannot erase what power writes about (and *on*) their particular bodies; nor can they counter such descriptions with wholly uncompromised, authentic language of their own. But they can be *bricoleurs* who rearrange existing phrases and paragraphs to alter the received story.

However, as the metaphors of those last two sentences imply, any *bricolage* involving rearranging texts written onto human bodies would seem to entail a violent dismemberment. Acker's novels are very much concerned with the violence already done to various groups of human bodies by available representations of them. But the rhetorical practice these novels offer suggests that the answer may be to treat bodies as *always already* dismembered, always composed of partial and contradictory meanings. This dismembering applies to both human bodies (and the identity categories in which they get grouped—female, black, young, etc.) and the bodies of texts.

One of the ways of talking about such a dismembered self, stitched together from *re*membered scraps of text, is to call it monstrous. Monsters are half-and-half, borderline creatures who horrify precisely because they are at once human and not human, natural and unnatural.[5] Monsters are also traditionally often the product of human scientific endeavor and the highest aspirations of Enlightenment rationality. (I am thinking, perhaps obviously, of Frankenstein's creation.) In a playful scene in *Don Quixote*, Acker capitalizes on this image of rationality backfiring.

The passage comes from the middle section of the novel, "Other Texts," in which Acker's female Quixote retells a series of familiar stories. One of them is a Japanese monster movie. Two mutant monsters—Megalon and Godzilla—have emerged as a result of nuclear weapons testing (identified as a "rational" behavior).[6] As the movie's recounted plot reaches a climax with the monsters fighting to determine the fate of the earth, they pause, incongruously, to discuss human reason, which they agree is the root of oppression:

> "Anti-rationality."
> "In the modern period, exchange value has come to dominate society; all qualities have been and are reduced to quantitative equivalences. This process inheres in the concept of reason. For reason, on the one hand, signifies the idea of a free, human, social life. On the other hand, reason is the court of judgement of calculation, the instrument of domination, and the means for the greatest exploitation of nature. As in De Sade's novels, the mode of reason adjusts the world for the ends of self-preservation and recognizes no function other than the preparation of the object from mere sensory material in order to make it that material of subjugation. Instrumental or ossified reason takes two forms: technological reason developed for purposes of dominating nature and social reason directed at the means of domination aimed at exercising social and political power." (72)

As Daniel Punday has pointed out, "most of the philosophical reasoning in Acker's novels . . . is partially ironic," and this exchange is obviously no exception, as a critique of reason couched in exaggeratedly rational language.[7] By inserting the hyper-rational language of Western sociopolitical analysis—its "on the one hand" and "[o]n the other hand," its "signifies" and "inheres" and "adjusts"—into the middle of a low-budget, non-Western movie, Acker comically deflates this language's pretensions to being always and everywhere the superior and appropriate form of discourse.

Two things are particularly important about what the monsters have to say. First is that they identify reason as *the* central dynamic of "democratic" capitalism. This dynamic carries within itself its own contradiction: it is at once a universal leveling force, framing all things as "quantitative equivalences," and the source of social *in*equalities. In fact, reason enables "subjugation" precisely through its premise that all things can be judged according to one standard of utility. It provides supposedly neutral grounds for "free," unideological comparison, yet its product is domination. It encourages us to use one another and to use nature.

The second is that the monsters themselves are at once reason's progeny and its opponents. They depend on reason for both their language and their very existence. Without "technological reason" they would not exist within their fictional world, where they have been produced by atomic testing. As Cold War monsters, they also derive from the linkage of technology to "social reason . . . aimed at exercising social and political power." Yet their monstrosity challenges the manipulation of nature, by problematizing the idea of "nature" as "mere sensory material." And they likewise question social reason by suggesting that far from being universally valid, "adjust[ments of] the world for the ends of self-preservation"—such as the development of nuclear weapons—can turn against the manipulator in certain circumstances.

This brief scene embodies the paradoxes in Acker's own practice. It denounces the inequality and destruction at the core of society's current structure, but it depends on that society's products to do so. It raises the question of whether Acker, too, simply subjects all things (texts) to a single standard of utility—to serving her goal of subversive political analysis. Megalon and Godzilla only appear in Acker's novel because they are useful raw material. Again, her construction of a text out of existing images seems merely to extend (in a fashionably poststructuralist way) the "anything goes" tendency of capitalism since its Enlightenment beginnings.

Seeing the more materialist side of Acker's practice depends on the crucial difference between "exchange value" (what the monsters denounce) and use value. While the former presumes universality, the latter always has to consider context. A practice built on use value also "adjusts the world for the ends of self-preservation," but its criteria for utility are necessarily local and contingent. Whereas exchange value implies a strategy, use value depends on fleeting tactics.

READERS AS PART OF HISTORY

I described briefly in the previous chapter the ways in which Acker highlights the different meanings of a given text for different readers, especially female readers. Her novels emphasize the context of reception, partly by focusing on characters who have traditionally not been the implied readers of a mainstream textual tradition (whether literary *or* popular). To the extent that her novels have "main characters" (since even her narrators tend to shift identity and gender), in *My Death My Life by Pier Paolo Pasolini, Don Quixote,* and *Empire of the Senseless* they are, respectively, a (dead) gay man, a "mad" female knight, and a mixed-race cyborg terrorist and her drug-addict male "partner." Like Megalon and Godzilla, these characters tend to have a slightly skewed vision of the discourses that have at once shaped them and cast them out, designating them monstrous.

Again, this sense of the varied uses to which varied readers will put texts offers an answer to the problem of dehistoricization that purportedly accompanies postmodern textual practices. In the previous chapter I suggested that the lack of attention to readers' locations was a crucial gap in the model of history assumed by much theory aimed at historicizing postmodernism; but this is also true even of the historicizing of some critics who argue a hopeful—and feminist—potential for postmodernism. The oppositional practices of "other" readers in Acker's novels can supplement the sense of historical context here, too.

For instance, Linda Hutcheon's *The Politics of Postmodernism* has furthered thinking about postmodernist literature and its attention to historiography; my argument is indebted to her view of postmodernism's inevitably compromised position, its "double coding" as "complicitous critique."[8] But Hutcheon ends up deeply ambivalent about whether postmodernism can offer agency, precisely because she does not consider that a text's meaning is dependent on the context of reception. Rather, she has to invoke authorial intention to distinguish between politicized texts (which she claims for postmodernism) and indifferent ones. Thus she simply dismisses those "vague and unfocused references to the past" found on television or in shopping mall architecture as not postmodernism but mere "commercial exploitation," limiting her definition of postmodernism to the presumably more thoughtful appropriations of history in high culture.[9]

For instance, Hutcheon praises the "motivated historical echoes" and "respectful parody" of architect Charles Moore's design for the Piazza d'Italia in New Orleans.[10] But her analysis focuses on Moore's "respectful" intentions, rather than on exploring what his design's references to Italian history must be "motivated" *by*—which is his specific local *audience*, a community of Italian-Americans. Despite her concern with history and political action, Hutcheon's definition of postmodernism remains largely formalist and elitist. A postmodernist text becomes simply one that is self-reflexive and skeptical about its own use of history. It is hard to assess whether such ironic distance has any progressive potential without addressing the specifics of reception.

Hutcheon's model corresponds to only one side of Acker's practice, the poststructuralist emphasis on the total textualization of experience, including our relation to history: "We only have access to the past today through its traces—its documents, the testimony of witnesses, and other archival materials. In other words, we only have representations of the past from which to construct our narratives or explanations. In a very real sense, postmodernism reveals a desire to understand present culture as the product of previous representations. The representation of history becomes the history of representation."[11] This observation seems integral to Acker's novels, obsessed as they are with investigating the history of representation, particularly the representation of women. But their focus on historically excluded readers also enables the crucial insight that "present culture" is not only "the product of" historical texts; history is also produced *by* present culture, in the form of particular readers. Certeau comments, "Whether it is a question of newspapers or Proust, the text has a meaning only through its readers; it changes along with them."[12] People living in the present actively interpret the (textual) past according to their own locations—not freely or individualistically, but always from an identity that has been produced as *different from other present identities,* and indeed is multiple and fragmentary in itself. The present conjuncture, composed in part of divergent identities and acts of interpretation, is not monolithic but heterogeneous. Thus history's meaning is heterogeneous too.

Readers *of* Acker

Most critics writing about Acker up to this point have also emphasized the side of her work that is, like Hutcheon's description of history, most radically textual. This can at times lead to an account of the otherness produced by reading (in her novels) as an indiscriminate, ubiquitous otherness simply shared by all postmodern readers. Such accounts do not translate easily into a politicized reading practice.

The context of reception for Kathy Acker's work has changed quite rapidly in the past decade or so. While still by no means popular, her novels grew more widely available starting in the late 1980s and were increasingly reviewed in major publications in both the United States and Britain (where she lived for much of the eighties, returning there shortly before her death in 1997). Acker's own marketability as an *outré* media figure—publishing's "bad girl"—led to interviews in a wide (and illustratively bizarre) spectrum of journals, from *Poets and Writers Magazine* to *On Our Backs* ("Entertainment for the Adventurous Lesbian") to the cyberpunk glossy, *Mondo 2000*.[13] *The New York Times Book Review*, in whose pages Acker's work was damned as failed parody and labeled "abusive to women" in 1984,[14] was by 1988 installing her as the "darling of the mid-1980s downtown Manhattan arts scene," comparing her to Gertrude Stein, and paying tribute to "the seriousness of Ms. Acker's purpose."[15] This change of heart in the literary-critical establishment may indicate the extent to which she became a significant figure in at least certain circles of postmodernist "hip."

Born in 1947—although there is great debate about that[16]—Acker self-published her first novel, *Politics*, in 1972.[17] She went on to publish some fifteen books (novels; a book of poems; a libretto, "The Birth of the Poet," produced by Richard Foreman at the Brooklyn Academy of Music in 1985), several short stories, some journalism, and numerous critical essays (published in one volume shortly before her death). She moved to the major U.S. independent publisher Grove Press in 1993, which subsequently reissued a number of the earlier novels; to Picador in Britain in the following year, where the publication of *Blood and Guts in High School* brought her immediate literary celebrity; and eventually to corporate powerhouse Pantheon.[18]

There are several ways of reading this growing success, although it does seem (at least in part) to indicate "the ways in which capitalism informs publishing to the extent that a writer who 'blasphemes' against every conventional value imaginable can be safely incorporated into consumer culture."[19] Joe Moran, in his study of "celebrity" authors, argues convincingly that Acker became increasingly marketable—in both purely commercial and academic-critical terms—because both her novels and her public persona combined weighty poststructuralist intellectualism with streetwise, punk rebellion and the *appearance* of raw, confessional autobiography (particularly in Acker's depictions of sexual relationships and family dysfunction, often involving characters named Kathy). This combination of heady theory and painful experience, he argues, "suggests that the self can be reinvented at the same time as it points to the existence of an innate, deep-seated identity."[20] However, these two strains (in tension with one another) that Moran identifies in Acker's approach are not identical to the two forms of otherness that I have suggested feminist postmodernism necessarily negotiates and combines. The first, which Moran terms a "textual" approach to identity, corresponds with the generally poststructuralist-postmodernist account of otherness as a property of all subjects, rendering them fluid and fragmentary; but the second, "punk-confessional" mode, which Moran calls "essentialist," by no means necessarily links otherness to concrete social divisions.[21] In fact, many sympathetic critical readings of Acker's work run the two together in such a way that her novels seem *only* to describe a diffuse and generalized postmodern otherness.

The more essentialist moment in Acker's writing is manifested not just in her use of apparently autobiographical elements, but also in her frequent representation of acutely painful *bodily* desires as absolutely fundamental to her characters' social experience—and in her search for a language that can break free of existing codes to express those desires.[22] Such hungers point to a reality beyond the purely textual or linguistic—and in doing so they invite academic criticism that combines the insights of poststructuralism with a more psychoanalytic emphasis on desire that exceeds and disrupts language. This has been, I think, the predominant mode in Acker criticism. Acker herself, in interviews and in her work, appears also to endorse such an approach through her discussion not only of Jacques Derrida and Michel Foucault, but also the more overtly psychoanalytical theorists, Jean Baudrillard, Julia Kristeva, Gilles Deleuze and Félix Guattari, and indeed, Jacques Lacan. But for all its value, this critical orientation can tend to minimize discussion of the *historical* and *material* aspects of the reading practice Acker's novels might offer.[23] I am concerned to emphasize those latter aspects because they mark the ways in which this reading practice can be a feminist, as opposed to merely gendered, approach.

As critics' attention focuses on the reaching for a bodily "Real" in Acker's work, femininity becomes less a historical fiction (and a location *within* discourse) than a synonym for this desired, desiring, extradiscursive space—which is in turn allied with the internal otherness of all subjects. For example, Catherine Griggers finds in *Don Quixote* and in Acker's essay, "Realism for the Cause of Future Revolution," what Roland Barthes calls "the subjectivity of the nonsubject," marked by "amatory excess." Griggers also characterizes Acker's readers as "positioned by the text as heteronomous, nongendered, 'non-subjects' in the process of becoming."[24] Kathleen Hulley notes Acker's protest (in *Algeria*) against the white, masculine hegemony's transformation of both "'woman' and 'Arab' into the wholly imaginary signifiers of the Real"; yet she duplicates that elision, by saying of Acker's violent sex scenes, "This is not pornographic, and it surpasses the obscene. This is language scraping as close as possible to an unspeakable, and obliterating 'Real.'"[25] While I will later also defend these sex scenes as central to the search for an active female desire, it seems problematic to turn their images of violence against women into a *metaphor* for the psychosexual construction of language. (Sara Ahmed asks of such "postmodern" readings, "what violence is at stake in this non-reading of violence?")[26] Finally, Robert Siegle—whose comprehensive chapter on Acker's earlier work in *Suburban Ambush: Downtown Writing and the Fiction of Insurgency* was perhaps the first extended study of her oeuvre—suggests that in her texts, "we are all 'women' submitting to the paternal state."[27]

I am lumping together these relatively divergent analyses of Acker's work not in order to dismiss them, but to suggest that the tendency has been to emphasize her practice's affinity with post-*structuralism*. To move toward a political reading of post*modernism*, analysis is necessary of the local, historical contexts that allow the otherness in her texts to bring forth feminist tactics.

Rationalism and opposition in postmodernity

I began by suggesting that Acker's novels identify rationalism as the key dynamic underlying capitalist society and the oppressive inequality it manufactures. I don't want merely to replace one totality—the aspiration of language toward the Real—with another, as the unifying "theme" of her work. Nor, as the Godzilla-Megalon scene illustrated, is Acker's position in relation to rationalism as monolithic as simple opposition. Her novels recognize that opposition fails because of postmodern capitalism's ability to co-opt all direct challenges. Acker contests the extension of rationalized control enabled by the transition from modern, monopoly capitalism to its postmodern, multinational form; but she does so, in part, by working from *within* the specific worlds of various stories (literary and popular) that capitalism tells itself, stories that reinforce rationalism. Her novels see rationalism everywhere, but also suggest that it depends on constantly being reproduced through particular acts of telling and reading, which differ crucially from one another in their local context.

Rationalism has been central to capitalism since its beginnings, as a tendency toward systematization and abstraction that allows all things to be valued on a single, universal scale. Since the Industrial Revolution, rationalism has increasingly been applied to routinizing processes of production and marketing. If such a development is characteristic of modernity, it also continues to be—although differently—central to postmodernity.

Rationalism has faced major challenges from poststructuralist theory in the intellectual sphere, but also from procapitalist voices within the international business community. Nevertheless, I hope to establish that far from being in decline, capitalist rationalism is merely mutating in order to accommodate itself more effectively to the conditions of postmodernity. Ridding itself of its foundations in dualistic thought, rationalistic capitalism is extending its reach to incorporate those modes of living that formerly remained outside the commodity market and potentially oppositional.

Postmodern rationalism seeks to absorb areas formerly free from the market by becoming, in a sense, its own opposite. Contemporary theorists of capitalist management such as best-selling author Tom Peters have argued for what they call an *irrationalizing* of business in order to cope with the more rapidly changing postmodern market: "In a world driven by fashion we must learn to deal with the irrational. No! Exactly wrong. We must learn to revel in the irrational, cotton to it, take it to our bosom, smile at it, grin at it. It's not enough to 'cope with it' or 'deal with it,' though that's more than most of us, trained as administrators, engineers, or scientists, do. Welcoming, laughing at, enjoying: That's more like it!"[28] Peters proposes that businesses can essentially rationalize the "irrational" market by systematizing their approach to the rapidly shifting desires of consumers. Rather than behaving like "administrators, engineers, or scientists," businesspeople should behave like *image marketers*. By doing so, they will be able to create and manipulate consumer demands.

Thus rationalism's newly happy relationship with irrationality derives from postmodernity's reduction of all things to images and representations. Peters's rhetoric demonstrates how identities and discourses formerly outside the market, now that they exist primarily as representations, can be redeployed toward capitalist ends. The very title of Peters's *Liberation Management*—with its echo of "liberation theology"—borrows cheerfully from previously leftist discourses, putting them to use for corporate planners. Oddly (and apparently inadvertently) echoing Bakhtin, Peters suggests the metaphor of the carnival to characterize the ideal postmodern organization's "joyous anarchy" and localized, contingent marketing strategies.[29] He hopes to provide a "new definition of revolution": a revolution signified by the ability of one multinational to lay off thirty-eight of every forty employees as "excess baggage."[30]

In the spheres of production and distribution, the postmodern shift toward decentralization that Peters advocates represents not so much irrationalization as the fruition of Fordist rationalization (at the same time, I would argue, as it also indicates a new phase of capitalism). The Fordist era—approximately 1911–45 in the United States—was characterized by the rationalization of production, distribution, and state planning.[31] The weak point in the Fordist regime of systematization and control was the worker him- or herself; as Antonio Gramsci recognized early on, the mindless, repetitive tasks of the assembly line left workers' minds dangerously (from the bosses' perspective) free. Thus Fordism's historically new efforts to regulate the private behavior of workers were only in part aimed at instilling appropriate consumption habits; they were also geared toward containing the potential threat posed by workers' increased mental freedom.[32]

Postmodern rationalization seems to have solved that problem, by attacking the uncolonized areas of the worker's identity on two fronts: (1) by producing increased worker identification with the corporation, and (2) by multiplying the number of ways in which the worker as, also, *consumer* is interpellated by various products and services. On the first strategy, Peters cites a successful German firm named (appropriately) Rational, praising its exemplary rejection of management-worker hierarchies and its "small is beautiful" philosophy. A key to Rational's success is the flexibility allowed by the workers' "self-discipline" and desire for "self-actualization," which render rigid supervisory structures unnecessary.[33] In place of these structures, this firm, like many companies worldwide, has instituted procedures for encouraging worker input and innovation, ostensibly offering them more freedom and more active participation in the production process. By soliciting their workers' mental as well as physical investment in the work process, these companies cleverly frame increased unfreedom as increased freedom, thereby defusing the danger of worker sedition latent in Fordist organizational structures.

On the second front, postmodern capitalism adapts itself, under the paradoxical guise of *de*rationalization, to subtle nuances of taste and to the most microscopic shifts in consumption, enabling it to tap into new markets both domestically and overseas. What this means is that consumers, like the Rational workers, are increasingly the objects of rationalization. They become commodities for marketing divisions to consume. As one of Acker's narrators puts it, "I am the commodity. The commodity buys me."[34] This too signals both a fulfillment of Fordism and a departure from it. The very success of Fordism meant that by the mid-1960s, the domestic markets of industrialized nations were saturated and new markets had to be found or created.[35] Responding to this need, technologies of microscale market research and the willingness of producers to try what Peters calls "zany" marketing ploys (i.e., those that don't appeal to the mainstream consumer) have transformed the undifferentiated mass of the market into innumerable fragmented submarkets and target groups, extending capital's reach.

Thus, capitalism can now tailor itself to the most personal, formerly private identifications of a wide range of consumers. "Derationalization" allows rationalization to get inside the subject in a way not previously possible. Peters offers the buzzword "diversity" for this new colonization of foreign and nonmainstream-domestic markets: "The message of this section ["Fashion, Diversity, the Globe"] is fashion. Translation: diversity. The globe is shrinking. But as it shrinks, oddly enough, it is becoming more diverse, not less."[36] His appropriation of a term that has also become a buzzword for progressive multiculturalists is not coincidental. Theorists of the relationship of nonhegemonic groups to postmodernism have argued that the commodification of identity now happening on a broad scale has long been a fact of life for white women and for people of color.[37] Disempowered people have been offered on the market both as bodies to be consumed and as easily targeted consumers. It may be that postmodernity simply marks a generalizing of this commodification of identity to everyone, even formerly privileged or immune social groups. The new danger in this extension of personal commodification is that histories of oppression and ongoing struggles for self-representation get lost in postmodern capital's reduction of all identity differences to mere market "diversity."

Thomas Foster and others see, nonetheless, hopeful potential in the breakdown of otherness caused by postmodernity's commodification of all identities. While all identities are not commodified equally, capitalism's willingness to sacrifice the binary ideology of otherness to an extended market may signal a "crisis in dualistic thinking."[38] (I will draw on Foster's argument further to talk about the new permutations of identity Acker raises in *Empire of the Senseless*.) But this crisis of dualism also means that any attack on hegemonic rationalism that simply embraces irrationality as an oppositional stance will miss its mark in the postmodern arena.

Acker's antirational stance from *Pasolini* to *Empire of the Senseless* increasingly acknowledges this complexity, seeking a way out of the binary "rational/irrational." *Pasolini*, the earliest of the three novels, is the most simply oppositional, primarily interested in attacking rationalism. Yet it does so while recognizing that marginal subjects are somehow losing the ability to launch such attacks, as hegemonic "irrationality" leeches their opposition away.

Rationalized violence in
My Death My Life by Pier Paolo Pasolini

My Death My Life by Pier Paolo Pasolini (1984) dates from a period that Acker has characterized as her phase of plagiarism.[39] This period also covers the novels *Great Expectations* (1983), *Blood and Guts in High School* (1984), and *Don Quixote*, although virtually all of Acker's novels borrow previous texts to a certain extent, often using them to provide a ready-made plot structure. Whereas the titles of *Great Expectations* and *Don Quixote* indicate the primary text that Acker uses in each case to frame her own novel—and to hold together the multiple allusions and appropriations within each novel—*Pasolini* takes as its "originating text" the real-life instance of the brutal 1975 murder of the Italian filmmaker and poet. *Pasolini* is a murder mystery, with Pasolini himself assuming the posthumous role of detective, seeking to understand the complex forces that led to his death.[40] The mysterious historical facts surrounding the murder are reviewed briefly in the novel's introductory section. Acker reveals these so-called facts to be contingent on the competing theories of various parties (the police, the press, Pasolini's friends) about motives and culprits.

The pastiche structure of this novel involves fragments of a multitude of existing texts, from a James Bond movie to Joyce's *Ulysses*, several Shakespeare plays, and a history of the post-Revolution conflict between Robespierre and Danton. The narrator's identity shifts constantly—from male to female, omniscient to autobiographically confessional, literary to pornographic—leaping across centuries and genres as s/he slips from one pilfered text into another. The stolen text may be radically altered, as with a version of *Hamlet* in which Polonius is an incestuous drunk and Gertrude and Claudius are in jail with an Irish terrorist maid named Al'Amat. Or it may appear verbatim, as do scraps of *Ulysses*.[41]

This widespread plagiarism is a way to trouble the authority of writer over text, meaning, and reader. As Barthes and Foucault have famously noted, the contribution of authorial signature to a literary work is part of a societal dynamic of control, of limiting possible meanings.[42] Authorial ownership normally functions as a form of rational causality, determining meaning and thereby legislating a certain sense of how reality works. It is by now commonplace to point out that this sense of reality has tended to be male and otherwise hegemonic.[43]

In a sense, *Pasolini* is framed by *two* primary "texts," both of which share the goal of identifying a rational, causal pattern in human events: one is Enzo Siciliano's 1978 biography of Pasolini, from which Acker borrows extensively; the second is the genre conventions of the detective story. Acker uses both to explore and attack the oppressive workings of rationalism in Pasolini's Italy and her own United States. Rationalism connects the two "texts": it concerned Pasolini in his life and contributed to his death, and it gets continually reinscribed in the very form of popular stories. Disrupting it becomes a major focus in Acker's novel.

Conventional detective novels inscribe a world inherently reasonable, logical, and determinate—and kept so by the appropriate exercise of authority. Acker explores the implications of these assumptions, particularly the assumption of ordered causality. The problem with causality as an epistemological model is that it tends to be limited in focus to discrete, individual acts or events. In that sense, it is individualistic and dehistoricizing. *Pasolini* diffuses it across an entire tradition of texts, locating the causes of the filmmaker's death in social ideologies that are reproduced textually, in art and in mass culture. Acker broadens the narrow scope of normal causality in order to investigate how stories can become really fatal in the late capitalist world.

The historical Pier Paolo is an apt subject for this investigation, because of the slippage between his art (films, poems, radical journalism) and his life—and, especially, his death. The artist was reportedly killed by one of the ragged boy-prostitutes about whom he had always written (and whom he had long patronized), who "belonged to the Pasolini iconography" to such an extent that one of Pier Paolo's associates was convinced he had seen the boy in a Pasolini film.[44] But there was also speculation that this boy's subsequent conviction was another fiction—that the murder had been a political conspiracy, a way to silence Pasolini while simultaneously discrediting him by marking his homosexuality as sordid and self-destructive. Acker's use of the figure of Pasolini shows her concern with the meeting of the textual and the material: how texts become real history, even as they take their meaning from historical circumstances. Pasolini is a figure of this intricate and potentially dangerous symbiosis. In this narrative, the historical Pasolini becomes a fictional character in yet another layer of text.

Acker's radically fragmented narrative takes the profound rationalism of conventional mystery novels and turns it on its head. The conventional detective story is a paradigm of hermeneutic endeavor. One "true" interpretation is selected from among competing possibilities. Blame is assigned, order restored, and the reader can generally assume that the appropriate punishment will be meted out. While the murder mystery celebrates the containment and defeat of irrational violence, it legitimates the rational powers of the brilliant detective (and, by extension, the reader). It is founded on a fundamental dualism: order versus disorder, unreasonable violence (murder) versus reasonable violence (punishment), good versus evil. Simply put, "[d]uality is the basic principle of detection, since the sine qua non requirements of the detective story are a detective and a criminal."[45]

The detective story's ideological assumptions coincide with what Jessica Benjamin has said about the rationalization of violence and punishment under patriarchal capitalism. Benjamin—like other post-Lacanian psychoanalysts—identifies such dualism as the (psychosexual) root of domination. She argues that rationalism is gender specific: it "is in fact male rationality"—in her terms, a reaction to the male need for separation from and containment of the mother.[46] Rationalism is thus intimately connected with the myth of the autonomous subject; and consumer capitalism depends on this ideology of individualism.

In Benjamin's reading of the rationalization of domination in the pornographic classic, *The Story of O*, the connections become apparent between the ideology of the capitalist subject and the sexual violence that both Pasolini and Acker explore. Benjamin focuses on the ordered, intellectualized nature of the various masters' sexual commands to O: "Their acts are carefully controlled: each act has a goal that expresses their rational intentions." The masters must deny their dependence on O for pleasure, must avoid the danger "that the subject always becomes the object he consumes"—that object being, in this case, O's body.[47] Under capitalism, consumption defines identity—you are what you consume—yet in order for consumption to be attractive, the subject must *feel* that he is autonomous, expressing an authentic individuality through acts of purchasing. The only way O's masters can maintain this sense of autonomy is to deny that the pleasure they take from O *is* pleasure: to disguise it as a rational exercise of power. The more pleasure the subject experiences, the more powerful must be the framework of authority within which he contains this pleasure in order to prevent loss of self.[48] Benjamin argues that contemporary capitalism's ever-increasing offers of pleasure are bound to escalating structures of authority.

Pasolini's own later work traces the expansion of such a network of control, railing against both the increasing rationalization of sexuality in Italian society and the so-called "economic miracle" that moved Italy into the arena of multinational capitalism or postmodernity. Acker's novel, from the start, explores the links between such supposedly private and public concerns. It begins with two questions stolen from Siciliano's biography, but recast in the first person: "Did I ask to die? Was my murder a suicide by proxy?" The paragraphs that follow immediately cast these questions as wide-ranging and political in nature:

> In 1973 I [Pasolini] wrote: "Up until the 1970s the ancient world, the world which is daily life and thinking and loving, existed—but it was swept away. From the age of innocence we've passed to the age of corruption."
>
> The scene: Increasingly overt control of dynamic materialism by Multinationals in Italy expresses itself particularly in rise of terrorism (right-wing media strategy and expression of the populace's inability to act functionally and politically) and in Americanism, that homogenization of daily lives and identities.[49]

Clearly, causality (and fatality) is not a matter of individual psychology, as Sherlock Holmes would have us believe. Rather, the causes underlying both the patterns of daily life and the arbitrariness of death (terrorism) are economic and historical. The Italian public may commit "suicide by proxy," by tacitly accepting the lack of access to political power that motivates the terrorists who, in turn, kill ordinary citizens; nevertheless, ultimate responsibility must belong to the nebulous and faceless powers of the multinational-bureaucratic postmodern state.

Pasolini's diversion of causality also begins immediately on the narrative level. In the novel's introductory section detailing Pasolini's death, Pasolini's recollections of his just-finished film *Salo: The 120 Days of Sodom* are suddenly interrupted by another narrative, an ultraviolent detective tale about a girl named Sally (Salo?) that sounds like an American B movie from the 1970s retold by James Ellroy. The private eye narrator relates how Sally is raped by her stepfather, runs away to join a biker gang and then "the Jesus Freaks," conspires with her biker boyfriend (whose name is J. Habermas) to fake her own kidnapping, and ultimately is killed by her incestuously jealous stepfather, whose own abusive childhood is revealed after his arrest (178–83). This narrative is interwoven with the thoughts of the previous narrator ("Pasolini") about his murder, and with theoretical speculations on the nature of language. *Salo* shares with the Sally story a concern with the connections among sexual desire, control, and murderous violence; already we see how any investigation cannot be contained, is implicated with other texts and formed by larger structures such as language.

Acker's Pier Paolo writes of *Salo* that "human male sexual desires especially homosexual and sadistic are raised both within the movie and in the movie's audience at the same time that I'm showing the close connections between these desires and fascism. Because the state's now fascistic, sexual desire is totally reasonable that is separate from caring. This is great for a pornographer to say" (178). Strange slippages, both historical and political, occur in this description. An openly gay, Marxist "pornographer" links his own sexuality with fascism, and a film set in the short-lived fascist republic of Saló (established by Mussolini in 1943) is also described as being about the fascistic state "now"—an ambiguous reference to either 1975 or the mid-1980s of the narrator's posthumous "incarnation." Readers familiar with Pasolini's final film may make their own sense of the politics of these contradictions.[50] But within the context of Acker's fictional narrative, these comments also function as a *mise-en-abyme* helpful to grasping her use of history, especially the highly contingent politics of her layering of texts and historical periods.

The potential usefulness of comparing historical fascism to today's "fascistic" state, as both Acker's Pier Paolo and the real *Salo* do, lies in becoming aware of both similarities and differences. The continuities are important for gaining a sense of the sustained *strategies* of hegemony (such as rationalization). But representations of the past that function only as metaphors for the present make the shared features of the two eras seem inevitable. Agency lies in the ability to see the *differences* in given social structures over time, and thus to develop appropriate tactics.

This axis of continuity-and-difference becomes apparent in Pier Paolo's skepticism about the political meanings of homosexuality and his ironic self-characterization as a "pornographer." Whereas Nazi fascism was murderously heterosexist—and therefore, to be homosexual in that context functioned as a dangerous act of resistance—both Pasolini and Acker suggest that even then, homosexuality was not *only* an oppositional identity category. *Salo* suggests that even synchronically—in the fascist era—its meaning depended on one's political position. Fascism offered, in part, an alternative to the alienated identity offered by unrestrained international consumerism (what Gramsci terms Americanism), through appeals to nationalism and self-discipline; thus *Salo*'s bourgeois sadists, whose positions of power in the local fascist bureaucracy protect them, may in part enact homosexuality as a misplaced attempt to dissociate themselves from heterosexuality's involvement in the dynamic of reproduction. (This connects back to Benjamin's comments on sadism as denial of consumption.) Their brutally rationalized consumption of the bodies of peasant children, needless to say, utterly disqualifies this sexual practice as a "resistant" strategy.[51]

For Pasolini and for Acker's Pier Paolo, this complex political valence of homosexuality—its ability to be aligned with oppression *and* resistance, depending on context—is a connection between the fascist period and the present. In *Salo*, Pasolini explores a certain amount of disillusionment with the politics of homosexuality for which he himself suffered so much. What is specifically disillusioning about "now" is the increased commodification of the homosexual body as late capitalism expands its markets and recognizes a hitherto "untapped" clientele. Thus Acker's character can refer bitterly to himself as a pornographer, recognizing that he sells the arousal of (male) audience desire even as he raises problems with that desire. (I will explore in my chapter 4 whether the same can be said of Acker herself.)

Pasolini also offered in his 1973 newspaper columns an analysis, reminiscent of Foucault, of the extended control and punishment of homosexuality that goes with this market expansion.[52] An identity position need not become hegemonic or even "acceptable" in order to become marketable. So the historical analogy between the two periods—fascist and "fascistic"—seems to rest on the similarity that at both times, homosexuality carries both oppositional and co-opted meanings, dependent on the immediate context. The historical differences lie in the specific contexts available in each period. Although any connection between homosexuality and fascism remains, for me, problematic, it points to the central "lesson" of Acker's approach to history as pastiche.

Perhaps this acknowledgment that rationalized power destroys even as it legitimates leads Acker to assert, in a parenthetical aside halfway through the book, that "Pasolini died by suicide" (273); all too easily, marginal groups' efforts toward representation and greater visibility are turned toward greater regulation and repression. This version of the "crisis of representation" springs from the ability of postmodern capitalism to digest and exploit images at an unprecedented rate. To explore how such domination increasingly exploits *texts*, Acker's narrative continues its investigative pastiche, independently of its apparent originating motive to solve the murder.

One of the things Acker's pastiche does is to refuse any separation between art and politics. By placing fragments of "high" culture next to "low" culture's scraps—versions of *Hamlet* alongside scenes from the biker story—Acker shows how remarkably *similar* they are, in terms of both texts' suggestion that the dynamic of control between fathers and daughters (Ross and Sally, Polonius and Ophelia) gets played out in incestuous attempts to monopolize the daughters' sexuality. High culture is by no means innocent of the discourses of exploitation supposedly particular to mass-cultural "trash" fiction.

Acker rewrites classics and pulp texts alike in a flat, deaestheticized style that becomes, in a sense, the common thread among the texts. Rather than functioning as a reinstatement of the unifying authorial voice, however, this deaestheticization marks an irruption of the irrational, challenging the normal rules of reading. As far as there *is* one narrative voice among all the permutations of texts, it is the voice of a stubborn misreader, a reader who consistently focuses on the wrong things and fails to notice the things to which she is supposed to be paying attention. The narrative voice of Acker's novels sees nymphomania in *Romeo and Juliet*, and an exploration of the logic of nuclear weapons testing in *Godzilla*. She is Bakhtin's carnival fool, whose "stupid" insistence on supposedly minor or self-evident points reveals the fundamental contradictions of hegemonic ideology.[53]

Acker's strategically stupid style refuses attempts to compartmentalize (rationalize) thought and speech into monologic units. Here, art cannot be so easily separated from the worlds of politics and economics. The rhetoric of rational argumentation and the discourse of romantic courtship intersect with profane slang:

> Romeo: If you were the woman I worship, my lips would be pressed on the dripping red-violet of your cunt-lips.
> Juliet: So you don't love me. (*Takes in this fact.*) You're supposed to be pretending you love me and the more you don't, because love is confusion, the more love you're feeling for me. In this way pretense becomes reality. (210)

When the narrator comments on a previous sentence, "I like this sentence cause it's stupid" (249), she is rejecting the rules of art and their role in forcing all speech to repeat permitted meanings: "Schools teach good writing in order to stop people writing whatever they want the way they want" (251). Art as a category separates political analysis from desire, separates public and private discourses so that the personal cannot be identified as political. This silencing separation also creates the myth of human freedom: "Art proposes an interiority which no longer exists for all of us are molded" (246). Or, as Mikhail Bakhtin puts it, "the unity of a style thus presupposes on the one hand a unity of language (in the sense of a system of general normative forms) and on the other hand the unity of an individual person realizing himself in this language."[54]

Pasolini not only rejects aesthetic style, but also attacks the fabric of language itself. If the novel's rejection of rational (monologic) causation is played out on the structural level as pastiche, on the linguistic or microlevel it becomes nominalism. The novel's introductory section concludes: "I, Pier Paolo Pasolini, will solve my murder by denying the principle of causation and by proposing nominalism."[55] Nominalism, the theory that abstract principles exist only in language and have no objective reality, suggests that meaning—causality—is a function of language and not prior to it. Nominalism is a counterrational position because it resists the view of language as inert matter to be subjected to a user's will.

Nominalism identifies causality at work in language itself, in the movement from signified (cause) to signifier (effect). That movement—meaning—must be blocked in order to break control. The power in naming, the power available to those who define which signified belongs with ("causes") which signifier, becomes apparent in Acker's reading of the James Bond movie *Live and Let Die*. Bond, working in partnership with the CIA, wins control over the irrational and deadly forces of Voodoo (i.e., "No cause and effect, baby. Voodoo. Nominalism" [292]) by *renaming* his enemy. Bond manages to define the mysterious Black voodoo priest as a materialistic heroin dealer, thus rendering him controllable within the Anglo-American legal system—and understandable within the discourse of profit (292–94). Bond's ability to extend the domain of late capitalist rationalism is his ability to name, to connect signified and signifier. This is the power to define the Other as criminal.

To disable such hegemonic meaning-making, Acker turns in a middle section of *Pasolini* to strategies of radical syntactical disruption reminiscent of Gertrude Stein's more experimental work. Apparently meaningless clusters of two or three words are repeated dozens of times. Some seem related by sound, some evoke possible meanings, but none are clear. At the end of this section, we are told, "Don't make anything out of broken-up syntax cause you're looking to make meaning where nonsense will" (246). This strategy seeks to deny language its illusion of transparent referentiality and to focus attention on the materiality of the signifier. It insists that signifiers, in their material uniqueness, cannot be subjected to rationalized principles of exchange. Acker's character Emily Brontë (also referred to as "Kathy") elaborates: "Postcapitalists' general strategy right now is to render language (all that which signifies) easily manipulable. . . . In the case of language and of economy the signified and the actual objects have no value don't exist or else have only whatever values those who control the signifiers assign to them. Language is making me sick. Unless I destroy the relations between language and their signifieds that is, their control" (300–301). The paradox Acker captures here is that while the relation of signified to signifier is arbitrary (nominalist), the forces of hegemony manage to control through language by maintaining the illusion of a real, natural connection—the illusion that the names and definitions they give are the only possible ones. As Robert Siegle explains, "*How* meaning has been used is the problem, and the narrator's hope is to turn it back from a semiotic category assimilated to ideological ends toward the organic, bodily, sensory domain of use value."[56]

Nominalism, as a reading practice, becomes a significant tactic of resistance against late capitalism.

However, like any tactic, this one's life span is limited. The "meaningless" section of *Pasolini* lasts only a few pages; even the directive, "don't make anything," marks a return to syntax and some kind of communication. Acker cannot wholly reject meaning since that is the domain of power. The point *Pasolini* makes so insistently—and which distinguishes it from some poststructuralist positions—is that, arbitrary or not, language's fictions have real effects. "Emily Brontë" explores the paradox that meaning is a fictional construct, yet equals control:

> I don't mean. I am meant. That's ridiculous. There's no meaning. Is meaning a post-capitalist invention?
> The shits have made me. The shits have determined the sick bad relations of these parts sexually to each other. What I'm trying to say is that I can't just say, well human lives have always been miserable pain is just another event like shitting. Be above it (no meaning).[57]

By removing oneself from the activity of using meaning, one loses a major area of contestation. To reject the heritage of Enlightenment reason—as how "human lives have always been"—by embracing irrationality is not enough; one must also understand the varied means by which that heritage has been perpetuated upon specific people.

The helpless ahistoricism resulting from any rejection of rational language suggests why some poststructuralists' celebratory identification of "woman" or "the feminine" with ruptures of meaning is dangerous unless grounded in an awareness of how just such ideas have historically been used to *disempower* women.[58] Acker explores this problem further in her three rewritings of *Macbeth*, toward the end of *Pasolini*. Acker transposes the setting of the play from Scotland to Ireland, and makes Shakespeare's "Porter," the working-class drunk, into her stand-in for Macbeth ("Thane of Cawdor Glamis and the head of the IRA").[59] Each version pits Ireland as irrational and female against England as the male and rational. Ireland and the Porter always lose.

The three witches, or "blabbing bitches," as they become in Acker's rendition, exist on the edges of language and society. They speak in prophecy, a form incomprehensible to rational thought's focus on the causal connection between *past* and present (323–24). Hearing them, Banquo, who sides with the English colonizers against the Porter's struggle for home rule, makes explicit the connection between domination (England), masculinity, and the rejection of women-as-irrationality: "'I never believe in cunts or holes. Females always lie cause all they do is talk from feelings. All of my friends, cause all are English, are male'" (325). The bitches lack power if they are no more than "holes" in language.

Mrs. Porter makes the mistake of dedicating herself to "Irrationality, Animalism, and Night," valorizing the position in which "English" rationalism has placed her (326). The problem with her simple inversion of the rationality/irrationality binary is that it leaves her unable to understand her suffering as both colonized subject and (doubly colonized) woman: "'No causation for us. We can do whatever we want. Anything including hypocrisies and lies are just tools. Every event's unreal and separate from meaning. If this' all true, why am I feeling so much pain?'" (333). She bases her rejection of the rational on the assumption that rationality always operates in the same way; this leaves her unable to analyze the specifics of her own historical position.

However, Acker's *Macbeths* also supply a slight, hopeful sense of the possibility of agency and change by dialogizing Shakespeare's text, both among other texts and within itself. She intersperses each version with details from different moments in Ireland's history, from Edward I's conquest to Daniel O'Connell and the 1845 potato famine (she refers readers to Sean O'Faolain's book on O'Connell [372]) to the IRA's quest for aid from Nazi Germany in 1939. These specifics suggest that the conventional tragic form of Shakespeare's play—archetypal, oriented to the heroic individual—is inadequate to addressing the various political situations in which desperate tactics such as the IRA's arise. Again, Acker updates the individualist analysis of evil and violence by replacing it with a more historical and textual model of the causes of inequality and revolt in postmodernity.

Acker foregrounds Shakespeare's collusion with the imperialist ideologies of his England by moving *Macbeth* from a temporally distant Scotland to Ireland, where contemporary tensions make it harder for her twentieth- or twenty-first-century readers to accept that England's victory is, if personally tragic, a desirable restoration of order.

Acker's pastiche supplies the sense of historical context—the importance of readers' positions (including Acker's own position, as reader-writer of the texts she uses)—that can save the antirational strategies of a Mrs. Porter from slipping back into a simple reinscription of hegemonic binaries. Her formulation moves beyond the binary model of repetition versus silence or incomprehensibility. The workings of pastiche and plagiarism in *Pasolini* suggest that to repeat (sometimes word for word) patriarchal language may not result only in one's co-optation by existing structures. At first glance, Acker's recontextualization of primarily male-authored texts "in quotation marks" does suggest that excluded subjects are utterly determined by discourse. (Everyone, in fact, is discursively constructed; this is as true for the powerful as for the weak, but those in power get to repeat a text of privilege and pleasure.) Yet despite, for instance, the Porter's thrice-repeated death—his inability to escape the ending Shakespeare wrote—Acker's dialogized plagiarism argues the presence of both determinism *and* agency in reading.

Acker's project at this point (1984) remains primarily oppositional, often still searching for a sustainable position outside the framework of rationalism, to the extent of even questioning syntax. But as Acker's writing advances into the Reagan years, she moves somewhat from challenges to the signifier and narrative causality, toward a focus on disenfranchised readers themselves. In *Don Quixote*, a novel that can be seen as all about reading (as was Cervantes's original), Acker approaches the mythologies of a distinctively American rationalism—ideals of political freedom and personal desire—through the eyes of a female reader who has been at once written into such ideologies as their Other and barred from full access to them.

REALPOLITIK IN *Don Quixote*

If much of the textual strategy in *Pasolini* was concerned with aggravating the otherness inherent in language—thus disrupting the seamless identity of signifier with signified—*Don Quixote: Which Was a Dream* turns more toward *social* otherness, the otherness thrust on particular historical groups. (Acker's attention to textual disruption by no means disappears, however.) Quixote's tactic is not to reject rationality entirely, but rather to undermine its basis in dualism. This dualism, which divides the world into self and Other, also structures representation. While still analyzing the power invested in discourses of rationalism, *Don Quixote* suggests that as a site of contestation, rationalism itself may be less important than its representations, its myths. In a postmodern context in which representation is the primary arena of exchange and of power, it is also through images and stories that ideas of difference are created and dualism enforced.

The narrative structure of *Don Quixote* challenges the division between the rational and the irrational by tracing a hero's rational (i.e., goal-driven) pursuit of an irrational goal. Like *My Death My Life by Pier Paolo Pasolini, Don Quixote* is the story of an absurd, impossible quest. The quest is again plagiaristic, pursued through texts; this time it takes readers through Giuseppe di Lampedusa's *The Leopard,* Frank Wedekind's Lulu plays, a Japanese monster movie, Cold War foreign policy statements, and historical documents from the early days of the New England colonies. The quest is unlikely (or highly irrational) for a number of reasons.

Like *Pasolini,* it begins with the protagonist-quester's "death" but, undeterred, proceeds temporally forwards and hermeneutically backwards from there. *Don Quixote* opens with the female protagonist about to undergo an abortion. The utter loss of control entailed by this experience marks the death of her identity: "When a doctor sticks a steel catheter into you while you're lying on your back and you do exactly what he and the nurses tell you to; finally, blessedly, you let go of your mind. Letting go of your mind is dying. She needed a new life. She had to be named."[60] She renames herself "Catheter" (Kathy for short) or "Don Quixote" and, in painstakingly reasoned language, decides on a quest:

> she conceived of the most insane idea that any woman can think of. Which is to love. How can a woman love? By loving someone other than herself. She would love another person. By loving another person, she would right every manner of political, social, and individual wrong: she would put herself in those situations so perilous the glory of her name would resound. (9)

Her quest, like that of her Cervantesque namesake, is insanely romantic and frequently parodic. She sets out to right the wrongness of heterosexual love that has brought her to this painful situation, by battling the world's "evil enchanters"—from Ronald Reagan and "the editors of *TLS*" to Andrea Dworkin (101, 102).

This idea is impossible at its origin: "conceived" at the moment of abortion. But it is especially unlikely because of Quixote's gender, for women's socially defined identity does not include the active expression of desire. While women's historic association with irrationality also identifies them with unrestrained desire, their desire is conventionally figured as unfocused and turned in upon itself, rendered articulate (meaningful) only when given shape by male desire. Without the directive forces of male reason and language (this argument goes), desire fails to signify; it has meaning only when it becomes desire *for* something.

Acker's female characters tend to inhabit fully this stereotyped position as the raw signifiers of desire and, therefore, otherness. *Don Quixote* in particular explores the historical creation—through stories, texts—of a female identity that, synonymous with female sexuality, is incomplete, lacking, more object than subject. But by adopting just such an identity in her text, Acker emphasizes its instability, the aching desire in it that threatens to disrupt the very binary system that establishes it. I shall talk more about the disruptive function of desire in chapter 4; but Acker also undermines gender dualism in other ways here. And *Don Quixote* also dissects the flipside of the gender-power binary: the power that accrues to those (men) who are able to represent *their* desires as rational.

As the failure of *Pasolini*'s Mrs Porter illustrated, merely reversing the rational/irrational binarism by rejecting language and logic leaves the marginalized no way to combat their own positioning. Don Quixote's approach is rather to move among the locations that binary offers. Acker's knight tells the dog who stands in for Sancho Panza as her faithful and pragmatic sidekick, "I'm your desire's object, dog, because I can't be the subject. Because I can't be a subject: What you name 'love,' I name nothingness. I won't not be" (28). She locates her "identity" in this double negative, a tactical position that confounds dualistic strategy by showing that even denials can be used to affirm. She challenges gender dualism by variously appearing in the text as "knight" and "night": the former identity goal-oriented, hierarchical, and male (desiring subject); the latter dark, unknown, irrational, and—by extension—female (desired object). She adopts this not-so-much irrational as *a*rational gender position to enable her quest for love: "Finally Don Quixote understood her problem: she was both a woman therefore she couldn't feel love and a knight in search of Love. She had had to become a knight, for she could solve this problem only by becoming partly male" (29).

A similar blurring of binaries takes place in one of the book's most playful sections, an early interruption of the narrative entitled "INSERT." In it, Acker or an omniscient narrator advocates electing Prince (a.k.a. The Artist) to the Presidency, "because he's part black part white which is part good part evil" (21). He disrupts the dualistic assigning of evil to the Other through his body and his behavior: "The Prince believes in feelings, fucking, and fame." Like Machiavelli's prince, he "doesn't have any morals." But while Machiavelli's treatise on statesmanship was designed to give more power to already powerful rulers, the same strategies in the context of Reagan's United States can challenge the ideology of control. Prince rejects the morality that enables exploitation: "The Prince isn't moral: he doesn't give a shit about anybody but himself. The Prince wouldn't die for anyone, whereas Our President will always die for everyone while he's garnering in their cash" (21).

Acker even troubles the binary between human and animal, by her transformation of almost all the book's characters into dogs. Not only the knight's companions in her quest are canine; Richard Nixon and Henry Kissinger, among others, "woof" and "bark" and are referred to by the nonhuman pronoun, "it." This "it" both points to their dehumanization and bypasses gender dualism.

Acker makes these gestures toward nondualistic representation because dualism is the component of rationalism that allows for the establishment of hierarchies, a world divided into "us" and "them." Representation plays a crucial role in creating such divisions. In the Godzilla scene from which I previously quoted, the monsters suggest that rationalism produces inequality first by moving all things, objects and individuals, into the arena of representation. "Mere sensory material" enters the signifying system of commercial exchange, where it comes to *represent* a certain monetary value. As the monsters add later, such a process of turning things into signifiers has escalated as capitalism develops, until now it "pervades all the spheres of human life" (72). This "reduction of reality" to images, which in turn produce a fundamentally "manipulable other," means that in postmodernity, human inequalities are produced through one group's power to manipulate representations of another group for profit.

Ellen G. Friedman provides a historicizing sense of why this analysis should come from the unlikely mouth of Godzilla: "Designed by Japanese filmmakers to make big bucks with a cheap monster movie pandering to the 1950s atom bomb and cold war fears, Godzilla represents the exploitation and commercialization of those fears."[61] Godzilla, fictionally a product of the subjection of the atom to "technological" reason, is historically a product of the reduction of political tensions and human fear to the status of marketable commodities, objects to which a price tag can be affixed. The monster thus becomes a glaring example of the flattening out of history and personal pain—the Japanese people's very recent experience of the atomic bomb—in the international business of marketing representations. If profit demands that the Japanese film promoters elide historical abuses of power—or defeats—by representing the atom bomb, and the destruction it brings, as an invention for which *Japanese* scientists are responsible, so be it. Godzilla represents a particularly postmodern form of rational domination: the erasure of the suffering of "mass" humanity—its monstrous displacement—as it enters the field of representation.

A section of the book entitled "Don Quixote in America, the Land of Freedom," investigates one specific instance of how representation has become central to the perpetuation of power imbalances in the contemporary world. Here, Acker employs the figures of Richard Nixon and Henry Kissinger in order to dissect their practice of realpolitik—a particularly postmodern manifestation of rationality, because it operates through the control of representation. While realpolitik itself predates postmodernity, the Nixon-Kissinger version (to which I will be referring when I write "realpolitik") derives from a new, post-World War II emphasis on the utter divorce of national interests and morality.[62] What matters now to the realpoliticians is credibility or the regulation of images, a nation's *appearance* of power. This emphasis on appearances is a reaction to specific historical conditions, as Walter Isaacson's biography of Kissinger suggests:

> As the world groped its way into the nuclear age, the traditional methods of asserting national power—such as controlling more territory, forging new alliances, and adding to arsenals—were becoming less meaningful. The main way that a nuclear power could enhance its global clout was to increase the *credibility* of its commitments. Power thus depended more on perception—about a nation's will and the believability of its threats—than on military might.[63]

Nixon and Kissinger, therefore—setting the stage for U.S. presidents since—were engaged in manufacturing representations, the simulation of dominance that becomes dominance. That this simulation has its own consequences, Isaacson's account of the 1970 invasion of Cambodia makes clear: "Because Nixon as well as his critics portrayed the invasion as a bold and brazen expansion of the American war effort, it became so."[64] Such appearances must then be sustained, for credibility's sake, by further actions.

The effects of realpolitik as practiced by Nixon and Kissinger demonstrate, like the opportunistic timing of the Godzilla movies, that a reduction of historical conflicts to manipulable images does two things: it erases the pain of their victims, while simultaneously consolidating the power of the dominant side (or of the people in power *within* each warring side). Acker quotes Nixon's 1968 campaign pledge to support the struggle for Biafran independence, then imagines how internal power politics kept the Nixon administration from intervening to prevent the subsequent massive-scale starvation of Biafrans. Acker's character based on National Security Council staffer Roger Morris claims that Kissinger "had no rational reason to let those kids starve; it just did cause it was scared to alienate [Under Secretary of State] Richardson cause it and Richardson have other fish to fry."[65] Unfortunately, the need for good relations between Kissinger and Richardson is an entirely "rational" reason for allowing starvation, as far as realpolitik would define "rational." Kissinger is willing to intervene on the Biafrans' behalf as long as his negotiations remain secret from the State Department—since, being invisible or outside the realm of representation, these negotiations have no reality effect or existence for Richardson. But when a gesture or appearance of alliance between the two men takes precedence, the Biafrans must (literally) disappear and become *unrepresented*. Realpolitik, as the extension of rationalization into the realm of appearances, allows for the power of life and death to be wielded through the ability to control representation.

Acker recognizes that this problem goes beyond Nixonian realpolitik to the fundamental American myth of personal freedom. The Biafran tragedy prompts "a bitch" to ask Nixon, "'What was the American Revolution? What's this American freedom? Commerce's thriving in this country: the Heads of Commerce're getting wealthier. Reagan barks commerce's thriving in this country. Free trade, freedom: what're they? In peace as now: freedom is starvation. What if freedom revolts . . . and wants to name itself . . . ?'" (107–8).[66] She makes the point that without access to representation (naming), a belief in freedom only furthers free trade, the freedom to be a commodity, to be ultimately disposable.

Acker invokes the master rationalist, Thomas Hobbes, to explain how the ideology of personal freedom plays into the dominating logic of rationalism. Hobbes, the acknowledged forefather of realpolitik, visits Nixon and Mrs Nixon in their bedroom in the guise of the Angel of Death, claiming that Nixon has summoned him.[67]

Nixon has invoked rationalism, embodied by Hobbes, to justify the death of the Biafrans. As the president is "fucking Mrs Nixon," Hobbes talks through his philosophy and comes to the conclusion that humans ("dogs") operate like machine parts, which need to be in a dualistic relation to one another in order to function: "The operations of machine parts depend not only on power but also on unequal power relations (a definition of power)."[68] Therefore, "[t]he life of a dog, even if the dog's dead like me, is solitary, poor, nasty, brutish, short. The condition of a dog is a condition of war, of everyone against everyone: so every dog has a right to everything, even to another dog's body. This is freedom" (114). The ideology of individual freedom, so central to American politics, operates harmfully to enable the rationalization of the right to destroy another's flesh.

So any apparent opposition between rationalism and (irrational) idealism turns out to be more complex and perhaps not the point at all, especially because realpolitik operates in the realm of representation.[69] Idealism and realpolitik depend equally on telling an appealing story. The important question for Don Quixote, if she is to disrupt the rule of rationalism, becomes how to intervene in such stories, to stop their perpetuation of inequalities: "Don Quixote realized that defeating Nixon isn't defeating America and that to defeat America she had to learn who America is. What is the myth of America, for economic and political war or control now is taking place at the level of language or myth."[70] There can be no freedom without representation (taking control of language and myth); and yet, representation is an especially problematic place for *women* seeking freedom. As Quixote's narrative travels through plagiarized texts have already shown, women have such a history of *over*representation in men's texts that there seems to be no space left for alternate stories. And where would such new representations come from if "the history of women must define female identity" and history is only the sum of existing texts (29)?

But as the novel draws to a close, Quixote develops two tropes, two images of freedom that already exist in mainstream stories and that *define* freedom as the ability to use others' property (hence, others' *stories*) in "monstrous" ways. Those tropes are voodoo and piracy. Both also embody the central tension in Acker's work between a free-for-all world of ready appropriation and a more binary vision of excluded readers for whom there is *never* a home in existing texts.

Voodoo has appeared in Acker's work as far back as *Kathy Goes to Haiti* (written in 1978); in *Don Quixote*, it is a figure for the disruption of rationality through *bricolage*. It is also an image of Acker's text itself, which turns consumer commodities (texts, literature) against themselves. Quixote remembers visiting a Haitian church, where "the priests use nailpolish bottles, raw rum, and whatever they can get their hands on for everything" (193). This recollection comes during a battle scene that Acker has herself appropriated from Cervantes, although it is recast in a desolate inner city: the mad knight attacks a procession of "Religious White Men" who appear to be carrying off the image of a woman (which is either the Virgin Mary or, as Quixote claims, Queen Guinevere). Here, the battle metaphorically becomes an attempt to liberate the *image* of woman from patriarchal control—but for Quixote, there is no difference between an image and a woman, a text and the flesh whose meaning it determines. She tells the dogs, "We must turn to madness, or Voodoun, in order to set Queen Guinevere free" (191).

So on the one hand, voodoo is identified with a chaotic disruption of rationality ("madness") and of ownership, in a world where there is nothing outside texts. There is some danger in this approach that when Acker "gets her hands on" voodoo, she may be appropriating the cultural practices of people of color under the guise of shared otherness; white postmodernist feminists have been called to account for such *in*difference to the specifics of "difference."[71]

However, voodoo also seems to represent a liberated space of pure articulation *outside* the textual economy of patriarchy. The church Quixote describes is a kind of anarchic paradise, where desire speaks and acts without restraint: "Being Haitian it held all practices including every sort of fucking and Voodoun. All ways were allowed: all cultures: aloud."[72] In this second vein, which is closer to what Moran calls the essentialist moment in Acker's work, her version of voodoo may be no less an *in*different appropriation that has little to do with what "Being Haitian" has historically meant. It does seem to speak a desire for a unified community of outsiders, sharing together their exile from conventional power. It also risks simply reproducing the condition of indiscriminate otherness produced by dualistic thought.

The same ambivalence is evident in the ideal of the pirate that Quixote and her dogs proclaim. Part 2 of *Don Quixote* had ended with a scene of Wedekind's Lulu by the seashore, saying: "Now I must find others who are, like me, pirates journeying from place to place, who knowing only change and the true responsibilities that come from such knowing sing to and with each other" (97). Lulu's speech itself expresses both an awareness of a (postmodern) world in which all is flux, and the belief that being an Other in such a world produces both "true" knowledge and the promise of authentic community.

The image returns in the book's last few pages, as Don Quixote dies (for the third time, and it is still not apparently fatal) and her canine sidekicks declare themselves pirates. Here, one of the dogs gives a description of piracy as free-floating and unrestricted otherness:

> In this total devastation of the heart which is the world, the landlords rule. There is no way we can defeat the landlords. But under their reins and their watchful eyes,
> I sail as the winds of lusts and emotions bare me. Everywhere and anywhere. I who will never own, whatever and whenever I want, I take. (199)[73]

Yet this freedom to "poach" on the dominant text (to use Certeau's term) also derives from an otherness seen as permanent and total. Just as future victory is inconceivable for this dog, there has never been a place where her existence was possible within the mainstream society: becoming a pirate makes her "[n]o longer a poor woman: a woman dependent on the kindnesses of men in a land where there are no kindnesses for there is no land in sight" (199).

Acker attributes specific gender to the permanent exile of piracy, more than to voodoo. Quixote suggests, again in a sort of essentialist mode, that this female place-lessness can be the basis for a different community and language:

> Even a woman who has the soul of a pirate, at least pirate morals, even a woman who prefers loneliness to the bickerings and constraints of heterosexual marriage, even such a woman who is a freak in our society needs a home.
> Even freaks need homes, countries, language, communication.
> The only characteristic freaks share is our knowledge that we don't fit in. Anywhere. It is for you, freaks my loves, I am writing and it is about you. (201–2)

This passage seems to capture the paradox at the heart of Acker's twin approaches to text and identity: even those women who reject the identity (as man's Other) offered them by existing texts, and are thus condemned to be *even more* "other"—to never "fit in. Anywhere"—need access to representation in order to have any notion of self or of shared identity. Yet the only "writing" that Quixote/Acker can offer her "freaks" depends on the existing texts. This paradox, I think, usefully keeps the glorification of a kind of absolute otherness, which certainly creeps into this passage, from becoming the basis of resistant politics in Acker's writing.

I would argue again that the moments in Acker's novels when she moves *beyond* the mutually undermining tension between radical textuality and essentialism are those in which the historical or material, *local* differences between experiences of otherness come into consideration (which is why I want to emphasize this local, historical element in my readings of her work). To return to voodoo, what (I think) saves Acker's use of this trope from charges of appropriation here is that even while she blurs historical categories of difference to incorporate voodoo into her own *bricolage*, she grounds her appropriation by not ignoring race—as one of the key differences *within* "Difference." Quixote's battle with the Religious White Men suggests, in fact, how gender and race interact in the dynamics of oppression. In the semicomic mode typical of philosophical discussions in her work, Acker relates the kidnapping by these "penitents" of the image of ideal womanhood to their racially dominant position. An exchange between Quixote and a dog suggests that it is precisely these men's entrapment in dualism (which is described as a modernist phenomenon) that inspires their exercise of dominance. The knight asks:

> "Why are they ashamed and miserable?"
> "They're repenting that they're white. Any thinking human does this. Don't you read your own history books? So if you attack those miserable moderns or modernists, knight, you'll be making a miserable historical mistake. You will be preventing whites from hating their own whiteness."
> Don Quixote finally refuted the dogs' attack on her attack: "Liberalism has never stopped me from doing anything," said the night. (179)

In this situation, white liberal men compensate for their racial self-hatred (penitence) by exercising increased power over white women, and both the guilt and the power depend on dualistic identity categories. A specifically feminist-postmodernist voodoo dissolves such clean divisions between self and Other by highlighting the multiple forms otherness takes (racial and gendered, among more)—while always remaining otherness. So a postmodernist practice of history (a historicizing postmodernism) need not bog down in either self-hatred or denial of responsibility, but can match its tactics to specific situations.

Don Quixote doesn't fulfill her quest for true love, but maybe she learns how to forge brief moments of solidarity. If both rationalism and its excluded Others must jockey for power in the same realm of representation, *Don Quixote* concludes with the knight seeking ways to at least prevent any monopoly on representation. No less an authority on patriarchal representation than the voice of God speaks to Quixote, confessing his (or, the voice suggests, why not "her"?) imperfections and warning that there are "no more new stories" (206–7). The voice tells Quixote that since God is dead, she will have to "Make Me up" (207). Paradoxically obedient, the knight agrees to do just that, but refuses to claim the monopoly on truth that others who have made up stories of God have arrogated to themselves. Within the ongoing quotation marks that highlight Quixote's act of narration (and therefore reveal her, in this case, to be lying), she promises that she will "never reveal the reality God had just revealed to me about God,—the gossip,—to anyone" (207). Rejecting God as the authorizing force behind her fictions, Quixote also makes that authority impossible for others to claim any longer, by spreading the story of God's imperfection and death. If there are to be "no new stories," Acker's novel seeks to ensure that the old ones no longer pose as whole truths. Instead, they become the raw materials from which new stories can be "made up" according to the changing needs and histories of specific Others.

Empire of the Senseless, REALM OF THE MULTINATIONALS

Acker's next novel spins out the implications of the death of God, extending it to the overturning of *all* patriarchal claims to control over language and representation. In *Empire of the Senseless*, Acker suggests that conventional models of authority—and therefore, of resistance—no longer pertain to postmodernity. In particular, Acker's recurring dyad of the rapacious father and self-destructive, rebellious daughter gives way to a search for less-dualistic narratives. In the novel's vaguely futuristic world, the postmodern extension of rationalism is fully realized: its ability to incorporate flux and subsume irrationality, which in turn allows capitalism to insinuate itself into the "personal" space of different bodies. Purely oppositional strategies are helpless to contest this empire, both because those who would oppose it are already compromised (in their very bodies) and because power is a matter of images, and therefore very difficult to target.

While *Empire* is by no means a conventional narrative, its structure is more readily apparent and more chronologically consistent than in the works from Acker's plagiarism period. There is, nevertheless, still plenty of plagiarism in this novel. Acker's own summary suggests that the narrative structure of *Empire* attempts to work through issues of dualism and opposition:

> it was the structure which really interested me—the three-part structure. The first part is an elegy for the world of patriarchy. I wanted to take the patriarchy and kill the father on every level. And I did that partially by finding out what was taboo and rendering it in words. The second part of the book concerns what society would look like if it weren't defined by oedipal considerations and the taboos were no longer taboo. I went through every taboo, or tried to, to see what society would be like without these taboos. Unfortunately, the CIA intervenes: I couldn't get there. I wanted to get there, but I couldn't. The last section, "Pirate Night," is about wanting to get to a society that is taboo, but realizing that it's impossible.[74]

This structure becomes an unresolved dialectic, representing perhaps the inadequacy of dialectical accounts (such as the oedipal model) when power is now better represented by pervasive underground intelligence networks (such as the CIA) than by any definable figure such as a father or a state government.

Two characters narrate *Empire of the Senseless*: a woman, Abhor, and her on-again-off-again male "partner," Thivai. Their world is only a slight distortion of our own, emphasizing postmodernity's newest elements: pervasive and invasive technology, the global hegemony of multinational corporations, the decline of the nuclear family, and the redrawing of international boundaries by the rise of both postindustrial capitalism and minority liberation movements. Cyberpunk novelist William Gibson sees such articulations of a possible future as merely highlighting conditions that already exist; it is no accident that Acker borrows heavily from Gibson's *Neuromancer* in setting up Abhor, Thivai, and their environment.[75] Abhor and Thivai are secret agents and/or revolutionaries, ultimately pursuing only their own survival in a world of shifting alliances and ambiguously aligned intelligence networks. Their primary allegiance is not to any one organ of power, hegemonic or oppositional, but floats in the changing field of representation. They search for the various secret "codes" they need in order to survive: the texts with which and through which they can negotiate a workable identity.

Each subsection of the novel begins by identifying its narrator, Abhor or Thivai. Part 1, "Elegy for the World of the Fathers," opens with Abhor speaking "through Thivai": he assumes her first-person voice, to recount to us what he knows of the childhood of Abhor, whom he describes as "my partner, part robot and part black."[76] This is the world of patriarchal representation, where the female has no voice.

Part 1 explores the production of gender in the interconnection of two dualistic structures: patriarchal language and the nuclear family, especially as dissected by Freud and Lacan. The seemingly inevitable implosion of the family into father-daughter incest reveals the power structures at work in language. The mother, excluded from even the ambiguous power bestowed on the daughter by her status as the father's creation, is removed from the scene by separation and suicide.[77] Abhor's father indulges his narcissism by making his daughter utterly like him: "I looked like him. I smelled like him. I learned like him. My father had propagated" (9). His denial of Abhor's difference is paradoxically characteristic of dualistic thought, which sees in the Other only the mirror-image of the self.[78] It is therefore only "natural" that the father would be aroused by this perfect woman, this image of himself that reaffirms his own centrality. As he rapes the teenage Abhor, he sees himself as the very paradigm of the created world: "I am fucking God and I made God!!"[79]

However, this dualistic denial of real difference breaks down when it encounters the diversity of the postmodern marketplace. And when the family collapses, so does conventional language. Abhor's father "goes too far": he relinquishes even the structure of sex-within-the-family and slips into an underworld of brothels and simulated sex shows. While the sex industry may be renowned as the world's oldest, it too has its specifically postmodern form—marked by, on the one hand, a greater specialization and diversification (to encompass the greatest number of bodily practices) and, on the other, a professionalization characterized by increasingly centralized control of formerly "freelance" workers.[80] When the father encounters this intensification of sex-as-exchange-value, he finds that language also collapses, having lost its foundational assumption of inherent value and its clear binaries. "His language went through an indoctrination of nothingness, for sexuality had no more value in his world, until his language no longer had sense."[81] Now, during sex with Abhor, he cries out in a bizarrely fragmented Spanish.

This potentially liberating breakdown in patriarchal language is also signified in *Empire* by the appearance in the text of Arabic as Algerian rebels begin to take over Paris. Arabic, the language of the West's increasingly focal Other, signifies the absence of meaning to Acker's English-speaking westerners. Abhor speaks to her boss in Arabic when she realizes that communication with him has become impossible (56–57). Later, when Thivai has been imprisoned, his English is interspersed with Arabic as he tells the tale of Sinbad the Sailor and of Scheherezade (Shahra'zad) (148–62). The meaning-disrupting speech of the Other becomes a source of alternative models of subjectivity (the sailor or pirate) and of narrative itself (a woman's subversive storytelling as an act of survival and as a rejection of sexual victimhood).

What dualistic thought, with its two options "my meaning" or "no meaning," cannot account for is a third option: that Arabic is not meaningless—as Thivai's retelling of stories from Arabic shows. There is a shift in Acker's strategy between *Pasolini* and *Empire*. Abhor (possibly speaking for Acker) explains:

> Ten years ago it seemed possible to destroy language through language: to destroy language which normalizes and controls by cutting that language. Nonsense would attack the empire-making (empirical) empire of language, the prisons of meaning.
> But this nonsense, since it depended on sense, simply pointed back to the normalizing institutions.
> . . . [A]n attack on the institutions of prison via language would demand the use of a language or languages which aren't acceptable, which are forbidden. Language, on one level, constitutes a set of codes and social and historical agreements. Nonsense doesn't per se break down the codes; speaking precisely that which the codes forbid breaks the codes. (134)

Acker has shifted her focus from a rather abstract and generalized opposition to language itself, to those stories and ways of *using* language that have been outlawed under historically specific circumstances. She now seeks not to destroy the realm of language and representation but to expand it, to exploit its own contemporary dynamic of expansion. This explains her project in part 2 of the book,

"Alone," where she explores and violates taboos. "Alone" covers the period of Abhor and Thivai's separation following a revolution in which the Algerians (enacting a script borrowed from Toussaint L'Ouverture's Haitian slave rebellion) take over Paris and—supposedly—destroy the structures of oppression.

Thivai's first subsection of "Alone" disposes of any number of sexual taboos: child prostitution, intergenerational sex, interracial sex, brother-sister incest, homosexuality, rape, etc. But Thivai is still (literally, for a while) carrying his father around on his back—the father at whose behest Thivai murdered the female members of his family—and his postrevolutionary world is still a sexist, dualistic one. It ends with a filthy youth who proclaims "I'm free. We've had a revolution" forcing himself on a girl who wonders "Whose freedom is dirt?" (108).

Abhor, however, recognizes that the revolution against the sexual, racial, and economic structure of the Fathers is not only insufficient, but may be anachronistic in the postmodern world. The revolution may be inevitable—and even *necessary* for the Algerians—but it is not a sufficient form of resistance against the current hegemonic forces, for it misrecognizes the forms that power now takes. It is aimed against a monolithic racial identity as the source of oppression: whites, and especially, wealthy whites. But Abhor realizes that (racialized) "fatherhood" has been replaced by a more diffuse system, and specifically by multinational capitalism, as the locus of oppression in the world.

> My father's no longer important cause interpersonal power in this world means corporate power. The multinationals along with their computers have changed and are changing reality. Viewed as organisms, they've attained immortality via bio-chips. Etc. Who needs slaves anymore? So killing someone, anyone, like Reagan or the top IBM executive board members, whoever they are, can't accomplish anything. (83)

The multinationals and their international defense body, the CIA, are able to operate and to rebuild power in postrevolutionary Paris because they do not depend on any national government such as the one the Algerians destroyed. Now, in this Foucauldian world, power is everywhere. It fights from within and can only be fought from within.

I mean this "within" quite literally: postindustrial power permeates the body itself. In this novel, more than ever, bodies are Acker's battleground. But here, bodies are not essentialized as the site of truth, as Moran suggests they tend to become in Acker's work.[82] Abhor, the "part robot" cyborg, literalizes the internalization of technological power. This power of the multinationals exists as "implants" in her body. Thivai, too, is a part-human, part-manufactured "construct": he is a junky. His blood is poisoned with heroin, and he will die unless he replaces it with an "enzyme."[83] In a discussion of the Gibson character on whom Thivai is modeled, Thomas Foster cites William S. Burroughs, also an important influence on Acker: "Burroughs argues that drug addiction is the most advanced form of capitalism because 'the junk merchant does not sell his product to the consumer, he sells the consumer to the product.'"[84] Watching Thivai shoot up, Abhor thinks: "These days the principal economic flow of power takes place through black-market armament and drug exchange. The trading arena, the market, is my blood. My body is open to all people: this is democratic capitalism."[85] When the CIA returns to Paris, it is by infiltrating the blood of the underclass; they set up a secret drug-testing operation in a brothel, using the johns as their guinea pigs. Again, capitalism (which it is the CIA's job to promote) extends its reach by catering to the bodily desires of a specialized subsection of the rationalized market.

But if Abhor's body is the pure product of her father's desire for self-duplication and her society's power to render itself internal to the subject, she is also a disruptively Frankensteinian monster. Acker suggests that especially with new body technologies, the binary opposition of nature and culture has collapsed. Permeable postmodern bodies do not offer a "ground," a space outside discourse and power. This fact has an ambiguous value. Abhor has learned young that she cannot rely on her body for any kind of truth value; her sexual attraction to her father despite his raping her has taught her that desire speaks a learned language, not an essentially liberating one. But if her body is contested ground, she fights for it and with it. Abhor's body is a site of gender conflict, and of conflict between the definitions white/black and human/machine. Her identities are multiple. By keeping these categories in play, she keeps ownership of her body unsettled.

To do so is an important strategy for women and other historically oppressed people because it acknowledges that ownership of one's "own" body is not an option—and has never been, for many people. Again, through this denial, the monstrous body puts the lie to the concept of human freedom so central to rationalism. Thomas Foster argues (of cyberpunk fiction in general) that this crisis of bodily autonomy "calls into question the privilege of the white male individual and therefore may enable the recognition of other forms of historical experience."[86] These other histories have been excluded from the textual corpus of History by the representation of that body, and all bodies, as possessing an organic and causal unity.

Abhor's cyborg body emphasizes the constructedness and polysemy of both historical bodies and the body of History. Donna Haraway's "Manifesto for Cyborgs" claims the cyborg as the image of the resistant postmodern subject, and as a model of subjectivity especially appropriate for the postoedipal world, where to turn against only the literal father is to mistake the enemy. Haraway's cyborgs are "the illegitimate offspring of militarism and patriarchal capitalism, not to mention state socialism. But illegitimate offspring are often exceedingly unfaithful to their origins. Their fathers, after all, are inessential."[87] The strength of the cyborg body is its evasion of (dualistic) origin narratives, its failure to evoke any stable, recognizable identity category. How can one speak of a cyborg body like Abhor's? How can one find the terms for its race (already mixed) or its gender when such categories only pertain to human beings? Can a machine have race or gender? What about a half-machine? The cyborg-monster questions the organic unity of History, by revealing the blurred categories on which such a narrative depends. It also denies the rational separation of the material world from the human utilizer of that world. In the cyborg, "technology no longer plays a dialectical role as the Other of humanity; instead that otherness exists within the 'human.'"[88] Yet this commingling serves as a reminder that hegemony now has the technological means to penetrate bodies both figuratively and literally.

Abhor's recognition that the contemporary diffusion of power has made bodies into heteroglossic texts provides the focus of her section of "Alone." While Thivai uses his postrevolutionary time indulging in male heterosexual fantasies, she explores a manifestation of the cyborg body: the tattooed sailor. While Thivai bemoans the fact that "[t]oday there's no more pirates therefore I can't be a pirate," Abhor finds her modern pirate in the person of Agone, a gay Cuban sailor who runs drugs.[89] Abhor, cross-dressed as a boy sailor, follows Agone to a seedy tattoo parlor, where he decides to make his own body a forbidden text by becoming tattooed. The tattoo, like Don Quixote's image of the "freak," and in some ways like the label "queer," is a term of exclusion that has been claimed by its intended victim as a mark of defiance. Originally a hegemonic possession, it becomes resistant in other historical hands. Abhor relates the history of tattooing, which was first used "to mark and identify mercenaries, slaves, criminals, and heretics," but which, among the stigmatized early Christians, "actually served to enforce their group solidarity. . . . Tattooing continued to have ambiguous social value; today a tattoo is considered both a defamatory brand and a symbol of a tribe or of a dream" (130). Here is one occasion where a marginalized subject, while he cannot avoid being a signifying surface, can at least direct the movement of the pen. That the pen is *not* a pen, but is a needle or (here) a knife suggests how painful and ambiguous is the inscription of one's own self as text. In getting the tattoo, Agone recognizes that one or other social text *will* penetrate his flesh, making it a sign for others to read, and that this will always involve pain; he claims, at least, the right to exhibit an awareness of this sign-making—and the right to introduce a "personal" or secret meaning, troubling any act of reading his body.

Agone's experience of being tattooed is entwined with the enactment of homosexual desire. The tattooist seduces him, and the two active rejections of hegemonic masculinity blur and become analogies of each other. Both experiences (in this context) are about interfering in the transmission of hegemonic meanings, making penetration something other than one-way domination. Agone loses his sense of reality and identity when the tattooist touches his penis: "For the first time he had to hold on while the seas started to rise. He knew, from experience, though he didn't know from where the experience had come, that he was about to no longer know where he was" (137). He has left the known port for the shifting sea of unfixed identity. The tattooist's lips on Agone's penis are "waves which had parted to let the kid walk safely through this monstrous ocean. The father parted himself, all of His world, all of being, to let the child walk in safety" (137). This is not the oedipal father-God, nor the accompanying model of conflictive oedipal desire.[90] With the painful decision to rewrite his body, to take the tattoo upon himself and claim "the power of those who chose to live beyond the norms of society," Agone also chooses to rewrite the script of sexuality and take pleasure in what is called "outlaw."[91] Abhor, in drag, looks on and learns.

That Agone, not Abhor, receives the tattoo is significant.[92] In their reading of tattooing and gender, Frances E. Mascia-Lees and Patricia Sharpe argue that tattoos may in fact function to close down polysemy, especially for women. They warn that because of the historical association of women's bodies with the nature side of the nature/culture binary, tattoos on women may only reinforce the notion of the female body as an originally pure space, affected by culture only on its surface. Tattoos may thus play into "the predominant Western cultural metaphor of writing on the body . . . in which the woman is envisioned as the blank page awaiting inscription and the male as the writer."[93] Even among groups of men, tattoos may be used to evoke or externalize an "essential" identity, as among male prisoners who "see their tattoos as marks of identity which cannot be stripped from them as their clothes and other personal possessions have been."[94] But the evocation of an essential identity can have different, more dangerous, implications for women. Women are already overassociated with an essential bodiliness that men are usually assumed to transcend. Noting this discrepancy, Daniel Punday suggests, "It is appropriate, then, that Acker describes tattooing on the male rather than female body, since for her tattooing is a form of representation that has the power to reveal the material where it might otherwise go unnoticed."[95]

In contrast to the bodily materiality emphasized by Agone's tattoo, Abhor uses precisely the clothes that could be "stripped from" her as her tool for emphasizing bodily *constructedness*. Her cross-dressing prevents her female body from being reduced to a gendered univocality in the way that even tattooing might encourage. The necessity of this difference between her strategy for disrupting bodily meaning and Agone's (even as a marginalized male, a gay Latin-American criminal) is emphasized by her subsequent experience of the relation between body and text for women writers.[96]

Abhor's utopian moment of witnessing a body claiming the right to write its own definition is only temporary. She subsequently finds that as a woman and a (part) black, she has less power of self-definition than Agone. She finds herself again having to negotiate with patriarchal texts, and with their denial of women's power to write themselves. Part 3 is largely a plagiarism of *Huck Finn*; in it, Thivai's version of the pirate myth and Abhor's collide. Thivai is Huck, for whom it is all something of a romantic adventure; Abhor is Jim, the illiterate black whose body is in danger. Their final adventures demonstrate the extent to which dualism persists in a heritage of familiar narratives.

Abhor's dreams of the open sea have found material form in the dirty waters of the Seine/Mississippi. A river flows in one direction only, confined by banks. Abhor may have moved beyond dualistic versions of gender and race, but she still has to deal with Thivai's notion of rebellion, which is firmly patriarchal and Eurocentric. His pirate narrative is that "[b]y murdering raping and looting men get gold 'n jewels 'n engraved stationery 'n corporations 'n hospitals."[97] Being a pirate means being a man, in a strictly binary system that sees women as "the same as loot" (189). Abhor does not meet this story's definition of femininity, which seeks to naturalize gender. Abhor's cyborg body threatens this naturalizing: Thivai complains, "nothing (not even womanhood) was natural in her" (193). In order to reduce Abhor to the appropriate role of object, Thivai has her arrested so that he will have to rescue her. The textual impediments to Abhor's pirate dreams are enforced by the male-invoked power of the state—now once again reified in the form of the Revolutionary Algerian Police.

Here, Acker reexamines the relationship between body and text when that body belongs to a woman in a sexist society. Thivai and his gay biker friend, Mark, visit Abhor in prison and decide to make her "into a great writer so that she'd have a reason for being in jail for the rest of her life. And at that time, society needed a great woman writer" (203). Thivai and Mark cut Abhor's fingertips and force her to write in her own blood, because "[w]riters need disability or madness they can overcome in order to write" (203). The essentializing of art, as an act of individual and unique heroism, goes hand in hand with the naturalizing of gender. Haraway offers an anatomy of organic origin myths such as those embodied in Thivai's sections of the narrative: "Every story that begins with original innocence and privileges the return to wholeness" and focuses on "war, tempered by imaginary respite in the bosom of the Other."[98] Such stories, she points out, also maintain the nature/culture binary in seeing writing as a "fall," a (necessary) corruption of the blank page of nature. Writing must therefore be a heroic and original effort, a labor painful to the body—and especially to the female body, which requires a more violent effort to separate itself from nature—*not* the playful pilfering and mixing of existing codes suggested by a cyborg text such as Acker's. In both cases, writing and identity, the dualistic myth of the organic "body" is used to prevent the pirating of power away from hegemony.

Empire ends with Abhor again stealing a text and using it to confound rationality. She escapes from prison, finds an abandoned motorcycle, and rides it in defiance of Mark and Thivai. When Thivai tells her she can't ride without knowing the rules, she finds a copy of *The Highway Code* and performs her own "stupid" (in the Bakhtinian sense) reading of it. She weaves a narrative around the list of warning signs in the *Code*, signs saying "radioactive," "spontaneously combustible," "compressed gas," "oxidizing agent," "corrosive," and "toxic." Signs invented for destructive commodities that embody the worst excesses of instrumental reason, the subjugation of raw material to the demands of human financial profit, become the basis for a tale of liberation, of outlaw Arabs and motorcycles. Abhor takes the rule book and makes it her own, as she takes the phallic sexual power of the motorcycle and the outlaw status of the biker and makes of them her dry-land version of the pirate.

But *Empire of the Senseless* concludes on a provisional note, as Abhor receives another reminder that she cannot, in rejecting rationalism, risk falling into its dualistic opposite, irrationality. Irrationality cannot acknowledge the power imbalances rationalism has created. After Mark tells her how sexually violent biker men are against women, Abhor gives up her biker dream of an alternative community. Each useful myth must be discarded as its context changes. Abhor begins again the difficult and constant struggle to fight hegemonic rationalism while maintaining a nonessentialist insistence on gender differences. That these differences are textual and contextual is underlined by the drawing of a tattoo that is the book's last image. It is a rose pierced by a knife, wrapped by a banner upon which is written "DISCIPLINE AND ANARCHY." The tension between the discipline of life in a dualistic, gendered body and the anarchy enabled by recognizing that body as a construct pervades Acker's vision of a postmodern feminist subjectivity. This is also the tension between the discipline of the hegemonic text and the anarchy of the contextual mutations that can be made from it. This tension, permeating the cyborg-pirate's skin, is a fruitful one that keeps blooming—and changing—as it bleeds.

Conclusion

I have called Acker's novels "unreasonable" (in my chapter title) because this word offers a third term, a way out of the binary opposition between the rational and the irrational. To be unreasonable frequently carries connotations of protest, of someone's stubborn refusal to acknowledge the superiority of the logic of the person using the term. The unreasonable person's position implies that rationality isn't everything, that other desires or even needs must also be taken into account. To be irrational, on the other hand, is simply to be incomprehensible or hysterical, to remove oneself from contestation entirely.

Acker's novels from *Pasolini* to *Empire of the Senseless* engage with a system increasingly able to incorporate both rational and irrational protests. These novels develop another strategy, an "unreasonable" manipulation of textual scraps that takes the very words and images that have inscribed women as powerless and irrational beings and turns them to women's advantage by tactically recombining them and pointing out their contradictions.

Only by understanding Acker's work as materialist, as concerned with historically specific circumstances, can the space for agency it offers become apparent. With my readings in this chapter and in chapter 4, I hope to counteract some previous critical treatment of her work. Approaches to these novels that draw on a certain universalizing tendency within poststructuralism find in them complex and interesting examples of either women's or, worse, all people's relation to a language that (universally and uniformly) fails to refer to anything but its own history. But these readings rarely see Acker's work as offering more than a critique, nor go far toward finding a way out.

Poststructuralism's notion that reality is only constructed through language, through texts, can indeed offer room for agency and change, *if* combined with an insistence on the dependence of this reality on particular readers who construct it differently according to their own historical positions. Texts only exist when read, and only historically specific readers read them. Acker's engagement with rationality, not simply as the inherent structure of language itself but as a changing material structure existing in specific forms of social organization, offers examples of how readers of the postmodern social text might capitalize on proliferating narrative possibilities in order to evade categorization and stay one step ahead of hegemony's ability to incorporate images to itself.

3
Angela Carter's War of Real Dreams

> One of the fighters bandaged his own wounds. The girl, naked, bathed in the river. The girl and the fighter fucked. The temple is decayed.
> —Kathy Acker, *In Memoriam to Identity*

> I led her to the bed and, in the variegated shadows, penetrated her sighing flesh, which was as chill as that of a mermaid or of the marmoreal water-maiden in her own garden. I was aware of a curiously attenuated response, as if she were feeling my caresses through a veil, and you must realize that all this time I was perfectly well aware she was asleep, for, apart from the evidence of my senses, I remembered how the peep-show proprietor had talked of a beautiful somnambulist.
> —Angela Carter, *The Infernal Desire Machines of Doctor Hoffman*

One would be hard pressed to find a style that differed more from Kathy Acker's blunt, street-smart polemics than the purple prose of British writer Angela Carter. Carter was a fabulist, a connoisseur of the fantastic, the Gothic, and the grotesque. While Acker strips the mystifying aestheticism from the patriarchal narratives she retells, Carter draws on all the rich resources of literary language to induce in her readers a claustrophobic awareness of the power of the aesthetic to construct compelling worlds. Stylistically as well as thematically in Carter's novels, the beauty of imaginary worlds is a powerful force, one not to be dismissed by those who would change society. Carter is more concerned than Acker with acknowledging and investigating the allure of images offered by largely masculine aesthetic traditions, as well as the political implications of that allure.

The two writers' approaches to literary history and its shaping effect on female social identity do have a great deal in common. Like Acker, Carter takes a postmodernist view of history as the transmission not so much of facts but of texts. Literary and artistic texts are very much a part of this body of history, both products of their historical moment and integral to defining that moment. That the images of reality and social identity offered by literary history play a significant role in shaping the present prompts both writers' obsession with reworking existing texts. Carter's method is more allusive than Acker's direct plagiarism; she integrates borrowed texts into her narratives and into the very fabric of her language, a language dripping with "literariness." Both writers' quotational tactics suggest that literary meaning, rather than being autonomous and fixed, changes according to the circumstances under which a reader uses a text. Their novels' engagement with the history of literature thus becomes an examination of the history of texts' uses and effects, especially their often horrifying effects on women.

I have chosen Carter as this study's second exemplar of feminist postmodernism because her work shares with Acker's a central concern with reading as a location of agency. However, my focus is also on the intense aestheticism of Carter's works from the 1970s. I want to frame that aestheticism as a response to, and an intervention in, a different decade and a different set of national conditions from those faced by Acker in the eighties. Discussing Acker's work in the previous chapter, I was interested primarily in developing a theory of feminist-postmodernist rhetorical strategies, drawing on Acker's use of existing texts and how she changes the political meaning of various images by divorcing them from their original historical context and juxtaposing them with other images. In this chapter, I also want to historicize this strategy itself, to generate a sense of how it might adapt to a specific moment of cultural struggle.

What interests me is how Carter's treatment of existing representations intersects with the deployment of utopian images in various political discourses in Britain at the time. The 1970s were a period when the exhaustion of one set of ideological images in Britain led to the need for a new political imagery. This exhaustion of images made new cultural production particularly relevant to political debates. My readings of *The Infernal Desire Machines of Doctor Hoffman* (1972), *The Passion of New Eve* (1977), and *Love*—initially published in 1971, and revised from a later perspective in 1987—suggest that Carter's aestheticism, her elaborately stylized immersion in literary traditions, is a strategy for engaging with the contemporary politics of Britain in the seventies, including the decline of socialism and the evolution of the women's movement. Carter's novels of this period recognize that politicized desires compete and gain their power first and above all in the realm of representation. I will begin by arguing that Britain's economic and political crisis of the 1970s accompanied a crisis of representation; then I will examine Carter's novels of the period, as they both join in contemporary criticisms of existing political visions and utopias and create a space for theorizing how such images might be historicized and recombined in resolutely *non*-utopian ways as the basis for new political identities. I aim to develop a sense of Carter's work as both dependent for its meaning on the circumstances of the day, and itself an intervention that refigures the crisis.

Britain's crisis of representation

In my introductory chapter I added my voice to those theorists who argue that postmodernity in general is marked by an increase of political contestation on the level of images or signification. However, the unique conditions of this development in Britain in the past three decades or so have been shaped by the legacies of colonialism, the economic effects of World War II, class configurations "left over" from the nineteenth century, and Britain's reluctant acknowledgment of postwar U.S. dominance. These circumstances add up to a crisis of national identity.

Stuart Hall and Henk Overbeek, among others, have argued that the postwar social contract disintegrated in Britain by approximately the time of the energy crises of 1973–74, which brought down the (Conservative) Heath government. This social contract had been characterized by a widespread acceptance of limited state socialism within a capitalist frame, or social democracy.[1] Capitalist and conservative factions generally found Labour Party policies of nationalization and the welfare state acceptable because these policies sought also to rationalize and modernize British industry and the workforce. However, Overbeek argues that the subsequent breakdown was due to the fact that these programs never succeeded in establishing a Fordist "regime of accumulation" on the same level as had been accomplished in the United States by World War II or in Western Europe after the war.[2] Accompanying this policy failure was the British government's, industry's, and the public's failure to develop political visions appropriate to the new international circumstances.

The persistence of Britain's residual ties to its imperial history contributed to this failure of Fordism (as, also, to a lingering image of national identity based on empire); privileged trade arrangements with the Commonwealth nations created artificial supports for fundamentally inefficient businesses and helped dissuade the British government from entering into the more modernized European Common Market. Ironically, the relative lack of damage done to British industry by World War II meant that outmoded production systems were not replaced in Britain as they had to be in much of Europe. The war had also left British trade unions unscathed, compared to the wholesale repression they underwent on the Continent, meaning that class and craft divisions inherited from the Industrial Revolution persisted largely unmodified. And finally, the terms of Marshall Plan aid to Britain—the emblem of postwar U.S. global hegemony—required a moderation of some nationalization plans and a concentration of capital in finance rather than industry.[3] These factors combined to pave the way for the exceptionally heavy impact on the British economy of the global recession in the early seventies.[4]

To borrow from the title of one of Carter's novels, what resulted in Britain was a "War of Dreams"—a period, from approximately 1973 to Margaret Thatcher's election as prime minister in 1979, of intense contestation over the form the nation's future would take.[5] All the conventional options seemed to have expired in the postwar compromise that had brought down Labour and Conservative governments alike in a spiral of inflation, unemployment, and bitterness. The newer utopian visions of the sixties also rang suddenly hollow; as journalist Andrea Adam remembers it, the counterculture collapsed when "[e]veryone woke up one day and realised that they were nearly 30, without a job and that jobs were getting very scarce and that they were broke and there was no money coming from anywhere."[6] Socialism had suffered a series of defeats and disillusionments, some of them the result of the Labour Party's compromises with capital.[7] In addition, "the events of 1968"—the Prague Spring, the student uprisings in France, Germany, and Britain, and the increasingly violent protests against the Vietnam War in the United States and elsewhere—left British socialism split between a disillusionment with "actually existing" communism, on the one hand, and increased radicalism on the other. Many formerly socialist women were also growing disaffected with the male bias of the utopia they were offered, realizing that "Socialist men were just like men anywhere."[8]

Hall argues that the emptying out of the old visions meant that who would win this struggle "for the formation of a new hegemonic stage" turned to an unprecedented extent on the ability to articulate new political and social *images*.[9] Cultural and political control would go to that faction most able to provide stories and identities that could make sense of the new reality. His thesis is that the rise of Thatcherism as a new political solution, which ended this period of contestation, is attributable less to any real economic remedies than to a successful articulation of new political images. The crisis of the 1970s that Hall describes—a crisis of the social identities and political dreams available to Britons—underlies the concern of Angela Carter's fiction with the interrelation of aesthetic image and material reality. Carter's novels of this period highlight the bankruptcy of the political visions inscribed in existing literature and suggest how resistant groups, including women, might strategically recontextualize elements of familiar narratives to offer new images of identity.

Critical responses to Carter

Looking at the continual back-and-forth movement in Carter's work between the fantastic and the insistently material, critics have often suggested that her writing begs to be read allegorically.[10] That observation has occasionally led to rather reductive readings of her work as simply the direct translation of some contemporary ideological conflict (say, reason versus unreason, or cultural feminism versus socialist feminism) into a stylized setting—which, in turn, often prompts the critic to wonder *why doesn't she offer a solution?* I don't think that the allegorical element in Carter's work functions that straightforwardly—but nevertheless, the concept of a text that works on more than one level seems crucial for analyzing the sense that her writing (especially prior to the 1980s) often creates for *readers* of being both beckoned and alienated by the fictional worlds she offers.

Most critics and many other readers have, in fact, been more attracted than repulsed by Carter's novels and short stories, especially in more recent years. Since her early death (at the age of fifty-one) in 1992, there has been the usual ironic outpouring of both popular and scholarly attention to her writing, especially in Britain; but even in the 1980s, she had become a central literary figure in Britain and a frequent visiting writer at universities in the United States, and her early novels (with the exception of *Several Perceptions* [1968]) were back in print in the United Kingdom after a period of being unavailable. Even while Carter was still in her twenties, her second and third novels (*The Magic Toyshop*, 1967, and *Several Perceptions*; her first was *Shadow Dance*, 1966) won literary prizes. Between 1965 and her death, she published nine novels; three collections of her own short stories and one of translations; a collection of three radio plays; and a critical work, *The Sadeian Woman and the Ideology of Pornography* (in Britain, *The Sadeian Woman: An Exercise in Cultural History*). In addition, she wrote regular reviews and essays for *New Society* and other publications (and published two collections of these pieces) as well as editing three collections of fairy tales and women's short stories; and both *The Magic Toyshop* and her story, "The Company of Wolves," were made into movies (the former directed by David Wheatley in 1989; the latter, by Neil Jordan in 1984).[11]

In the United States, she has been less well known. Her three last and most cheerful novels—the widely acclaimed *Nights at the Circus* and *Wise Children*, and the 1988 revised edition of her earlier *Love*—and her 1979 collection of stories based on fairy tales, *The Bloody Chamber*, have consistently been available from Penguin, but until her death, her earlier novels were unavailable except from British publishers.

But despite Carter's greater popularity in Britain, not all British readers have seen her work as fruitfully engaged with contemporary politics. The dandyism of her style has proved highly disturbing to readers on both sides of the Atlantic. The controversy she has generated among critics is provoked not only by her preoccupation with violent or coercive sex, as I will discuss further in the following chapter, but by the apparent complicity with the ideology underlying those actions of her elaborate and seductively sensualized descriptions.

Often, Carter's work has been defended and attacked on the same grounds: for its aestheticization of violence. Recommending Carter to U.S. readers, Walter Kendrick situates her primarily as the inheritor of a high-cultural tradition of decadence. He praises her "ability to make gorgeous tableaux out of carnage," arguing that "the violence she portrays would be merely sickening, like Stephen King's or Clive Barker's, if it weren't described in rhapsodic, grand-operatic terms that in their very extravagance promise deliverance from evil."[12] For Kendrick, Carter's aestheticism marks her work's engagement with an *idea* of violence, which participates in a larger exploration of representation itself.

While Kendrick is quite right to situate Carter's aestheticism in the context of a high-cultural tradition, doing so does not entirely address the argument made against her work that representations of violence *should* be "merely" sickening, and that to cloak them in the promise of redemption (aesthetic or other) is implicitly to celebrate bloodshed. His defense leaves Carter vulnerable to the criticisms voiced by Robert Clark, who sees in the shimmering surfaces of Carter's fiction a deadening of affect and, thus, of moral and political judgment: "The brilliant and choice lexicon, the thematization of surfaces and odors, of beauty, youth and power, the incantatory rythms [*sic*] and tantalizing literariness, are strategies that bind the reader poetically, give the illusion of general significance without its substance, and put the reason to sleep, thereby inhibiting satire's necessary distancing of the reader from both the text and the satirized illusions."[13] Clark, like Fredric Jameson, sees this ethical neutrality as the necessary end product of postmodernist literature. He associates Carter's strategy with the techniques of advertising, arguing that both use floating signifiers of beauty to elicit a generalized desire—a desire that is then directed to the product at hand, be it a shampoo or a novelist.[14]

Clark's concerns, however, spring from an assumption that beauty can be transhistorical, that such a thing as floating signifiers of beauty—unattached to any society or any particular aesthetic tradition—can exist. But Carter emphasizes the traces of historical meaning that attach necessarily to the specific literary traditions on which she draws (the Gothic, surrealism, domestic realism, the picaresque, etc.). She denies the possibility of a privileged literary realm separate from history.[15] As Alison Lee puts it, "Even when Carter's novels are set in the future or in an unspecified time . . . , the historical perspective is maintained by a literary history that has been equally important in shaping how we view the world."[16] Far from keeping the reader on the level of enchanted surfaces, the jarring combination in her work of the almost excessively literary and the downright brutal can produce a vacillation between surface and meaning—again, the allegorical mode—that seems to beg for some material grounding.

But the most useful readings of allegory in Carter's work emphasize the fact that the reader cannot comfortably stay on one side *or* the other, reading her texts as mere fantasy or as plain historical realism; rather, the inextricable intertwining of the decorative and the material suggests that the imaginative realm is one place where real history is made. Carter's imaginary worlds do not point in only one direction, and this is made clear in part by the refusal of any image to connect to one referent only. This instability of reference is emphasized by the multiple allusions Carter incorporates; critic Linden Peach, for example, points out that in *Love*, a central character (Lee) is likened in a single sentence to "Billy Budd, or a worker hero of the Soviets, or a boy in a book by Jack London."[17] For Peach, such a mess of connections is "ahistorical" and even "dehistoricised"; but perhaps it also points to the possibility of recontextualization as a means of changing the historical "message" that the invoked texts have previously carried.

This may especially be true when Carter's allusive texts are read in the context of a historical moment when the nature of the new political imaginary and the new political formation was to some extent "up for grabs." In such a context, the referent of her stories may be the process itself by which storytelling (however fantastical) and concrete politics interact, in the production of visions with which readers might identify. What Alison Lee says of *The Infernal Desire Machines of Doctor Hoffman* may be equally true of all three of the novels I discuss here: "The novel is indeed an allegory, but one of reading, of desiring, and of desiring through reading."[18]

Postcolonial fantasies:
The Infernal Desire Machines of Doctor Hoffman

The Infernal Desire Machines of Doctor Hoffman provides an apt example of Carter's engagement with the early stages of the 1970s' political upheaval. With this novel, Carter turned from the claustrophobic domestic settings and sexualized family relationships of early novels such as *The Magic Toyshop* and *Love* to charting fantastical adventures on a grand, international scale. The narrative concerns a struggle (open to a number of allegorical interpretations) over who will rule a nation: whether the dominant regime will be based more on repressive, rationalist control or on the manipulation of fantasy and representation associated with the mysterious revolutionary, Dr. Hoffman.[19]

The war *Hoffman* chronicles, in a fictitious Latin-American nation sometime after World War II, is between the central government and the renegade physicist-metaphysician, Hoffman, who has found a way to make the contents of the human imagination become palpable and *real*. Hoffman is systematically undermining the distinction between reality and fantasy by flooding the capital city with concrete manifestations of the citizens' desires, dreams, and nightmares. The narrative, which purports to be a memoir written years later, follows the darkly picaresque adventures of its narrator, the cynical and disaffected Desiderio, an agent of the government Ministry of Determination, who sets out to destroy Hoffman but falls in love with his enigmatic daughter. Desiderio hunts Hoffman through a series of self-contained subcultures: a provincial town rife with sexual intrigue; the timeless traditional world of the river-dwelling "Indians"; a traveling circus; the sexual underworld of a sadistic aristocrat; a transatlantic voyage complete with an attack by pirates; an African coast metamorphosed into the phantasmagoric continent of "nebulous time," populated by Hoffman's mythic beasts; and, finally, Hoffman's own Gothic castle-cum-laboratory. The Doctor's daughter, Albertina, accompanies Desiderio in various guises through most of his adventures.

It is also possible to read the novel as *anti*allegorical, at least inasmuch as it warns against the reduction of any image to a single meaning: it seems to point out that no system, and certainly neither end of *this* political spectrum, can account for the local, concrete, and *varied* experiences of representations (in the plural) of diverse social groups. Specifically, neither warring party in *Hoffman* seems to see the differentiating effects of a history of colonialism and gender stereotyping when shaping its vision of a new regime. My reading of the novel will attempt to keep a balance between exploring its apparent historical referents and pursuing this antiallegorical emphasis on the multiple ways in which any single image takes on meaning for different readers.

The novel's central conflict, Hoffman's attempt to subvert the government, certainly evokes the movements for political and sexual revolution that had risen to prominence in industrialized nations in the 1960s but were already fragmenting and collapsing by the turn of the decade. Carter looks at Hoffman's "liberation" campaign through Desiderio and Albertina, both of whom are marked as racially different from the European colonial mainstream: Desiderio is the abandoned child of a white prostitute mother and an indigenous "Indian" father, while the "Mongolian"-looking Albertina was born to the (white) German Doctor and a Chinese mother. Carter suggests, ultimately, that the collapse of liberation movements may be attributable to their failure to acknowledge that their utopian visions are just as predicated on the racism and sexism of existing images and dreams (transmitted, in part, through literary traditions) as is the dominant culture.

This critique has its parallels to the Britain of the late sixties: for instance, while the "underground" magazines addressed to the British youth counterculture—magazines such as *IT (International Times)*, *Oz*, and *Frendz*—sought to offer a revolutionary alternative to the piecemeal and narrow-based reform proposals of the bourgeois, white establishment, all too frequently their visual and verbal rhetoric relied on and reinforced hegemonic taboos, offering images of naked women and "savages" as symbols of transgression. One 1970 issue of *Oz* featured an article by "Germaine" (Greer) denouncing the bourgeois base of the emerging American women's movement, which was accompanied, in the typical random-collage style of the day's underground press, by a photograph of a dark-skinned (probably Asian) young girl on the verge of puberty, wearing nothing but jewelry. The same issue illustrated *Oz*'s regular medical column, "Ask Doctor Hippocrates," with the image of a topless Black woman, sliced in half vertically to expose sketched-in viscera.[20] These images may have come across as funny and silly, as shocking, or as calls for a natural, liberated sexuality, but their participation in long traditions of using the sexualized and mutilated bodies of women of color to communicate the power desires of some white men to other white men undermines the counterculture's claims to represent—in both senses—a clean break with existing culture.

In fact, another possible "allegorical" reading of Carter's novel could see it, more generally, as a reflection of contemporary debates over the politics of representation—and especially, the rise of poststructuralism. Robert Clark, for instance, reads the central opposition between the Minister of Determination and the Doctor, the two men vying for control of the nation and for Desiderio's allegiance, as a stereotyped version of postmodernism debates. For Clark, the novel stages the struggle between "a humanist episteme founded on truth, reference, and reason" (although the Minister, who represents this position, admittedly employs "fascistic secret police") and "a relativizing episteme of constant flux between images." He identifies the novel as a literary engagement with "the crucial socioeconomic transformation of the post-war industrialized world."[21] In simplified terms, that transformation is the unprecedented concentration of political and economic power in the realm of representation. However, Clark concludes that *Hoffman* ultimately falls on the Doctor's—or poststructuralist's—side of the opposition, and that it thus shrugs off the question of history entirely. He suggests that Carter's highly crafted, seductively artful narrative itself dissolves into a meaningless rehearsal of literary images, "a parody that has no discernible point of departure or of arrival and seems always to verge on pastiche."[22]

But Clark's critique may have too much in common with the Minister in its suggestion that real history stops where symbolization begins. He ignores the novel's setting in a postcolonial nation that is *not* fully a part of the "industrialized world"; the *ideological* means and effects of this marginal position are central to the novel's political meaning. To suggest that *Hoffman* relinquishes political reality for textual play ignores the crucial connection Carter makes between the two.

Clark's reading situates *Hoffman* only in the macrocontext of a culturally uniform shift from an Enlightenment to a postmodern episteme. Such shifts do not occur uniformly; they are experienced differently and unequally by privileged sectors of society and those marginalized by race and gender. Rather than presenting an either/or choice between modernity and postmodernity, *Hoffman* addresses the role played in the formation of the emerging conjuncture by inherited images of race and constructions of gender. Far from wholeheartedly endorsing the indiscriminate flux of images, Carter's novel may serve as a warning that postmodern power factions will depend on the ability of the images they deploy to evoke a whole range of historical associations. Contrary to the assertions of some postmodern theorists that images today have been emptied of their history, Carter suggests that such associations, born from real relations of power, cannot be escaped; those who recognize this, and know best how to manipulate the loyalties and animosities various images evoke, will win the War of Dreams.

This reading again suggests Carter's complex engagement with the contemporary crisis in Britain, despite (or *through*) the obvious foreignness of *Hoffman*'s world. I want now to pause, and to summarize briefly the evidence of an intense contestation taking place in Britain over symbols of race and gender during the years leading up to the crisis of the 1970s. I do this not to suggest that Carter's novel simply *reflects* the situation, translating it into fantastical terms, but rather to bolster my argument that both race in particular and, to a lesser extent, gender were already providing a highly charged vocabulary of images—one that belies the notion of any uniform, indiscriminate postmodernity such as Clark's reading assumes.

The ghosts of Britain's imperial past remained an active influence not only in the form of the special economic relations with the Commonwealth countries that helped cripple Fordist reforms. Postwar British governments also wanted to assure voters of a continued claim to the "moral leadership" they exercised as "the mother country."[23] This necessitated keeping Commonwealth residents in Britain's sphere of influence by continuing to extend to them the formal and legal status of native British subjects. When existing economic conditions in the former colonies (unequal land distribution and a heavy emphasis on export crops) combined with the acute labor shortages in Britain—brought on in the postwar years by "a massive backlog of postponed projects," reconstruction, war casualties, and emigration—these Commonwealth Britons took advantage of their lingering colonial status to immigrate to "the mother country" in unprecedented numbers.[24]

The reactions of white Britons to the influx of West Indian, Indian, and Pakistani Britons offered an early example of the means by which reactionary forces would eventually be able to win the 1970s War of Dreams by recombining *existing* political discourses as replacements for worn-out visions of national identity. Paul Gilroy traces a shift in anti-immigrant rhetoric in the late 1960s, exemplified most dramatically by Conservative Member of Parliament Enoch Powell's infamous "river of blood" speech of April 1968. Powell's speech was an open expression of racism unprecedented in recent years.[25] But it also combined an existing discourse, which based national identity on a shared legal system, with another discourse, dating from at least the nineteenth century, of urban youth criminality and illegality, in order to figure young black males as a criminal threat to British nationhood.[26] Clearly, the old, benignly paternalistic ideology of the Commonwealth was dead; the self-congratulating image of the dark-skinned, British-educated, gentleman "overseas" citizen was slain by visions of poor West Indian immigrants moving in next door and competing for resources in a rapidly declining economy. A significant number of white Britons, sometimes reacting to the new immigrants with a hostility bordering on panic, drew instead on the racist ideologies that had long been cultivated as a necessary, if hidden, underpinning to British imperialism. During the 1960s, first Conservative then Labour governments passed increasingly drastic anti-immigration laws. Popular racist sentiment took perhaps its most sinister form in the founding of the fascist National Front in 1966.[27]

The concern of Carter's novel with postcoloniality recognizes that a racial situation such as the new one in Britain provides potent weapons in a war of images. Postcolonial immigration enabled right-wing groups to replace the worn-out historical language of industrial classes with a new vocabulary of national identity whose *foundation* was the unspoken term of race. Gilroy cites an editorial from the Thatcherite journal *Salisbury Review*, looking back on the 1970s: "never before had it seemed so hard to recreate the verbal symbols, the images and axioms, through which the concept of authority could be renewed." Gilroy refers to this situation as a national "crisis of representation" and suggests that the Right's eventual solution was to make "'race' and nation the framework for a rhetoric of order through which modern conservatism could voice populist protest against Britain's post-imperial plight and marshal its historic bloc."[28] This new deployment of old, imperialist racial-national ideologies could unite the white working class with the traditionally middle- and upper-class Tory constituency in an entirely new political bloc. Arising in the moment when these repositionings were beginning to take shape but were not yet consolidated, Carter's novel addresses the powerful potential of race and postcoloniality as symbols onto which Britons could concentrate political desires, both reactionary and progressive.[29]

To a lesser extent, gender had also begun to emerge in public by the end of the 1960s as a discourse where the old identity options were apparently exhausted and where new meanings might be developed. The (second-wave) British women's movement, which would contribute in the seventies to the sense that existing political visions were bankrupt, arose in reaction to (although also on the shoulders of) the leftist initiatives of the sixties. Its growth was stimulated in part by the obliviousness of conventional socialism and national-liberation movements to the specificities of gender oppression, and by the ways in which leftist utopianism reproduced the sexism of dominant culture.[30]

However, gender as a political issue did not reach an intense level of public debate in Britain until somewhat later than the race/immigration crisis and later than the publication of *Hoffman* (although both struggles are, of course, ongoing). While historians of British women's rights activism in the twentieth and twenty-first centuries emphasize that feminism remains alive and well—and is perhaps more widespread than ever—mass organizing under the banner of Women's Liberation was "a particular phase of the women's movement that was a product of the 1960s, . . . peaked in the 1970s and faded in the 1980s."[31] A discussion of these "peak" years will come later, in reference to Carter's 1977 *The Passion of New Eve*. But when the sixties were melting into the seventies, British feminists were talking about gender primarily in terms of a blind spot in leftist visions.

In *Hoffman*, Carter highlights the material results of such a failure of the imagination by making apparent some of the effects on women of many (male) oppositional movements' conventional fantasies of gender; she does so through Albertina's sufferings as a supporter of her father's liberation project. These negative effects point to the more fundamental failure of leftist utopianism to recognize that all dreams are entangled in a web of power relations already existing in society. I say "more fundamental" because the success of the New Right a decade later rested on just this realization. What was at stake in the struggle over images of gender in the late sixties and early seventies became very apparent by the end of the 1970s. The New Right had by then also recognized the importance of images of gender and had managed to deploy them to its own advantage, marshaling voters around popular ideologies of family sex-roles and directing these already-existing myths toward attacks on the feminist agenda.[32] The familiar litany of challenges to abortion rights, cuts in welfare support to mothers, and other policies promoting women's marginalization in or elimination from the workforce were all couched in the rhetoric of the traditional British family. All this was far in the future as Carter wrote *Hoffman*, but the later success of the Right in manipulating existing gender and race ideologies to gain popular support points out how crucial it was for British women in the late sixties and early seventies to establish those dreams and myths as a central concern of the radical Left—not only for white women's sake, but for the configuration of the entire political landscape.

The existing dreams circulate in culture through many channels, literature and other forms of the written word having historically been among the most significant. Carter's layering of allusions insists on this intertextuality of lived experience, which shapes all political movements through a heavy and rich legacy of images. Elaine Jordan emphasizes the parodic and quotational form of the episodes of Carter's narrative, their extensive echoes of other texts. Among the sources of Desiderio's adventures she identifies are pornography, fairy tales, Rousseau, Lévi-Strauss, Freud, Sade, and Nietzsche; Suleiman points out extensive borrowing from *The Cabinet of Dr Caligari*, and Lee notes allusions to the work of various composers; I would add the existentialism of Camus and, for the centaur episode, that great exercise in antiutopianism, *Gulliver's Travels*.[33] The narrative emphasizes the often unacknowledged effects of each of these texts when used to shape a world. *Hoffman* suggests that neither side of the partisan struggles between proponents of the Enlightenment/modernist episteme and postmodern flux gets at the real issue; the novel's intertextuality argues that texts *do* shape our world, and that the real question is to discriminate among the different effects of specific images.

Granted, the simple allegorical reading of the Minister and Hoffman is initially available. Carter offers plenty of textual support for seeing the Minister as the embodiment of Enlightenment positivism, and specifically of realist attitudes toward signification. The Minister is a paragon of impassive order, the only man whose lack of imagination renders him immune to the hallucinations of "the Hoffman effect." His primary strategy against Hoffman is linguistic: a massive project of classification, of matching existing objects to their appropriate names in order to keep their identities from slipping or blurring. This means that neither language nor the reality it describes may deviate from historical precedent. Such a philosophy also has its political component:

> He called it his theory of "names and functions." Each man was secure in possession of a certain name which also ensured him a certain position in society seen as a series of interlinking rings which, although continually in movement, were never subjected to change for there were never any disturbances and no usurpation of names or ranks or roles whatsoever.[34]

For the Minister, language and images exist only in absolute correlation with material reality. His is certainly one of the worldviews, Lyotard's "metanarratives," that were challenged in the late sixties and early seventies.

Hoffman, too, can be located historically in the competing worldviews of the period. In the story of his rise to power we get one parodic version of sixties counterculture: a privileged child of white liberals, a bright university student who dabbles in radical theory and free sex, drops out of school, identifies and associates with the racially marginalized, and ends up a brilliant but eccentric recluse (26–27). More specifically, Clark identifies Hoffman with "Reich's then fashionable theory of the orgone box and the early Marcuse's belief that, in Carter's [actually, Hoffman's] words, 'By the liberation of the unconscious, we shall, of course, liberate man.'"[35] Hoffman's answer to the Minister's theory of signification is a caricature of poststructuralism: "the difference between a symbol and an object is quantitative, not qualitative."[36] Yet in his campaign to make symbols become palpable objects, the Doctor fails to recognize the qualitative differences *among* symbols, their different use values in political struggles.

The problem with both the Minister's and Doctor's utopian aspirations is that neither man adequately acknowledges the reality-effects of imaginary constructs—the ties between symbols and material conditions. This is why neither side holds up as the ideal (or possibly, even as the preferable choice) in an allegorical reading. The Minister simply "refuse[s] to acknowledge how palpable the phantoms" are, despite the fact that when illusory mendicants disappear from the city streets, they leave behind talismans they have carved from real wood (25). Desiderio wonders, "how could a knife of shadows cut real flesh from a living tree? Clearly the phantoms were capable of inflicting significant form on natural substances" (18). Hoffman, for his part, fails to see that the imagination is not a utopian space: the fantasy images he evokes may turn violently on those who imagined them. When Albertina and Desiderio are captured by centaurs during their travels in the Doctor's dream continent, Albertina is convinced that the mythical beasts are emanations of her own desires. Yet the captives "[eat] the bread of the centaurs and [are] nourished by it" (186), and when the centaurs come close to killing the pair, Desiderio notes ironically, "Whatever the reality status of the centaurs, they certainly had the power to deprive us forever of any reality at all" (190). The Minister's philosophy cannot account for the compelling power of the fantasies Hoffman offers, while the Doctor mistakenly believes that ideal images can be formed independently of the shaping influence that existing mythologies and material relations exercise over the human imagination.

That influence becomes very apparent in the extent to which the representations Desiderio and Albertina encounter differ in their effects according to established constructions of race and gender. The Minister's humanist ideology maintains that race makes no difference—or, rather, that racial difference is itself nonexistent. The white regime in the capital city where Desiderio lives would most prefer that people of color literally didn't exist: "The word 'indigenous' [is] unmentionable" and "the city fathers in their veranda'd suburbs [contrive] to ignore" the dark-skinned population of the city slums (16). Yet those people make the city and nation possible. Historically, the colonizers "utilized their labours to build the capital" (67), and their cheap labor remains crucial to the city's prosperity as they comprise the bulk of the "urban proletariat" (69). The society's solution is to obscure the facts of the history and present existence of people of color by rendering them anonymous symbols, mythic figures:

> [I]t was perfectly possible—and, indeed, by far the greater majority of the population did so—to spend all one's life in the capital or the towns of the plain and know little if anything of the Indians. They were bogeymen with which to frighten naughty children; they had become rag-pickers, scrap-dealers, refuse-collectors, and emptiers of cess-pits—those who performed tasks for which you did not need a face. (69)

This myth of absence—this absence in all but myth and cautionary tales—is determined both by the nation's history and by contemporary needs. In order to maintain their claims to governance and cultural hegemony in this postcolonial era, the colonizers' white descendants want to deny the existence of their nation's legitimate inhabitants; but they cannot afford literally to do away with them. Turning them into myth, as Roland Barthes has argued, deliberately retains their presence in representation while emptying it of the history that makes that presence threatening.[37] This representational strategy simultaneously creates white identity, by contrasting it with a mythic Other, and erases the identity of the native people.

This denial of the reality of racial difference in the Minister's world cuts both ways for Desiderio; at first, it "politely" renders his difference invisible, but eventually, it leads to a deadly denial of his reality. Desiderio manages to maintain his respectable position as the Minister's assistant because the nuns who raised him insist he is white.[38] This lie allows his colleagues disingenuously to ignore the evidence of his father's "genetic imprint on [his] face" (16). (He must be white, for he *has* a face.) But when he is sent undercover, outside the city, on his quest for Hoffman—when his government employer literally assigns him a fictitious identity—Desiderio quickly falls afoul of the Minister's own Determination Police, whose job is to test the "reality status" of suspicious objects and persons by subjecting them to the cruelest of tortures. The suspicious objects and persons rarely survive these tests. The leather-trench-coated Determination Police appear to have "been recruited wholesale from a Jewish nightmare" (22), and the history of the imagery they evoke is entirely appropriate to the destiny they plan for Desiderio; they attempt to erase the Other from the present entirely, relegating him to myth and the past. Now that the war of dreams is on, the Indian's semireal status marks him as a dangerous walking fantasy.

However, this official claim of race blindness is not the only popular representation of race in the fictional world of *Hoffman*. Carter emphasizes that, fortunately, various discourses are always in competition with one another to construct a given social group. In sixties counterculture, for instance, race was also constructed by the dream of "ethnic" authenticity, the attribution of innate wisdom and virtue to cultures believed to be uncontaminated by the industrialized West. In Britain this fetishization was directed primarily at the Indian subcontinent, surfacing in everything from Indian-print cotton dresses to a fascination with Buddhism and so-called Oriental mysticism to George Harrison's 1966 pilgrimage to visit sitarist Ravi Shankar. This primitivist valuation of non-European cultures could be employed progressively, to contest bourgeois-Christian values and white supremacy; but Desiderio's encounter with "primitive" people who seem to validate his preconceptions of idealized, uncontaminated otherness suggests, again, the need to be aware that no one discourse can ever completely control the meaning of a group identity. Any attempt at resistance or escape predicated on such a belief will be foiled by the changing meanings of a given identity (racial, sexual, etc.) in different contexts of power.

On escaping from the police, Desiderio takes refuge with his "own" people, the simple and generous river-dwelling Indians. During this "anthropological idyll,"[39] he tries to revert to some residual tribal self whose existence can be fully defined and delineated by a comfortingly consistent set of ancient beliefs and practices. He believes he can escape the war and wash away his urban identity in the heritage of his blood. His life with his new Indian family indeed seems simple and harmonious, until he acts as a mediator between the illiterate Indian traders and a white merchant who tries to cheat them.[40] Then, in accordance with their traditions, the river people determine to kill Desiderio and eat his flesh in order to absorb his special knowledge of the ways of the "shore-dwellers." They almost succeed in luring him to a ritual death by showering him with sexual attention from the family's women, playing upon his own primitivist fantasies of uninhibited and exotic native sexuality. Denied the luxury of indulging in Desiderio's dream of cultural innocence, the river people know they cannot survive economically in isolation from white society. Rather than rejecting or contradicting the dominant culture's equation of primitive with savage, they have embraced the "savage" elements of their tradition, adapting them to their new needs as businesspeople. They manipulate the ultimately racist and sexist images Desiderio has picked up as a largely assimilated Indian to serve their own material ends.

In this chapter, "The River People," and elsewhere, Carter's novel argues that the capacity to survive in postcolonial (and, by extension, postmodern British) society depends on the ability to manipulate representations. The book's most powerful characters are those who wield images most successfully. Here I am thinking of Hoffman and of the grotesque Lithuanian aristocrat in whose employ Desiderio and Albertina witness the horrors of the unleashed human imagination in the book's middle chapters, "The Erotic Traveller" and "The Coast of Africa." (The Minister, for all his authority, would ultimately be helpless against Hoffman were it not for Desiderio's eventual understanding of the power of representation. It is Desiderio, acting alone, who finally defeats the Doctor.) The Count illustrates the extremes of racist and sexist violence that can result from the unopposed dominance of one set of representations. Thanks to the increasing power of "the Hoffman principle" (the concretization of imagined visions and desires), and, more prosaically, to the Count's immense fortune, this aristocrat manages to inhabit a world he has constructed entirely from existing fantasies; he himself comes straight from the pages of Sade, and he exercises his passion on surreal, semihuman, mechanical prostitutes from the pages of Baudelaire.[41] The events that seem to emanate literally from his desires turn on his obsession with a phenomenally virile and cruel black pimp, whom he imagines to be his vengeful "twin." This shadow character eventually appears for the showdown in the guise of a cannibal chieftain on the coast of Africa—where the Count and our heroes have been shipwrecked—surrounded by huge female warriors and by "[i]ntensely black and perfectly naked" concubines whose breasts show gigantic bite-marks (158). All the most pernicious stereotypes of sexualized racism combine in the Count's dream finale, and the results are a wholesale bloodbath from which only Desiderio and Albertina escape.

If this is the ultimate flavor of a world shaped by one rich white man's catalog of favorite representations, the question of resistance becomes all the more crucial. To say that power derives from the ability to control representation is one thing; but how can the marginalized acquire such power, when they lack the economic means to beam electronic images across the nation (as the Doctor does) or (like the Count) to pay others to act out their dreams? How can they even begin to desire alternatives to dominant images, when it is clear that the structure of desire is itself a product of existing representations?

For Desiderio, resistance seems to derive from his position as a racial outsider. He manages to retain mental independence, never siding entirely with either party in the war but remaining cynical and detached. He explains, "I was a very disaffected young man for I was not unaware of my own disinheritance" (16). The place in society from which Desiderio has been disinherited is in part a place in the public store of images, in representation. In other words, Desiderio's resistance derives from a racial identity conceived not essentially—as an Archimedean viewpoint on society, uncontaminated by ideology—but as a particular relation to stories. He recognizes himself as not entirely real in the white imagination, and he eventually reacts against the consequences of this: "I possessed a degree of ambivalence towards the Minister's architectonic vision of the perfect state. This was because I was aware of what would have been my own position in that watertight schema" (60). While the Minister panics at the prospect of Hoffman's dream images breeding with real humans and spawning a generation of half-real creatures, Desiderio feels that he is himself "a half-breed ghost," part mythical bogey-man (19).

Desiderio's reactive disaffection endows him with a remarkable ability to escape, to evade the dangers of his place in (or absence from) other people's utopian visions. Evasion and escape are dominant structuring motifs in his adventures; each episode ends with a skin-of-the-teeth getaway. His marginal status in representation allows him to slip with relative ease out of various narratives. The paradoxical advantage of occupying the representational position of myth is that while, as Barthes argues, the object of myth (here, the Indian as signifier) suffers an emptying-out of historical meaning as it enters myth, it also opens up to a certain fluidity; it can in fact serve various myths, depending on changing historical circumstances.[42] Richard Rodriguez has theorized the potential benefits of "*El fatalismo del indio*," the passivity and indifference that supposedly result from being relegated to a timeless, mythic past in the popular imagination; he suggests this apparently neutral state allows the indigenous person to adapt the various shapes of the colonizer's imaginary quietly to his or her own purposes.[43] Desiderio's narrative escapes can be read as an ability to leap from one person's (or group's) vision into another, to play them off against one another, exploiting the variation among them. Although Desiderio's very name marks him as the object of others' (narrative) desires, being the archetypal "desired one" means that he is impossible to pin down; he will be different things to different people. He finds agency in the unstable meaning of racial identity as constructed in various dominant discourses.

Appropriately enough to the early stage of the real (British) War of Dreams in which *Hoffman* intervenes, this representational agency seems more developed around race than around gender. Desiderio, for all that he imagines himself to be apart from dominant narratives, remains blind to the ways in which he reenacts clichéd patterns of gender relations. Trapped in an age-old narrative of true love leading to death, Desiderio eventually kills Albertina. This outcome seems to be the product of an ideology that teaches male agency's incompatibility with emotional attachment to a woman. The ease with which such an ideology repeats itself in narrative is illustrated within the novel by the foreshadowing of the conclusion in an early chapter, in Desiderio's liaison with the disturbed teenager Mary Anne. Mary Anne carries a heavy legacy of literary history; she is the Sleeping Beauty and Tennyson's Mariana, a sleepwalker who lives in a house completely surrounded by briars.[44] She comes to Desiderio in her sleep, and the following morning she drowns herself. The false accusation of necrophilia with which Desiderio is charged after sweeping up her body in his arms is symbolically accurate, for his narrative of romance is entirely entwined with female death (62). Carter also offers another emblem of such romance, in Hoffman's love affair with his wife's embalmed corpse.

It may be the very ubiquity of women (or more accurately, fictional femininity) in representation that traps both Mary Anne and Albertina. While a myth of absence—arising from the threatening position of race in postcolonial society—paradoxically enables some fluidity in Desiderio's positioning as an "Indian," Carter's allusions to previous narratives point out the pervasive *presence* of Woman in representation. Yet this presence is limited to variations on a single role: the object of male desire. The love story is the common narrative thread that holds together Desiderio's picaresque adventures, even when his quest for Hoffman fades into the background. While Desiderio himself has demonstrated that the imagery of desire may, like other representations, be turned toward subversive ends, in the world of *Hoffman* there is as yet no sign that such contestation has begun around the roles of women. This is the world of sixties liberational discourse, where the sexual revolution means that "[b]y the liberation of the unconscious, we shall, of course, liberate *man*" (208; emphasis added).

Albertina's involvement in her father's war of dreams illustrates both the appeal of the realm of images—its political potential—and its great power to oppress. The war of dreams obviously engages Albertina's commitment; it seems to promise her power and freedom from the single image of sex object. It offers a world where she can play the powerful roles of Ambassador and "Generalissimo." Yet even as the appointed representative of liberated desire, she cannot be both woman and agent. As the mysterious Ambassador, she must literally assume male form if she is to activate familiar images of power and credibility (32–39). Similarly, she must go in drag as the Count's valet if she is to gain his confidence and escape the worst of his ravages. (As a boy, she still experiences the Count's rapacious desire; but his women lovers all end up dead.) She still operates in a world where the dominant desires belong to men.

This is particularly apparent in the differences between the novel's two harrowing rape scenes. First, Desiderio is raped by nine Moroccan acrobats, products of the Hoffman effect, whose stereotypically "dirty" Arab appetites again seem to demonstrate the collusion of fantasy and racism (117). His pain is "terrible." Yet when Albertina is later raped successively by every male in the centaur tribe, not only are her physical injuries nearly fatal, but she also suffers from the representation of female rape in discourses such as Freudian theory, a history of blaming the victim; she concludes that her rapists are "only emanations of her own desires, dredged up and objectively reified from the dark abyss of the unconscious" (186). If, as Albertina mistakenly believes, the liberation of dreams is a total liberation from history, one has only oneself to blame for what those dreams produce. But a vague memory that troubles Desiderio emphasizes Albertina's mistake: a memory of just such an eroticized scene of a young woman being trampled by horses that had been offered for the titillation of male visitors to the peep show where he once worked (180). The peep show's images—bizarre scenes of sex and violence, where the female orifice is a gaping mouth and the male member is "the key to the city"—had in fact been used by Hoffman as a set of prototypes for his manifestations of desire (44–46). Albertina's suffering as a woman has been thoroughly predetermined by the stereotypical form of male dreams.

The Hoffman camp's failure to acknowledge the differential effects of liberated desire is most acutely visible in Albertina's contradictory location as a woman of color. To me, the destruction of the revolutionary movement begins at the moment when the effects of existing representations of race and gender combine.[45] Looking at Albertina as the Generalissimo, the commander of her father's very real troops, Desiderio stops loving her for a moment, feels "an inexplicable indifference toward her"—and this begins the falling-away that will soon enable him to kill her and her father, destroying their movement in the process (193). In this role, she evokes images of race and gender conventionally marked as undesirable. She is allied with "swarthy, silent" mercenaries of a type Desiderio feels he has "seen very often before but only on newsreels"; she is no white Joan of Arc, instead rendered unattractive by the negative meanings such "swarthy" soldiers carry in official representations such as newsreels. And as the Generalissim*o*, she retains her own gender but, significantly, loses all her sexuality as far as Desiderio is concerned. He is turned off by the "crisp, antiseptic soldier to whom other ranks deferred," and particularly by the prospect of deferring to her himself (193). Desiderio experiences this sudden cooling as "inexplicable" because the images coming together at this moment in Albertina's person cannot be sorted out from one another. She becomes undesirable because she is unfamiliar, rendered contradictory by the "*indifference*" of Desiderio's (and her own) ideology to the differences in representation.

Critics differ in their readings of just how complicit Desiderio is with the narrative's events, and how much critical distance Carter expects her own readers to have on Desiderio's desires. This also becomes an important question for the other two novels I discuss here, both of which are narrated from what appears to be (although more ambiguously) the perspective of a male character. Most agree that Desiderio functions as a reader within the text, moving through stories of which he is not the author (although Sally Robinson suggests that *all* the desires made manifest in *Hoffman* are Desiderio's own).[46]

At one extreme, Aidan Day proposes that Desiderio represents Carter's own viewpoint almost fully, while at the other, Peach comments that it would "require considerable insensitivity not to be critical" of him and other male protagonists of Carter's.[47] I think our own awareness of Desiderio's critical distance—his ability to be "*in* the fictional illusion, but not *of* it"—is *one* step toward modeling the kind of reading practice this novel invites.[48] But passivity and indifference are so central to his character that he cannot stand, like Acker's protagonists may, as the figure of an active, tactical reader.

So I would argue that the model of rereading this text offers its readers derives partly from Desiderio's reservations, and partly from the awareness that Carter offers us of his blind spots—his failure to be sufficiently critical of *some* of the iconography of desire that Carter's text reproduces. Desiderio may read as a "disaffected" outsider, but he always does so as a heterosexual *male* outsider, who still has thoroughly conventional desires when it comes to women. Robinson has proposed that Carter's adoption of Desiderio as her narrative center means that "[t]here is, quite simply, *no place* for a woman reader in this text"; however, Robinson sees this "no place" as such a glaring absence that through it, the novel "paradoxically addresses the reader as *feminist* by denaturalizing the processes by which narrative constructs difference."[49]

However, Desiderio also begins to un-write this exclusion. The retrospective nature of the narration, established in the frame that opens and closes the novel, calls attention to the mistakes of Young Desiderio (as Old Desiderio calls him). Looking back from his much later position as autobiographer, Desiderio seems so disgusted by his own narrative that even he has moved some considerable distance toward recognizing the tragic absence underlying its construction. He is thoroughly unfulfilled by the reestablishment of the previous status quo, which has left him and his nation with no dreams, no contestation, no lively political imagery. This bankruptcy is evident in the weariness with which Desiderio seems to resign himself, in his introduction to the story, to the predictability of his narrative: "I will begin at the beginning and go on until the end."[50] He acknowledges that there are now only old stories, officially sanctioned: "you know very well already that it was I who killed Dr Hoffman; you have read all about it in the history books" (208). The subversive possibilities of Desiderio as representational escape artist have been reduced to "inert matter," officially conscribed in the sanctioned role of politician, "old hero, a crumbling statue in an abandoned square" (221).

But in the very writing of this narrative Desiderio not only creates an alternative image of himself (not just as a "crumbling statue"); he reminds his readers of the affective power of stories, the immense desire that images can provoke. Why else would anyone bother with a story that's been "given away" in the introduction, and why would Desiderio's fictional readers desire a tale they already "know very well"? Here, the fascination and undeniable beauty of all Carter's exquisitely crafted, hallucinatory episodes are central to the book's political import, reminding readers how compelling even old stories are. Carter, through Desiderio, holds out this allure as an incomplete promise, a tool that can be used for change.

More than simply offering his readers an attractive hallucination in which to indulge, Desiderio also raises the possibility of telling the familiar story differently (because he is now, in his old age, a different reader): "he makes it clear that his retelling of his story will be different from the official accounts."[51] The chief difference is the sense of loss and lack introduced by Albertina's absence. In both the introduction and conclusion to the memoir, the specter of Albertina comes, "unbidden," to haunt Desiderio. In fact, only his storytelling (the rehearsal of the male vision) keeps her at bay, for she returns the moment he stops writing. We might see her as Robinson's female reader who has "no place" in masculinist utopian visions except as ghostly, troubling absence. As such, she offers a fitting introduction to Carter's next novel, *The Passion of New Eve*.

THE WAR OF GENDER DREAMS: *The Passion of New Eve*

Despite the inadvisability of trying to fix one moment when the phase of feminism known as the Women's Liberation Movement peaked in Britain, it does seem safe to say that such a moment would have fallen sometime near 1977, a year that also saw the publication of *The Passion of New Eve*. Certainly by the middle of the decade, feminist activism had made gender a major issue of public debate. In late 1975, the Labour government had passed the Sex Discrimination Act after a seven-year battle; in that year, the 1970 Equal Pay Act had also taken effect.[52] Britain's first rape crisis center had opened in 1976. Nationwide "Reclaim the Night" rallies began in 1977.[53] And perhaps the first major signs of the movement's fragmentation surfaced in 1978, which Amanda Sebestyen describes as "a watershed year for the organised women's movement, with the last national conference," where deep divisions between socialist and radical feminists became apparent.[54]

When the national crisis, the crisis of ideology, came to a head with the fall of the Heath administration in 1974, women had already identified struggles over representation as a priority. By 1972, the WLM had its own journal, *Spare Rib*; it was followed in 1975 by the first feminist publishing imprint, Virago. Marsha Rowe, one of the founders of *Spare Rib* and formerly a central figure at *Oz*, recalls that the magazine grew out of women's frustration with the "dream world" offered by the sixties underground press.[55] Here, feminists saw only the same tired imagery they could find in the mainstream daily tabloids, with their topless "page threes." When the war of dreams developed, these women were ready to enter it not only as critics of male images and agendas, but also as active creators of an alternative political symbology.

This is certainly not to say that feminists ignored the *material* ramifications of the Left's limited conception of democratic revolution. Women, especially working-class women, had found that despite socialism's rhetoric of liberation and democratization, material gains achieved by the Left did not extend to them. For instance, amid the growing labor militancy of the late sixties, women machinists at Ford had to stage a separate strike in 1968 for pay equity. "At the same time, women who had their job expectations raised by the opening up of mass higher education"—the establishment of the "red-brick" universities—"found that they were discriminated against in favour of men when it came to career and job prospects."[56]

But feminists recognized that this material inequality had everything to do with images and ideologies. Filmmaker and theorist Laura Mulvey recalls that "[t]he women's movement discovered early on that images and representation were a political issue."[57] As a (male) women's libber put it in 1968: "Attitudes have got to be changed, and that is a task for propaganda and persuasion."[58] Rejecting the simplistic economic determinism of "vulgar" Marxism, the new women activists "insisted on the centrality of ideological struggle, which had been all too glibly nudged to the periphery of political struggle by much of the left." Many feminists were simply fed up with "traditional forms of political activity," and they focused much of their struggle on the level of images in part because of this profound disillusionment.[59] Largely symbolic actions such as the disruption of the 1970 Miss World pageant in London were as central to the movement's tactics as agitation for more concrete goals such as equal rights legislation. These symbolic interventions were a response to women's recognition that even leftist men often suffered a fundamental failure of the imagination when it came to rethinking gender.

When feminists in the 1970s turned to forging an alternative symbology, one form it took was a new "mythopoeic" feminism, which arose largely from the utopian visions of radical feminists but developed into a more widespread interest in revamping matriarchal and goddess myths (in the United States and France as well as the United Kingdom). At the time of Carter's writing, many feminists were exploring the possibilities of reclaiming female mythic/archetypal figures as positive images of female power. The decade began with Anne Sexton's 1971 *Transformations*, also producing such influential and diverse revisions of female mythic figures as Hélène Cixous's "Laugh of the Medusa" (1975), Mary Daly's *Beyond God the Father* (1973), and a host of mythopoeic works by feminist poets.[60] Most of these texts engaged in the double project of challenging traditional mythic images of women but then revamping them, uncovering the female strength latent in these figures.

Some feminists also sought to use representations to invest "the" female body with mythic significance and power. A 1974 article from *Spare Rib*, in which filmmaker Anne Severson describes making a short film comprised of shots of women's genitals, illustrates both the goals and the dangers of this version of feminist image-making. Severson recalls wanting to dispel women's shame about their imperfect bodies and about such stigmatized bodily functions as menstruation. She theorizes the power available to women who know and use their bodies, taking as an example a prostitute who appeared in the film, who had surgically modified her body, including her vagina and labia, in order to be more successful in her profession. The prostitute

> pointed out, and was intensely alive evidence for, the enormous power that comes from doing it the hard way, acting on your impulses, taking the consequences. If you choose to be at the bottom, or find yourself there, ain't nobody can shove you down. I might point out that she has Venus in Leo in the twelfth house: her love nature in the sign of generosity and expansion, in the house of karma and bondage, of salvation and secret undoing.[61]

The sudden shift in Severson's rhetoric, at the very moment when she begins to articulate a theory of women's sexuality and its political meaning, to a mythic Zodiacal discourse, functions to refigure the prostitute's power as the result of birth and fate, rather than agency. This rhetorical move leaves no room at all for addressing the significant differences between "choos[ing] to be at the bottom" and "find[ing] yourself there" as a result of forces beyond one's control. Severson's logic essentializes the "bottom" location assigned to women in patriarchy as the source of power, even while it defuses that power by confining its effects to the well-adjusted prostitute's individual psyche.

While Severson's article is not typical of the generally more materialist feminist discourse in *Spare Rib*, versions of its rhetoric were shared by a growing number of British and American feminists at the time. While this rhetoric rejected, and sought to invert, patriarchy's historically negative valuation of women's bodily "nature," it embraced the same dehistoricized and essentialist representations of what that "nature" might be.

The Passion of New Eve simultaneously critiques existing, worn-out representations of women and these feminist efforts to create a new political iconography. I see its agenda as unquestionably feminist, but like *Hoffman* this novel argues the need to take into account the cultural baggage that accompanies representations and makes them problematic tools for groups seeking to transform society. Women's ability to change the meaning of images is limited, because meanings will always be affected by the circumstances in which the image is received. In *New Eve*, Carter suggests that feminist projects to put new wine in old bottles—to revamp old gender stereotypes by inverting them, valuing what has been devalued as feminine—fail if they fall into the trap of essentializing their own images of "Woman" as men have done in the past. By accepting a single construction of femininity, even if they seek to change its popular meaning, they risk having that definition simply reappropriated by male hegemony. Feminist interventions in representation must be historically flexible, responding to the varying means of male power in specific local contexts (forms of the family, of sexual relationships, or of state/military power that differ according to race and class). Carter has written (in a much-quoted formulation), "I am all for putting new wine in old bottles, especially if the pressure of the new wine makes the old bottles explode"; but *New Eve* suggests she is *not* in favor of the consecration of that new wine as sacred.[62] What will explode the "bottles," the old images and forms of gender, is a multiplication of possible images, the introduction into gender narratives of an insistently relativizing and contextualizing—and thus resistant—impulse. Thus, as Carter also notes, a great deal "depends on new readings of old texts."[63]

New Eve opens at the movies, at a revival of an old film starring Tristessa de St Ange, a legendary tragic beauty from Hollywood's golden age. The movie provokes the narrator, a young British man named Evelyn, to think of Rilke's critique of the expressive inadequacy of modern symbols:

> But, no. He was wrong. Our external symbols must always express the life within us with absolute precision; how could they do otherwise, since that life has generated them? Therefore we must not blame our poor symbols if they take forms that seem trivial to us, or absurd, for the symbols themselves have no control over their own fleshly manifestations, however paltry they may be; the nature of our life alone has determined their forms.
> A critique of these symbols is a critique of our lives.[64]

In *New Eve*, Carter addresses particularly the inadequacy of the system of symbols that comprise gender. She situates her exploration in an apocalyptic version of the contemporary (1977) moment: a post-Enlightenment society riven by warring social factions, each defined not so much by an agenda as by a motivating set of myths. Or rather, as in her other apparently fantastical works from the seventies, Carter explores in *New Eve* how a set of myths *accompanies* and *promotes* a material agenda. Here, perhaps more than in any other novel, she considers what to do when all the myths are bankrupt and analyzes the means by which some political faction may, nevertheless, be able to deploy its set of images to determine the new political formation that arises out of this bankruptcy.

Carter's narrative strategy in this novel is to explore the various ways in which each faction, each locus of power, tries to render its own representations exclusive and universal. She demonstrates that these universalizing projects are doomed to failure—even, to an extent, for the most powerful groups. The novel implies both the broad reach, the global pretensions, of hegemonic Western culture and its current level of exhaustion; Carter chooses the United States as its setting, and the British narrator progresses from East Coast to West, ending at the Pacific Ocean—following the historical trajectory of westward expansion, of the search for fresh territory and a space free of the Old Ways. As he travels, he encounters increasingly violent and chaotic struggle between opposing elements of an exploding society. This struggle eventually erupts into a full-scale, multiparty civil war in California. Evelyn has naively come to the United States seeking to escape the cultural dissolution and leftover dreams of the Old World, but what he finds is the dual movement of postmodernity toward transnational homogenization and local factionalism (10). In New York, he finds the same racial polarization, urban violence, and economic breakdown as he left "at home" (33). He also finds the same movies playing.

New Eve suggests that the kind of economic collapse experienced by the citizens of Carter's New York provokes a crisis of cultural symbols, including those of gender; and American culture, as the contemporary apotheosis of the Old World's images and dreams, represents the westernmost point of exhaustion of those symbols. Evelyn is the emissary of an obsolete culture; he has come to New York as a professor, and from the range of his literary quotations it seems reasonable to guess as a professor of literature. But the university has been closed by militant blacks, a coup made less significant by the fact that European culture is available in Americanized form through Hollywood anyway; the great movies of Evelyn's idol, Tristessa, are *Wuthering Heights, The Fall of the House of Usher, Marguerite,* and *Emma Bovary*. Like a perverse system of mirrors, Hollywood reflects a distorted European culture back to the Old World, so that Evelyn has childhood memories of eating peculiarly English food while watching these American movies with his nanny in England (8). He finds that national culture has been supplanted by American (multinational) culture, but that following the crisis of the capitalism of which this culture was emissary and justification, this global imaginary is everywhere breaking down in context-specific ways.[65]

New Eve reveals the imagery of gender to be among the most successful in its pretensions to universality and permanence. Hegemonic images of gender do show some signs of breaking down, in the presence on the violent New York streets of the leather-clad radicals, The Women, who deride and terrorize men. But Evelyn's relationship with the black exotic dancer, Leilah, points not only to the economic incentives that work to keep existing gender relations in place but also to the pervasiveness of this particular system of mirrors, of representations which function as self-fulfilling prophecies by their ability to shape consciousness.

Leilah is dependent on existent fictions of femininity for her livelihood, for the money men will pay her for being attractive. Particularly in the deindustrialized economy of Carter's postmodern New York, marketing the female body as a representational commodity is one of the only ways to get cash. (And soon, thanks to a small example of the increased unemployment of educated men in such an economy, Leilah is supporting Evelyn, too.) These economic conditions provide some historical specificity to John Berger's argument that women experience themselves not as something that exists in itself, but from the alienated position of watching themselves turn themselves into objects of the male gaze.[66] Leilah embodies this condition. Evelyn describes her dressing to go to work:

> Her beauty was an accession. She arrived at it by a conscious effort. She became absorbed in the contemplation of the figure in the mirror but she did not seem to me to apprehend the person in the mirror as, in any degree, herself. The reflected Leilah had a concrete form and, although this form was perfectly tangible, we all knew, all three of us in the room, that it was another Leilah. Leilah invoked this formal other with a gravity and ritual that recalled witchcraft; she brought into being a Leilah who lived only in the not-world of the mirror and then became her own reflection.[67]

Leilah makes a living selling herself as the image of desire, but in becoming a reflection of an imaginary image of sexual woman, she loses her fully human status. Evelyn's initial description of her, during a highly erotic pursuit through the city streets, is in terms of animals or of mythic figures of enchantment; she is a cat, a racehorse, a fox, a siren, and a witch (18–20). This chase scene, Susan Rubin Suleiman notes, is lifted from the surrealist Robert Desnos's *La Liberté ou l'amour*, an allusion that emphasizes Evelyn's view of Leilah as no more than a concretization of his own images of desire.[68]

The excessive richness of Carter's descriptions of Leilah highlights her position as the focal point of a multitude of sexual fantasies, racist as well as sexist. She is less a real being to Evelyn than a collage of representations of the ideally sexual woman. Not coincidentally, she pauses at one moment during the protracted chase/seduction beneath a poster of Tristessa, the perfect celluloid female.[69] When the chase culminates in Evelyn telling us, "My full-fleshed and voracious beak tore open the poisoned wound of love between her thighs, suddenly, suddenly," it is all too apparent that he sees his "prey" through the filter of his education in the language of soft-core pornography—or perhaps D. H. Lawrence (25). He sees Leilah as a "succubus," a creature existing only in fiction (27). His references to her as "mud Lily" and "night-blooming flower" demonstrate that this mythic image of the ideally sexual woman is also a racialized one, dependent on a metaphorics equating darkness with vegetable nature and earthy sexuality (29, 28). The idealized image naturalizes itself, in part, through the historical entanglement of the discourses of race, gender, and nature. These references, coupled with his endless descriptions of her makeup and clothes, make it less than surprising that Evelyn callously rejects her when she becomes pregnant and sick. Poor Leilah has conformed herself so perfectly to the exoticized image of desire that she has entered myth, the dehistoricized realm of representations that have become so widespread in the imagination as to seem inevitable, natural. When her material needs—including money for an abortion—assert themselves so abruptly, Evelyn reacts with anger to this return of historicity and contingency.

Leilah's downfall makes it all the more problematic that the radical separatist Women—whom Evelyn subsequently encounters when he is taken prisoner at their underground commune in the desert—seem to accept and further mythologize the same ideal images of women. Their plan is to revive the ancient myths and bypass heterosexual models of creation: they will surgically transform Evelyn into a woman, Eve, then impregnate him with his own sperm. But in molding Eve into their perfect, primal woman, they seem to have nothing to draw on but the same hegemonic images of femininity. The women of Beulah (the commune) create their new Eve from a number of sources: from Hollywood, from art history, and from Christianity; Eve is both her namesake and the Virgin Mary, and has her own parodic Annunciation (66). "Beulah" itself carries echoes of the Book of Isaiah and the utopias envisioned by Bunyan and Blake.[70] Drawing on this history of male representation, the Women teach the new Eve to be ideally feminine—that is, passive and long-suffering—and defined by her sexual/maternal function. Evelyn is accustomed to his new femininity by watching videotapes of all Tristessa's movies, from which he learns how much "beautiful" suffering and tragedy it takes to be a desirable woman. This image of woman as masochist has been naturalized by dominating representation for a long time; Carter suggests that its history stretches back at least to the novels of Sade, from whose *Philosophy in the Bedroom* Tristessa gets her surname. Stretching even further back, Eve's next tutoring comes in the form of a video of "every single Virgin and Child that had ever been painted in the entire history of Western European art."[71] Carter parodies these representations of "natural" female behavior and beauty by showing that they can be taught and surgically produced.

But the Women and their imposing black leader, Mother, also seem smart about their use of myth, recognizing it as a response to historical circumstances. Mother and her single-breasted warriors—a parody of militant feminist utopias such as Monique Wittig's 1969 *Les guérillères*—effectively mix ancient myth with modern technology in their underground fortress-cum-laboratory; in this aspect, they astutely modify essentialist visions to fit contemporary conditions. Their chanted litany of names of the mother-goddess is modernized by the stereo system that produces the accompanying fanfares. Mother's body itself, surgically altered to sport two rows of swinging breasts, is an example of her treatment of myth as "a made thing, not a found thing" (56). She is "her own mythological artefact," deploying the power and fear associated with the "monstrous" position of the sexual Black female body in the white male imagination (60).

The Women's separatist strategy is a response to two historical developments in both the fictional world of the novel and the world of its contemporary British readers. The first circumstance is violence against women. In the novel, this is figured by the rape Leilah and Evelyn observe on the lawless New York street, by Leilah's bloody illicit abortion, and in the person of the mad survivalist Zero, who will later kidnap and rape Eve. This sort of violence was nothing historically new in the mid-seventies, but feminists had suddenly drawn it into public discourse, establishing rape crisis centers, getting legislation passed to protect raped women's rights, and staffing a network of shelters.[72] What had previously happened privately could now be the basis for public action; for instance, in 1978 the National Women's Aid Federation could state, "battering has only recently become 'An Issue for Public Concern.'"[73]

At the same time, the rise of new reproductive technologies (beginning with the Pill in the sixties) seemed to make permanent separation from men and their violence a scientific possibility. The Women's project for their underground utopia echoes Shulamith Firestone's prescriptions for the liberation of women in the popular *The Dialectic of Sex*, published in the United Kingdom in 1971. In Coote and Campbell's summary, her argument sounds very much like the strategy of Carter's revolutionaries: Firestone "recommended that women should fight back *at a biological level*. She advocated 'not just the elimination of male privilege, but of the sex *distinction* itself.' And finally she proposed the development of artificial means of reproduction, together with a form of communism described as 'cybernetic.'"[74] In this sense, Mother's use of the myths of femininity is motivated by historically new needs and possibilities.

However, while myth is, as Barthes points out, always historically motivated, it operates by attempting to freeze history at the moment of its deployment.[75] In this, it is fundamentally suited to hegemonic purposes, as hegemony's interest is to preserve things as they are, while resistant groups such as feminists fundamentally desire change. The Women are operating (as is Carter) at a moment of intense contestation, of the fragmentation of political visions; in this context of the war of dreams, their attempt to fix gender under a single representation removes it from the struggles for new alliances that will determine the new shape of power. A more successful strategy is to recognize the multiple desires that can cohere around images of women, and to invite and deploy those desires according to the specific situation.

By attempting to revalue the traditional image of woman, the Women ultimately play into men's desires. Sacred Eve emerges from under Mother's scalpel as an uncanny reproduction of a *Playboy* centerfold.[76] As soon as Eve leaves Beulah, where the Women can exercise an artificial monopoly on the interpretation of her image, this activation of male desires results in her rape and enslavement by the vile Zero, the one-eyed, one-legged poet who keeps a harem of silent wives. Zero laughingly reminds Eve that in the real (i.e., male) world, for every Eve there is an Adam to rule over her (91). Zero's presence in the narrative emphasizes the extent of male control over the meanings of representation. While he writes incomprehensible poetry, he literally denies his wives access to representation by barring them from using language (87). His power derives not so much from his guns and knives as from his wives' indoctrination (during their own childhoods of brutalization), which leads them to believe men's version of reality (99). Like Eve/Evelyn, and like the Women, Zero has built his dreams around the image of Tristessa—but for him, she represents women's threatening power, his suspicion that female sexuality might not solely exist to glorify men. He believes her celluloid image has unmanned him, left him sterile. He calls her "Public

3 / ANGELA CARTER'S WAR OF REAL DREAMS

Enemy Number One," the "ultimate dyke," and is obsessed with destroying her (91). When Eve falls straight from her "birth" at the Women's hands into the hands of Zero, it serves as a reminder that a direct inversion of male images and values cannot be maintained in a society where men have far more power than women to assimilate meanings to their own agendas and desires.

If Carter's textual strategy bears a certain resemblance to Mother's, inasmuch as both use scraps and echoes of existing texts to build a resistant political position, they differ in this awareness that texts cannot be made to signify in isolation from historical circumstances. Whereas Mother's project is to cleanse her materials—drawn from the Bible, Hollywood, or wherever else—of their historical associations, the many allusions in Carter's text function to reconnect these representations with the material effects they have had and continue to have on women. Thus, she juxtaposes the Women's utopian evocation of Madonna and child with the later appearance of the same religious iconography as the rallying point of the Christian Right, in the form of a platoon of boy soldiers who "rescue" Eve after she and the aging Tristessa have escaped Zero's planned apocalypse. These blond, gun-wielding children, off to usher in the Christian millennium in California, evoke Hitler's youth brigades and an even earlier precursor, the Children's Crusade (159). While they ascribe to Eve the same sexual purity and sacred maternity as the Women intended, Carter uses them to drag up the historical baggage that accompanies those ideals (including a brutal homophobia that leads to Tristessa's death). In this sense, the boy soldiers are much closer than the Women to knowing how to use images effectively in the war of dreams.

New Eve delivers its final blow to feminist attempts to essentialize gender through Eve's meeting with Tristessa. Tristessa, Hollywood's ideal of suffering femininity, the image on which so many women have based their constructed selves and so many men (Evelyn, Zero) have based their ideas about women, turns out to be a biological male:

> *That* was why he had been the perfect man's woman! He had made himself the shrine of his own desires, had made himself the only woman he could have loved! If a woman is indeed beautiful only in so far as she incarnates most completely the secret aspirations of man, no wonder Tristessa had been able to become the most beautiful woman in the world, an unbegotten woman who made no concessions to humanity. (128–29)

Yet Carter does not allow this revelation to suggest that over and against Tristessa's "fake" femininity, a real gender exists. For "woman" is a construction in a mirror, "the secret aspirations of man"; the symbol *is* the gender. When Zero forces Eve and Tristessa to perform and consummate a vicious mock wedding, neither "woman" (Tristessa-as-bride nor Eve-as-groom) is authentically female. Eve assures us that Tristessa's representations of femininity have in fact "achieved a more perfect degree of authenticity" than anything real could, because of their effects on audiences around the world (122).

Tristessa's existence confounds not only specific myths of gender, but the smooth functioning of narrative itself. Eve struggles for pronouns, producing such phrases as "he showed no signs of running away herself, he was too dazed" (137). After meeting—and falling in love with—Tristessa, Eve no longer peppers her narrative with comments on its own structural inevitability (as, for instance, "our destinations choose us, choose us before we are born" [39]). How *can* the narrative stay the same when it is no longer narrated by the same person (Eve, rather than Evelyn) and the object of narrative desire (the celluloid Tristessa) is not the same as it started out to be?

In fact, *The Passion of New Eve* goes nowhere; it ends strangely and inconclusively, as Eve heads out into the Pacific in a tiny boat, pregnant from her tryst with Tristessa. *The Infernal Desire Machines of Doctor Hoffman* closed with a foreboding focus on the dead Albertina, an image I have taken as Carter's call for women to contest their doomed role in existing utopian visions and narratives. The final sentence of *New Eve* seems much less sure of what the past demands of the future: "Ocean, ocean, mother of mysteries, take me to the place of birth" (191). These two endings seem emblematic: in 1972, Carter could focus solely on the effects of masculinist representations; in 1977, her project had become much more complicated by the need also to challenge some feminist representational strategies, to contest any attempt to restore a definitive form to the missing woman. Eve has left the dominant image of the father dead behind her—on her way to the coast, she came upon "an honest redneck paterfamilias" who had shot his whole family and himself in despair at the political upheaval—but now Mother's resistant efforts also seem to have failed (167). Her *guérillères* have left their desert hideout to engage fully armed in the battle for California. Mother herself has retired in exhaustion, recognizing that "History overtook myth . . . And rendered it obsolete" (172).

3 / ANGELA CARTER'S WAR OF REAL DREAMS   141

But *New Eve* does leave us with some hints toward a positive feminist strategy, one that relativizes representations and contextualizes their usefulness. Leilah, the black dancer, reappears in California as a guerrilla commander, choosing down-to-earth action over her mythic resonances as Mother's (literal) daughter. While, back in Harlem, militant resistance had been polarized into "the Blacks" and "the Women"—leaving Leilah's role divided and ambiguous—she now commands a multiracial, mixed-gender band of uniformless fighters, operating out of a bombed-out mall. The "Benito Cereno shopping centre and Relaxarama," with its kitsch "Spanish-style bowling alley-cum-bar-cum-restaurant," exemplifies hegemonic postmodernism's ability to cheerfully make all cultures into representations conveniently available on the commodity market (171, 168). Leilah and her gang have in turn appropriated this facade-world of relativized dreams to their own uses, adding their own revolutionary hopes to those the mall promises to fulfill.

Of all the possible approaches to the crisis of representation in *New Eve*, Carter seems least skeptical of this strategic mashing-together of various cultural fragments. Eve suggests to Leilah that perhaps the appropriate attitude toward all "symbols" is to "[p]ut them away, for a while, until the times have created a fresh iconography" (174).

Carter provides a last ironic variation on the image of the archetypal matriarch, poised on the sunset edge of Western culture's progress. Eve meets an old woman, blissfully drinking while she awaits her death on the Californian beach. In her, mythic elements are reduced simply to signs of age and decay; like Tiresias she is blind, with "sunken dugs" (as in *The Waste Land*), and her dirty hair is like an ex-Medusa's, "a nest of *petrified* snakes" (190; emphasis added). Eve takes the woman's little plastic boat, giving away in exchange a small bar of alchemical gold that has been a recurring symbol in the novel, an image of the ceaseless human attempt to create something timelessly valuable and authentic. Then Eve steals the old matriarch's canned food, leaving her just her vodka, and sets sail. Let myth die, Carter seems to say; let it drink and sing itself happily into oblivion while we focus on what we need in this specific moment. What we need for survival is not gold but plastic; not the permanent, but that which was intended for consumer culture desires and can be turned instead into an escape, a vehicle to somewhere new. Perhaps Eve's baby will be born in the plastic boat, a child bred of Hollywood and Christianity and literature whose father was a woman and whose mother was a man. Carter keeps things in the plural, letting no textual parent dominate the emergent imagery of a new political era.

REREADING *Love*

Carter's *Love* is able to fill in the space left vague and undefined at the end of *New Eve*, the space of the future political formation. *Love* supports Carter's conclusions in *Hoffman* and *New Eve* about the danger and inadequacy of attempts to universalize representations—here, inherited images of gender and class identity—and moves forward into the years after the crisis of the seventies to offer more detailed examination of which strategies have proved successful. *Love* is especially useful to my attempt to historicize Carter's interventions in the postmodern war of dreams because she has, in a sense, historicized it herself. The 1987 reissue of this 1971 novel includes an eight-page afterword that brings the novel's characters up to date, filling in the details of their fictional lives in the years since the events of the original narrative.[77] The afterword is spoken in the voice of the author, Angela Carter, but I would argue that it is an integral part of the fictional text, rather than a nonfictional commentary thereon. (For one thing, the narrator here still acts as though the novel's characters really exist and its events really happened, thus speaking from *within* their level of reality.)[78] This afterword functions as a playful reassessment of the earlier events and characters, suggesting how each character might have fared through the disappointment of revolutionary student politics in Britain and the rise of the women's movement.

Love is at once later and earlier than the previous novels I've discussed here; the afterword tells us that Carter wrote the first version in 1969.[79] The general tendency among critics is to situate *Love* not with her dystopian picaresques of the seventies but with the more realist "Bristol trilogy" of the sixties, which also includes *Shadow Dance* and *Several Perceptions*.[80] However, I want also to position this novel as usefully bracketing the war of dreams in Britain, which both *Hoffman* and *New Eve* have (on one level) offered ways of reading. Again, I wouldn't want to reduce the 1987 *Love* to merely a reflection of a historical moment (or, in this case, to an allegory-in-hindsight); it is also, self-reflexively, very much about the politics of fantasy and of representation itself.

The juxtaposition of Carter's earlier text and the new afterword highlights two different ways of reading; the afterword is, in effect, a rereading of the novel, and the novel itself is very much concerned with how the characters read the world (of inherited images) around them. What strikes me as a key difference between the characters' ways of reading in the main portion of the novel and that practiced in the afterword is that while the former seem almost morbidly *determined* by class relations, the latter suggests a more fluid and flexible *set* of social identities from which any given reader can approach his or her own story (including class, but also gender, sexuality, and to some extent race). The afterword represents the characters' identities not as essential and permanent, but as a set of interlocking and conflicting images and signifiers to which they can give varying emphasis.

So I do think that *Love* is "about" class, at precisely the time when class had become, thanks to the mutations of capitalism since the Second World War, an insufficient category of analysis. As Gilroy has argued, along with Ernesto Laclau and Chantal Mouffe, among others, when class identity could no longer serve as a reliable predictor of people's economic circumstances, new axes of identity—race and gender, along with nation, sexuality, positions on peace and the environment—began to seem more real, to offer more convincing narratives explaining one's place in society.[81] Thus the War of Dreams.

But *Love* crucially points out that class identity is not simply an objective social and economic location, but also a matter of a certain relationship to representation. A "class society" offers a set of stable positions from which to develop a way of reading the signs of society in order to make sense of the world and of oneself. Carter's novel shows the chaos when these class positions have broken down to a certain extent, but most of the characters have not yet learned to view signification in a "postmodern" way—that is, as a matter of tactics rather than truth. In that sense, this is again a novel centrally concerned with reading, an activity that is always "situated at the point where *social* stratification (class relationships) and *poetic* operations (the practitioner's constructions of a text) intersect."[82]

The fates of the three characters who comprise the household at the core of the original novel—Annabel, Lee, and Buzz—vary according to their respective practices of reading. Carter weaves a web of complex but compelling connections between those practices and their class backgrounds. Annabel is a middle-class art student, an unusual, eccentric young woman who is also deeply immersed in the romantic traditions of her bourgeois background. Lee, who becomes her husband, is a teacher at the local secondary school, a working-class orphan raised by a staunchly Marxist aunt. Lee's half-brother, Buzz, the bastard offspring of a passing American GI, is an artist and a scavenger, one of the new bohemians who wear gaudy clothes, use drugs, and occasionally go off without warning to Marrakech. Annabel and Lee consistently misunderstand one another; Lee has an affair, and when Annabel discovers it, she attempts suicide; Lee tries to take care of her but Annabel conspires with Buzz, who resents Lee for bringing Annabel into their household, and together Annabel and Buzz seek to dominate Lee entirely; the two of them have a brief affair, and Annabel kills herself.

Annabel, with her drawings of dragons and unicorns and her literary echoes of Poe's "Annabel Lee" (she even has "highborn kinsmen" who take her away at one point), holds what I would characterize as a romantic theory of the relation between representations and reality. Utterly uninterested in the physical world except as it reflects or augurs her own inner state, she uses words and pictures only to absorb external objects into her private and highly subjective mythology. She pays no attention to events or objects as material signifiers, only to their subjective and immaterial significance; she is "like a blind man at a firework display who can only appreciate the fires in the air by interpreting their various degrees of magnificence through the relative enthusiasms of the noisy crowd" (24). Her relationship with Lee is mediated by her changing representations of him: "as she drew him, so she saw him. He existed for her only intermittently" (35). He exists not as a thing in itself, but as the signifier of Annabel's feelings.

Annabel's is clearly an outlook based on material privilege, which sustains her ability never to think of other people "as anything more than facets of the self" (110). At Annabel and Lee's wedding, her parents ironically speculate that she might have been better off with Buzz, the bohemian, who might "grow rich for they [have] heard how photographers are the new aristocracy" (37). The narrator (who usually seems closely allied with Lee's viewpoint) comments, "No wonder the daughter saw only appearances" (36). Although here the signified (money) is clearly quite material, Carter suggests that Annabel has inherited from her parents the habit of seeing the world in terms of her subjective investment.

This is a twisted version of the legacy of Romanticism but, more broadly, Annabel becomes fatally trapped in the narratives provided for her by a romantic-aestheticist tradition. As the devotion of the narrator-lover in Poe's poem is cemented forever by his beloved Annabel's death, Carter's Annabel believes in the dreams that tell her she can "play games with death," using her own body's fragility to blackmail Lee into eternal loyalty (76). She responds to evidence of his unfaithfulness by attempting suicide, thinking she will "be able by these means to turn an event that threatened to disrupt her self-centred structure into a fruitful extension of it" (45). Even death is a signifier to her, not a fact. Lee has given her a print of Millais's "Ophelia" because it reminds him of her, and in her eventual successful suicide, she is described as feeling "like Ophelia" (109). The solipsistic, aestheticizing dream of reality to which she has subscribed takes its logical course.

This old dream to which Annabel subscribes is also, of course, fatally gendered. To say that Annabel is killed by her theory of signification would be simplistic; the afterword suggests, in fact, that she was simply "mad" and nothing could have saved her (113). But the *form* her self-destruction takes nevertheless suggests that a fatal interplay among class position, myth, and female body was there, awaiting her. Despite her self-absorption, "she had never learned to think of herself as a living actor," and when she does start to do so, it is only as an actor upon her own body (30). She makes of herself an aesthetic object like the beautiful, immobile Annabel Lee and Ophelia, or like the "whore" in the pornographic photos Buzz has given her, in the hopes of gaining the power of these lifeless images. Carter suggests (here and elsewhere) that there is little difference between "high" literature and pornography in terms of the images it offers women. Annabel dyes her hair, paints her face and nails, disappears into the realm of the perfectly artificial and thus becomes "omnipotent" (104). But the perfection of this change can only be sealed by death; her next step, her "ultimate, shocking transformation," is to become "a painted doll, bluish at the extremes" (112).

Lee's story of the world and of the relation between representation and reality is almost as class-bound as Annabel's, so the way they both take their class identity as their primary lens on the world contributes to the fatal lack of comprehension between them. Lee (his full name is Leon, for Trotsky), who considers duplicity the exclusive preserve of the bourgeoisie (and therefore fails to see his own), presumes a clear-cut opposition of right and wrong and an absolute correlation of signifier to signified—like a linguistic version of base and superstructure or class and class consciousness (22). He "always [speaks] the truth"—or so the sympathetic narrator tells us—and he thinks "a door must be either open or closed" (22, 23). He suffers from an eye disease, a sign of both his lack of vision and his working-class sentimentality, for it makes him weep frequently. He tailors his emotions to the disease: "since he had the simple heart of one who boos the villain, when, as he often did, he found he was crying, he usually became sad" (26). His efforts to match signified neatly to signifier are the symptoms of a world-view in which nothing means more than one thing. And in his romanticized Marxist conception, most things mean "class."

Like any inflexible way of interpreting phenomena, Lee's theory of signification eventually encounters things it cannot understand. (This blank incomprehension may have something to do with what critics have called the novel's lack of affect, its detachment from the events portrayed.)[83] The specificities of gender—as both material fact and as a particular relationship to images—are beyond Lee's ken. Annabel's place in representation is not only middle-class, but also accords well with John Berger's famous maxim, that "men act and women appear."[84] Lee's emphasis on the truth value of signifiers enables unambiguous action but leaves him utterly unable to comprehend her passivity and role-playing. The only thing he can think to do is "rescue her," not realizing that for Annabel, it is impossible that someone who exists only because of his relation to her could become her rescuer (70). Yet the rescuing hero is a figure Lee has picked up from Annabel's imaginary world, not his own; the working-class women in this novel emphatically don't need rescuing. For him as a lover from outside Annabel's class, the hero myth makes no sense.[85] Lee is divided between his resentment of Annabel's powerful self-containment and his impulse to pity and protect her. He cannot theorize such internal division; so he makes the disastrous choice of using an affair with another woman to reassert his autonomy and then deceiving Annabel in order to "protect" her from the truth.

Buzz is profoundly sinister and the novel's least likable character, but he has the most flexible and timely relation to symbols and signification. While he has the same class background as Lee, his relation to class is more tangential and his outlook, different. For one thing, Buzz's class consciousness is crossed by an awareness of race in a way Lee's is not. Buzz's lost father may or may not have actually been a Native American, but what matters is that Buzz believes he has always been treated as a dark Other, and himself makes this central to his identity (11). He has taken the Saturday-afternoon Western image of the Apache and created himself to mimic it, to match his "pictures of Red Indians cut out of books" (31). Buzz's performance of himself seems to assume that signifiers are not in any necessary relation to signifieds, that they can be played with and manipulated. His obsessive photography, his need to see everything through the lens of representation, "at second hand, without depths," illustrates his awareness that power and meaning lie not in things but in the malleable images of those things (25). He is a man with "opaque eyes which [are], in no sense, the mirrors of his soul" (67).

Buzz is also a member of a historically new "class," the young, urban bohemians. This is a social group whose status derives not from inheritance or money but from cultural capital. The creation of youth culture and of this "class" in the sixties—although it began to emerge with the Beat culture of the fifties—was in part a symptom of postmodern capital's need for consumption based on taste and fashion to become more widespread than before, less confined to the traditional moneyed classes. It also owed something to the rapid growth and commodification of the art market, creating more opportunities to make even a meager living as an artist than had previously existed.[86] While the preconditions for the existence of this "class" are largely economic, membership is based primarily on the ability to manipulate signs.

From the perspective of the late 1980s, Carter's afterword suggests that Buzz's relation to symbols and identity may be a fruitful model for postmodernity, in that it represents a practice of manipulation with certain goals in mind. It is also more widely available now, to other characters beyond the new bohemians; as Certeau reminds us, new reading tactics always depend on "a transformation of the social relationships that overdetermine [readers'] relation to texts."[87] The political value of Buzz's reading practice, however, is ambiguous, and depends very much on the goals it serves. Such a strategy can simply aid in self-advancement; this is clear, for example, in what has happened since 1969 to the rather creepy psychiatrist who treated both Annabel and Lee. She has become very wealthy by combining popular media psychology with roles on the boards of directors of drug companies and detoxification centers; she might be the very model of postmodern capital's manipulation of media to create or implant consumer "needs" and then capitalize on them.[88]

Buzz's story, too, is of a cynical success moving within postmodern capitalism. Carter writes, "In 1969, Buzz was still waiting for his historic moment, which is why he is the least resolved character in the novel" (116). Buzz takes the emergent world of bohemian art/youth culture to its logical capitalist conclusion. He becomes an enormous success as a Malcolm McLaren-esque punk rock entrepreneur, managing bands and clubs, and moves to New York where he dabbles profitably in real estate and graffiti art. Himself the subject of art images by Robert Mapplethorpe and Wim Wenders, Buzz (now Buzzz) "now lives a life of paranoid seclusion in a midtown penthouse, surrounded by a covey of leather-clad acolytes" (117).

But other characters show that a relationship to identity as a malleable set of representations can serve the political agendas of feminism and class struggle if combined with specific material goals, rather than with a Buzzian nihilism. (For if Annabel is Poe's Annabel Lee, Buzz is the "raven named Nevermore" [69].) Joanne, a working-class teenage student of Lee's with whom he had a brief affair, first capitalizes on her sex appeal by getting modestly rich in the newly burgeoning sex industry. But she subsequently recognizes—on having an abortion and quitting "the business"—that despite her money, her gender can also function as a source of oppression. She "becomes radicalized," participates in demonstrations in the early eighties at the women's peace camp at Greenham Common and for the miners' strike in 1984, and runs for office with the Labour Party (115–16). Whereas she used to foreground only her sex, Joanne now juggles multiple allegiances and alliances. At Greenham, she might emphasize her identity as a woman whose presumably innate nurturing power challenges the military-industrial complex; in her more mainstream political campaign, she might deemphasize women's difference from men, and instead highlight the bases of cross-gender working-class solidarity.

Lee, the would-be rescuer, is himself rescued in the afterword by a second wife, a pragmatic radical named Rosie. Rosie, through her involvement in the women's movement, teaches Lee to "read" his life with Annabel through their gendered power imbalance, rather than through the sole lens of class. As in Joanne's epilogue, Carter is careful here to trace Lee and Rosie's changing relationship in the context of contemporary events. They have their first daughter in 1972, when a Conservative government has come to power and Rosie has "reluctantly [come] to the conclusion that the revolution [is] not imminent in Britain" (118); rather than fight in the streets, the two settle down for a protracted struggle over the future, and their daughter functions as a mark of their recognition that this struggle will be played out as much in the "private" realm of family as in traditional political forums. Rosie then leaves Lee, at the darkest moment of economic collapse under the Heath government; at that point, history (the nation's and Lee's personal history) seems too much for the present to bear (118). But she returns "in the period of muted and, as it turned out, illusory optimism following the Labour victory in the 1974 elections," and after that she stays, because Rosie understands the terms of the war of dreams (119). She stays with Lee in part because of his remarkable beauty—although their radical friends would disapprove of such motivation (119)—but she values it not as the expression of his essential identity as the "worker hero," but as an image that can usefully activate desire, her desire to make their radical family work. In this sense, she allows Lee's and her own sexual identities to serve the strategic needs of their class and gender struggle. Their success derives from the combination of the real historical gains of the women's movement and Rosie's shifting tactics, based in her sensitivity to the power of surfaces and of the conflicting discourses that comprise identity.

Thus the revised edition of *Love* frames the period of the 1970s war of dreams that may have marked Britain's entry into postmodernity, by examining both the "prewar" period—"those days of social mobility and sexual license," when worn-out images of reality were failing to account for new crossings of class and gender allowed by mutations of capitalism (113)—and the "postwar" period when the ascendancy of Thatcherism and the New Right had demonstrated, as Stuart Hall argues, the power of those political interests that were able to articulate together diverse strands of class and national identity in new images of the future, the family, and the nation. The choices of characters in the afterword suggest hopefully that the material changes engineered in the 1970s by the women's movement can combine fruitfully with this new fluidity or fictionalization of identity to enable subversive positionings on the part of women.

Limiting my discussion to Carter's novels published in the seventies has meant that I must reluctantly give up any treatment of her more playful and bawdy, less grotesque (although no less politically grounded) novels of the eighties and nineties, *Nights at the Circus* (1984) and *Wise Children* (1991). Perhaps the only positive effect of Carter's premature death has been a huge increase of attention to these texts, as part of a critical attempt to assess her work's central importance for postmodern fiction. After *New Eve*'s injunction to put away our old narratives and symbols "until the times have created a fresh iconography," these two novels make a stab at that fresh iconography, at elucidating the fruitful role fictions can play in a politicized postmodern self. They offer, especially, new models of female powers of self-representation and of "family values"—that charged term of the late 1980s—as a matter of making do and making it up.

I have chosen this temporal limitation, however, because the seventies in Britain offer such a vivid illustration of the interrelation of fictional worlds and political realities. This decade's struggle to rethink national and factional identity, worked out in one way in Carter's novels, provides a case study of the material position of postmodern fiction(s)—as Elaine Jordan puts it, "the real material world of fantastic appearances."[89] In this light, Carter's deep engagement with the aesthetic realm can be understood not as escapism or apolitical dandyism, but as representative of the significant material contestation that takes place in that realm.

4
Reading Feminism's Pornography Conflict

A Canadian Supreme Court ruling in early 1992, which paved the way for increased restrictions on pornographic and obscene expression, offers an instructive illustration of the stakes of recent feminist debates about the explicit representation of sexual acts. That ruling, known as the Butler case (after the hapless Winnipeg adult-video dealer in question), has led to both domestic prosecutions and a significant increase in seizures by Canadian customs officials of materials entering the country, primarily from the United States. Seized texts have ranged from *Hothead Paisan* comics to works by Marguerite Duras, Oscar Wilde, Dorothy Allison, David Leavitt, Audre Lorde, Kathy Acker, *anti*porn activist Andrea Dworkin, and Bell Hooks—the last not for sexual obscenity but for alleged "hate speech," also open to restriction according to Customs interpretation of the Butler ruling.[1] Canada's crackdown has provoked much wringing of hands on the U.S. side of the border also, not only among civil libertarians but among guardians of culture such as the *New York Times*, which ran the headline, "Canada's Morals Police: Serious Books at Risk?"

The temporary confiscation of Dworkin's books underlines the ironies of feminist antipornography efforts better than perhaps any incident since the strange alliances of the 1986 Meese Commission on Pornography. For the Butler ruling had been, in part, based on the definition of pornography formulated by Dworkin and legal scholar Catharine MacKinnon, which has shaped recent efforts at antipornography legislation not only in the United States but in Canada and in Britain.[2] MacKinnon, working with the Canadian Women's Legal Education and Action Fund (LEAF), drew on the Canadian constitution's guarantee of equal gender rights in arguing that pornography, as "sexually explicit material that involves violence or degradation," violates women's rights by creating an environment hostile to them.[3]

The confiscations and prosecutions following the Butler case contribute a very practical angle on a number of theoretical issues surrounding pornography and censorship debates. Among these issues: the blurred line between fictional representations and real acts of hatred or discrimination; the difference between pornographic trash and "serious books"; and the apparent divergence between the interests of "women" and the interests of gays, lesbians, and people of color. This last problem is evinced by the fact that the majority of books listed in reviews of the post-*Butler* seizures—works by Wilde, Allison, Leavitt, Lorde, and Hooks, and Diane DiMassa's *Hothead Paisan*—primarily address gays, lesbians, and/or people of color. Owners of gay and lesbian bookstores allege that they have been "singled out" for harassment, prosecution, and fines; Customs officials have argued that this is due not to direct prejudice but to the practical fact that the generally small size of shipments from gay and lesbian publishers makes them easier to examine in detail.[4] A lawsuit challenging customs actions against one Vancouver gay and lesbian bookstore has gone all the way to the Canadian Supreme Court.[5]

I have begun this discussion of the antipornography movement and feminist postmodernism by reviewing the repercussions of the Butler case because all the above issues are also, I propose, questions central to postmodernism. The Butler case, and feminist debates about pornography, frame these problems from a slightly different perspective from many nonfeminist theorists of postmodernism, but if I rephrase them as (1) the textualization of reality; (2) the absorption of high culture by the terms of mass/consumer culture; and (3) the proliferation of otherness, they will start to sound very familiar to readers of this study.

In fact, the seizure of writings by Kathy Acker under the Butler precedent, although an unhappy moment, is fortuitous for my argument about feminist postmodernism—if not for those Canadians who would have liked to read or sell her work. This incident provides a concrete illustration of the political implications of interpretation—of reading a text as pornographic versus, say, postmodernist. Part of the reason I originally chose Acker and Angela Carter (who has been memorably dubbed "the high priestess of post-graduate porn") to illustrate this study's model of feminist-postmodernist reading was that both had, on occasion, been labeled pornographers.[6] While I believe this label is misleading—for it conflates the discrete stylistic conventions and contexts of reception of the popular genre (or range of subgenres) properly termed pornography with those of Acker's and Carter's difficult and not exactly best-selling novels, which enjoy the legitimacy of major publishers—it says a great deal about the anxieties shared by antipornography feminists and those critics who deny the possibility of progressive uses of postmodernism.[7] I also find this labeling representative of a disturbing and debilitating misunderstanding within feminism, on the part of critics of pornography, of the potential of feminist postmodernism to offer solutions to such anxieties over the status of feminist organizing in the contemporary context.

The debates among feminists over pornography that sprung up in the late 1970s, escalated in the 1980s, and continued through the 1990s, debates so fierce they have come to be called the "sex wars," *are* debates about postmodernism.[8] Their subtext is the question of how feminists ought to respond to this slippery phenomenon. While Craig Owens and others have pointed out the potentially productive intersection of feminist critiques of patriarchal representation and the postmodern crisis of representation, pornography has become the site at which feminism and postmodernism diverge. Antipornography feminism seeks to reject the existing regime of sexual representation entirely, seeing it as inherently masculine and therefore inimical to women's interests; postmodernism, on the other hand—at least, as I construe it—maintains that cultural and political contestation is inextricably bound up with existing representations. I want to argue that antipornography feminism is on the losing side of this divergence, fundamentally misrecognizing the fact that contemporary feminism has no choice but to function in postmodern conditions.

Any feminist interventions in postmodernity are inevitably staged within an active and fluid circulation of representations and identities. For all their materiality, positions of "difference" (and differences of positioning) are increasingly realized within and through representation. By rejecting the existing regime of representation, antipornography feminism stands to lose an ability to conceive of the multiple differences within each gender: the differences of race, class, and sexual practice among women, but also similarly varied relations to power among men. Not only does the concept of sexual pleasure become severely constricted if one eliminates all sexual practices found in male representation; more importantly, the concept of "women" grows equally exclusive if defined solely through its opposition to a monolithic notion of hegemonic (i.e., white, straight) masculinity.

Nevertheless, the attackers of pornography do raise very important questions central to feminist theorizing—about the role of representation in shaping lived conditions and about the possibility of agency in a male-shaped system. They recognize correctly that they have hit on an immensely compelling issue for many women, able to command a wide public forum. I will argue that antiporn feminism builds on the important insight that representation is a crucial site of feminist struggle; but I am concerned that its response to this recognition takes harmful forms.

Because of the issue's power, anticensorship feminists—however tired they may get of refuting the claim that porn is the paradigmatic example of sexism and oppression in contemporary culture—have also felt compelled to talk and write prolifically about pornography (and sex).[9] Carla Freccero exhibits some fatigue with the topic in entitling her article about it, rather optimistically, "Notes of a Post-Sex Wars Theorizer." But Freccero ends with perhaps the crucial question that must be answered before feminism in the United States and Britain can really get to that "Post" position: "Feminist movement and feminist thinking have the potential to conceive action and analysis in staggeringly revolutionary terms, and there are tactical priorities: imperialism, class stratification, the conditions of the neediest women in the United States. Many of the current conflicts in feminism continue to evade these questions. Why?"[10] In this chapter I want to stage the pornography controversy yet again in order to posit an answer to that "why?" and to suggest the kind of strategy that might help feminism address and move beyond the evasions and anxieties—evasions of internal divisions of economic and racial "otherness" among women, and anxieties over the ability of representations to shape the world—that have diverted much attention from the priorities Freccero cites.

When feminist antipornography work leads (albeit unintentionally) to the blacklisting of writings by not only gay men but white lesbians and women of color—when women have to choose one identity over the other—the need for a politics based on multiple categories of otherness becomes impossible to ignore. Postmodernist approaches can offer such a politics. Postmodernism conceives of subjectivity as constructed through acts of representation and reading; feminist postmodernism suggests that readers occupy complex and multiple positions in relation to any text. A feminist

4 / READING FEMINISM'S PORNOGRAPHY CONFLICT

postmodernist theory of readership can challenge monolithic constructions of the act of reading pornography as the duplication of male oppression and, in the process, suggest how various groups of diverse and perverse others might turn texts to their own purposes without having to resort to asking the state to intervene.

Disagreements over pornography thus provide particularly useful material for evaluating the benefits of adapting postmodernist theory to feminist struggles. In this chapter, I aim to demonstrate those benefits by drawing on both historical and theoretical arguments. I will propose that antiporn feminism's theories of the material effects of representation were in part an effective response to historical conditions arising in the 1970s, fundamentally postmodern developments that resulted in the fragmentation of the women's movement and the expansion of the pornography industry. The latter factor is symptomatic of postmodernity in two ways—as an illustration of postmodern capitalism's ability simultaneously to legitimate and to exploit the new identity positions arising from liberation movements, and, in the rise of legal pornography as a topic of "serious" discussion, as an example of the breakdown of divisions between high and low culture, a breakdown feminism had itself encouraged. Feminist critiques of representation were thus a first step toward developing a feminism fitted to postmodernity.

However, I find in the rhetoric of antipornography critiques, specifically of Acker and Carter, that the tendency to treat all representations as necessarily reproducing oppressive consciousness results in a static, oppositional model of difference that leaves women without agency and threatens to erase the differences among them. I will propose that antipornography feminism arrives at this impasse because of the assumptions about pornographic reading, as ingestion and reproduction, on which it bases its generalized model of reading; the second half of my discussion develops an alternative model of the pornographic reader—one based on the use-value of texts—as the type of the postmodern reader. I will focus on the feminist-postmodernist models of reading offered by Acker and Carter—especially evident in their treatment of explicit erotic representations—in order to suggest a contextual theory of how various readers might use different texts in different circumstances. Such a theory eliminates the need to see (male) representation as necessarily inimical to women; with the elimination of that binary structure, feminists need not treat internal differences among women as a threat.

Proliferating Identities in the Sexual Marketplace

I want to begin my argument by framing the rise of antipornography feminism as a postmodern development. Doing so allows me to situate this discourse as a response to a specific historical context, to pinpoint which of its assumptions—drawn from earlier humanistic discourses—become threatened and untenable in this new context, and to evaluate its effectiveness at rethinking those assumptions. In other words, antiporn feminism is a reaction to postmodern conditions; but the question remains as to whether it recognizes those conditions *as* postmodern, or rather attempts to reinscribe them into a humanistic frame of action. I propose the answer that while antiporn feminism effectively recognizes the increasing role of representation in shaping postmodern political conditions, it also requires a self-defeating withdrawal from the arena of representation. Such a withdrawal seems necessary because antiporn rhetoric defines feminism as an oppositional movement, and opposition disintegrates into diffuse and multiple categories of identity when it enters the postmodern realm of representation. Antipornography feminism fails to rethink opposition as the only model of political intervention, and therefore, I will argue, cannot offer a strategy—either of reading or of political action—fully adapted to postmodernity. I want first to establish that the threat to oppositionality inheres in postmodernity.

I have argued at a little more length in my chapter on Angela Carter that second-wave feminism grew, in part, out of a political environment in the 1960s that was essentially oppositional. The now-dated term *women's liberation* carries that implication, a vision of women's oppression as something entirely separate from them, from which they could be removed and set free (into some other conceptual space). Before Anglo-American feminism had had more than a few years to establish itself, however, it was faced with the loss of the oppositional model. Postmodernity challenged that opposition in two central ways: by fostering the internal fragmentation of the women's movement into further identity divisions, and by incorporating feminists' critique of the politics of representation into a general trend to foreground representation as the *only* site of interest, power, and identity-definition—thus reframing the demands of feminism as a set of desires that could be contained and addressed within an expanded representational marketplace, and positioning social transformation as a matter of commodity diversification. For instance, when women claimed the right to express and pursue their own fulfillment in sexual relationships, the pornography industry reflected that demand back to them as a call for the availability of more and better representations of female sexual pleasure. In this dual movement toward fragmentation and co-optation, any clear distinction between feminists and "society" was assailed both from within and from without.

Capitalism, far from reeling from the blows dealt it by the various countercultural movements, embraced them as new marketing opportunities, eagerly reaching out to newly articulated identity groups such as youths, blacks, and women, encouraging them to define themselves through material signifiers (such as clothing and hairstyles) and patterns of consumption (from rock concerts to drugs to vegetarianism). The opportunity to develop these new consumer markets offered a means to offset the effects of the global economic crisis of the early 1970s. But postmodern market diversification extends beyond the integration of newly existing social groups to their creation—to actively encouraging the atomization of formerly shared identities.

David Harvey sees this movement toward the subdivision of existing social groups as a feature of deindustrializing postwar economies. One of the features of the new post-Fordist phase is greatly intensified market targeting, a new emphasis on market research and specialized advertising aiming to exploit every nook and cranny of the domestic consumer base, creating new "needs" and desires and encouraging consumers to locate their identity in a variety of new lifestyle "niches." The greater the number of highly specialized identities the market can address, the more fully each consumer—who may identify with a number of these subgroups—can be interpellated and "milked."

Of course, the internal divisions that threatened to undermine the category "woman" almost as soon as it had been articulated as a political identity were not only caused by the new configuration of capitalism. They also owed (and owe) a great deal to a phenomenon that predates these changes, what Donna Haraway refers to as "the worldwide development of anti-colonialist discourse, that is, discourse dissolving the West." Haraway concludes, "As Orientalism is deconstructed both politically and semiotically, the identities of the Occident destabilize, including those of its feminists."[11] While the first internal disputes in the British and American women's movement concerned questions of sexuality (straight versus lesbian) and, relatedly, strategy (liberal versus separatist versus socialist), as the 1970s progressed, increasing challenges raised by feminists of color to the construction of feminism as "white feminism" erupted into very serious divisions over the movement's racism. In 1977, Barbara Smith could point in print to the lack of any "political movement to give power or support to those who want to examine black women's experience."[12] In Britain, the beginning of the eighties witnessed Afro-Caribbean and Asian British feminists forming separate organizing groups from white feminists; an indicative moment in the United States was the formal objections of women of color to racism (and, to a lesser extent, classism) at the 1981 conference of the National Women's Studies Association.[13]

The racial and national liberation movements on which these challenges drew are not peculiar to postmodernity, but rather, are consistent with the liberal-democratic tradition central to modernity.[14] However, they undergo alteration in the postmodern context in that they, like feminism, can no longer function as an oppositional voice *outside* the marketplace. The potentially anticolonialist image of a black, African soldier can today crop up in a Benetton ad, implicitly contributing an air of hip "danger" and worldliness to an international corporation. (Henry A. Giroux mentions just such a photograph in his analysis of Benetton's marketing of the *image* of "difference.")[15]

My point here is not to argue that the formerly oppositional identities offered by feminist, anticolonial, and racial liberation movements have been totally co-opted and neutralized by postmodern capitalism. Rather, the location of resistance has changed. Giroux, while he reads very pessimistically the transformation of "insurgent differences" into signifiers of "harmony, consensus, and fashion" for the worldly "Benetton Youth," draws the conclusion that those of us who wish to resist many aspects of postmodernity need to broaden the scope of our attention from the traditional sites of knowledge production. He admonishes, "the struggle over identity can no longer be considered seriously outside the politics of representation and the new formations of consumption."[16]

The pornography industry, which grew exponentially during the 1970s, represents precisely one such recently emerged formation where "struggle[s] over identity" take place in a context that is no longer oppositional, and where resistant identities become co-opted images. The enormous surge in pornography claiming to address the "problem" of women's pleasure is perhaps the most egregious example of the co-optation of feminist rhetoric as a means to sell commodities to newly constituted consumers.[17] Following a relaxation of obscenity prosecutions in both Britain and the United States, various forms of pornography achieved new legitimacy; new forms sprung up to address wider audiences than just the traditional target group of straight males. Linda Williams cites the emergence of the feature-length X-rated movie in more-or-less legitimate movie theaters as a dramatic example of these changes. Writer Nora Ephron's much-quoted comment about the first of these movies, *Deep Throat* (1972)—"Not to have seen it seemed somehow . . . derelict"—suggests just how significant were the porn industry's inroads into mainstream culture.[18]

Some feminists saw this expansion as a direct backlash against women's struggle for equality. For instance, even anticensorship feminist Melissa Benn, in her study of attempts to ban the topless photographs of women known as "page threes" that are published daily in British tabloid newspapers, assumes that "[i]t is certainly more than a co-incidence that the first Page 3 picture appeared in the *Sun* in 1970, which was also the first proper year of women's liberation in [Britain]."[19]

However, that "co-incidence" might have broader sources and more meanings than Benn implies. I would propose a more complex model of causality, one that sees the growth of the sex industry not as a simple product of backlash, but in the context of general trends in postmodern capitalism: its increasing dependence on marketing representations, and on marketing them to as diverse a range of consumers as possible. Contemporary capital needs to expand the field of representation to include as many new topics and as many new ways of forming individuals into consumer groups (i.e., audiences) as it possibly can. In her study, *Hard Core*, Williams reads the porn industry's expansion—à la Michel Foucault—as a stage in, and product of, the increasing constitution of sex as a new object of public discourse in the twentieth century. Representations of sex have come to seem increasingly worthy of social attention (or, as the academic protagonist of David Lodge's 1975 satire, *Changing Places*, puts it to himself as he sneaks into a strip joint, "a phenomenon of cultural and sociological interest").[20] Williams traces the liberalization of U.S. obscenity laws, arguing that the more sex was considered a controversial issue in society at large, the harder it was to demonstrate that even X-rated materials were without meaningful content or, in the Supreme Court's words, "redeeming social value." While this argument suggests that feminism's vocally framing sex as a political concern was actually one of the causes of the pornographic explosion, it also proposes that the industry's response was not necessarily hostile; Williams sees it as more an economic response than a deliberately political one. As Laura Kipnis puts it, "In social history terms we might note that *Hustler* [magazine] galumphs onto the social stage at the height of the feminist second wave, and while the usual way to phrase this relation would be the term 'backlash,' it can also be seen as a retort—even a political response—to feminist calls for reform of the male imagination."[21]

The burst of new pornography was the market's way of exploring and exploiting some of the issues feminism raised. Recognizing a group of consumers interested in exploring their sexuality, porn increasingly tried to address women—and not only straight women, but, to a certain extent, other formerly marginal sexual groups such as gays, lesbians, and practitioners of S/M, whose sexual practices had become an object of public discussion thanks to the events listed above. As I will later argue that attacks on Acker and Carter illustrate, this loss of a clearly oppositional or uncontaminated subject-position for women in the area of sexuality may be what troubles antipornography feminism the most. Antiporn feminists' consternation is indicative of anxiety over the intrusion of commodity marketing into what had previously been oppositional spaces, for the pornography business proved able to draw legitimacy from feminism's insight that all representation carries political meanings. The porn makers embraced—in their own self-interested and cynical way—calls for a rethinking of patriarchal representations of sexuality and used them to frame women not only as consumables (as images for expanded male audiences, now that female sexual pleasure was a social problem) but as consumers (as themselves a new audience "deserving of" their own sexual fantasies).[22]

Feminist organizing against pornography offered a way to reassert the foundation of feminism in the absolute difference between feminists and the mainstream of culture, and thus to reinvigorate the movement at a time when feminism was suffering on both sides of the Atlantic from a decline in measurable gains. Pornography became a major issue in the U.S. women's movement around 1977. At that point, the women's movement had begun to lose momentum, suffering frustrating setbacks on the Equal Rights Amendment and in the Supreme Court's refusal to overturn a ban on federal funding for abortions. The economic gains women had hoped for were also proving far slower to materialize than many had anticipated.[23]

The Women's Liberation Movement in Britain began to experience similar threats to its gains at about the same time: a bill attacking the liberal 1967 Abortion Act was introduced in Parliament in 1976, and conservative organizing against the Act intensified as the decade wore on. In Britain, the emergence of pornography as a new focus of feminist energy was evinced by both the "Reclaim the Night" rallies beginning in 1977, which frequently target "red-light" areas, and by a wave of discussions sparked by the government's (nonfeminist) Williams Committee on Obscenity and Film Censorship, which met from 1977 to 1979 and heard testimony from women's groups.[24]

Both Ann Snitow and Andrew Ross propose that pornography quickly caught on as a means of reinvigorating feminist efforts in the face of backlash partly because of the immediate emotional impact of some brutal and terrifying pornographic images, and partly because antipornography activists offered a clear moral division between men and women, in contrast to the blurring of sides and internal fragmentation that developed with postmodernity.[25]

This internal fragmentation can be read as a positive sign that the movement had acquired enough power and confidence, after the compulsive and impulsive push of initial actions, to begin a process of self-examination—and certainly, I do not wish to compose a narrative of feminism's decline. However, the emergence of internal differences may also have created a desire in some (mostly white) feminists for a new agenda that all women, under the umbrella of feminism, could unequivocally share. Campaigns against pornography seem to provide such a focus. In the face of setbacks and divisions, "[a]ntipornography theory offers relief in the form of clear moral categories: there are victims and oppressors."[26]

Antipornography feminism can thus be seen in the light of two characteristically postmodern developments—the fragmentation of the women's movement and the growth of pornography marketing—as an effort to defend a clear, oppositional model of difference against the threat of political paralysis posed by the market's diffusion and proliferation of categories of otherness—indeed, the proliferation of feminisms.

Reasserting Opposition — Refusing to (be) Consume(d)

Inasmuch as antipornography feminism recognizes and addresses the major threat postmodernity poses to political opposition, it might seem a successful feminist strategy for negotiating postmodern conditions. Focusing on the one issue of pornography enables feminism to take what's good about postmodernist thought, the view of representation as a crucial political arena, and reject what's bad—the loss of a fixed, shared identity from which to launch a critique of that power. Pornography provides the ideal focus because sexuality is the primary site at which women enter representation—sexuality is represented as women's (whole) identity—and because the object of pornography is primarily women, a position shared in this case (albeit differently) by working women, leisured women, white women, women of color, lesbians exhibited for male voyeuristic pleasure, and so on. Attempts to rally the feminist movement around the issue of pornography therefore appear to have the double virtue of retaining the critique of representation and preventing the cooptation of women into fragmented groups of representational consumers. These advantages account for many feminists' recent privileging of pornography as the term for a wide variety of representations, not only the girlie magazines and X-rated movies that conventionally comprise the genre.

Some feminists seeking to develop a critique of pornography draw explicitly on postmodernist theories of the politics of representation, in order to be able to generalize their critique to a whole range of texts, including some that purport to be feminist. I want to analyze one critique of Acker's work that can serve as an illustration of this tendency. The work of this critic, Colleen Kennedy, suggests why antiporn feminism cannot be a fully postmodernist rhetoric, instead collapsing in self-defeat.

Writing on the implications of explicit sex scenes by Acker and novelist Catherine Texier, Kennedy deftly draws on arch-postmodernist Jean Baudrillard to develop her critique. She argues that while Acker only *simulates* pornography in her novels, simulation is "a presumably 'unreal' action whose 'effect' is identical to the 'real.'" In other words, simulations, even those intended as critique or parody, cannot be distinguished from what they simulate, and Acker's fake "pornography" functions as, or *is*, pornography. The core of Kennedy's objection to Acker's work is that simulation "*cannot* be contained"; since, as Acker's pastiche strategy itself emphasizes, representations circulate in culture at large as part of a general consciousness, one author's intentions to turn them to feminist ends cannot determine how anyone will read them.[27]

I should emphasize that Kennedy is not alone in following this apparently postmodernist line of reasoning; her argument duplicates, on a metalevel, Catharine MacKinnon's contention that pornographic simulations themselves *are* acts of sexual domination against women (although I sincerely doubt whether MacKinnon would identify herself as a postmodernist thinker). In fact, Kennedy also makes that extra leap, when she equates reading one scene, in which Acker depicts a woman's lover nicking her genitals with a knife, with "witnessing the degradations of pornography" and then with "witnessing a woman having her vulva sliced with a knife."[28] Reading the simulation of porn equals reading porn equals standing by while real violence takes place. However, Kennedy's article is a particularly subtle example of this line of reasoning because she focuses on the dependence of representations on readers for their political import. Her trenchant critique is, in fact, aimed less at Acker and Texier—although she clearly considers their work dangerous—than at critic Robert Siegle, who sets himself up as what Kennedy scathingly calls "the 'ultrasophisticated' reader," who can explain to those more prudish readers who might be shocked by the sex in these novels why it is *really* politically subversive.[29] Siegle thus presumes to accomplish, and assumes that Acker can accomplish, the impossible: to contain simulation. Kennedy accurately points out that such a view of meaning as inhering in the text, waiting to be found by the good reader, completely ignores the context of a patriarchal society where men have historically had much more power than women to determine the meanings of representations.

Kennedy herself, however, then contradicts her own supposedly Baudrillardian position by implying that simulations ultimately *are* contained—by patriarchy. Far from being idiosyncratic, this move highlights the failure of much postmodern theory to follow through on the implications of the assertion that simulations do not mean inherently. Since simulations nevertheless do produce meanings somehow, this theoretical gap allows Kennedy and other antiporn feminists to assert that they do so according to a simple binary division: simulations always speak patriarchal power, and readers will respond either by being encouraged to continue "serv[ing] unreflectively the patriarchal establishment" or by finding them "offensive." Which camp one falls into will apparently depend on how one feels the "marked reality-effects" of such representations; presumably, men will feel their power validated, while women will feel victimized. One can accept representation and accept patriarchy; or one can oppose both.[30]

Thus while antiporn feminism recognizes the importance of contestation over images as the key location of postmodern politics, its strategy to counter the threat of political paralysis posed by the postmodern dispersal and proliferation of otherness (into diverse groups of consumers) is to reaffirm a clear division between patriarchy and its feminist opponents—those who stand at a distance from representation and refuse to consume it.

THE LOSS OF OTHERNESS AND THE LOSS OF AGENCY

I have already suggested, by referring to Canada's post-*Butler* situation, the profoundly negative consequences of this refusal of consumption or refusal to participate in the market of representations. This strategy cannot acknowledge that the material effects of pornographic (and all) representations differ according to factors other than gender. For instance, in gay male communities, and more recently and to a more limited extent among some lesbians, pornography has been instrumental in rendering visible the sexual practices central to both gay political organizing and gay oppression.[31] Some working-class women have found participating in the creation of pornography their best economic option and best route to autonomy.[32]

It stands to reason that if multiple categories of difference are created in part through the marketing of representations, to condemn that market wholesale is to lose the ability to theorize and mobilize various subject-positions—other than the two positions, inside and outside. And inasmuch as women always also participate in those categories—that is, inasmuch as women are always white women, black women, Latinas, indigenous women, Asian women, and so forth—they cannot remain in the outside location. For instance, while visible, white antiporn feminists have offered cogent critiques of the racism of much pornography, they fail to address the fact that they themselves evoke and circulate a representation with racial implications, the image of women as chaste and removed from (male-imagined) sexual desire. This construction revives a discourse whose price has historically been the *increased* displacement of sexuality

4 / READING FEMINISM'S PORNOGRAPHY CONFLICT 165

onto women of color.[33] And from the recent history of the American South to contemporary inner-city Britain, representations of women as innocent victims of male sexuality have resulted in the representation of black men as sexually rapacious.[34] In addition, Laura Kipnis has pointed out that the disgust and disapproval antiporn feminists exhibit toward graphic depictions of sexual organs and acts are emblematic of a fundamentally bourgeois desire to suppress and render "other" the unruly body, an attitude that has historically functioned to support class hegemony. Her analysis of *Hustler* makes the convincing point that, seen in this light, the advent and popularity of such a magazine is emblematic less of male resistance to women's sexual and social autonomy than of a specifically class-based resentment of the middle-class values feminism is seen as embodying and enforcing. These issues can easily be lost when antiporn feminists claim that it is possible for women not to participate in the field of sexual representations.

And in addition to these areas of contestation, agency itself is cast aside. While antipornography feminism posits a location outside patriarchal ideology from which women may recognize male representations as offensive, it cannot theorize that position, how one might get there or lead other women there. For identity is created and reaffirmed through representation, and can only be redirected by interventions in the available imagery. This is not to say that identities are not also profoundly material; however, material circumstances such as poverty, hunger, health, and skin color always undergo interpretation as they intersect with cultural discourses, such that they will carry different meanings for different bodies. For example, in this country white women experience poverty differently from white men—its gender distribution is deeply intertwined with ideologies of family and marriage, and where it does exist, it carries different forms of gendered vulnerability. This is increasingly true as more and more facets of previously "private" life enter the field of commercial representation. Feminist political action depends on deploying some representation of what female identity means in a given situation, and some representation of how that meaning might be different. Agency depends on participating in representation.

The crucial question then becomes, if antipornography feminists recognize that the social place of women is primarily constructed through sexual representations, what prevents them from intervening in those representations? Or more tendentiously, what assumptions of antipornography rhetoric preclude women's agency? These questions lead me back to antipornography critics' theories of readership, of the effects of texts on readers.

THE PORNOGRAPHIC READER AS POSTMODERN READER: TWO MODELS

Theories of readership are a prime site at which to evaluate whether antipornography feminism offers viable strategies for addressing the context of postmodernity, for postmodern subjects are above all constructed through reading. And when it comes to theories of readership, pornography again offers itself as a model for postmodernism. In the textualized world of postmodernity, the model of reading long connected to pornography seems to have become a generalized norm: the text acts directly on the reader, on his (as the theory goes) material world—not so much reflecting as creating reality. Literally, the pornographic text shapes the reader's body; it also shapes his future actions, the scenarios he needs to stage in order to achieve arousal. In this way more generally in postmodernity, fictions become reality. For example, if millions of West Coast television viewers during the early evening of a presidential election day hear that candidate X is winning by a landslide, that very statement will constitute an accomplished fact. According to the classic theory of readership, this is a pornographic scenario; offered a fantasy couched as a representation of reality, we act it out.

However, in its role as a fundamental assumption of antipornography feminism, this theory of pornographic reading as a duplication of the text cannot, by definition, be generalized across society. For if all readers/viewers duplicate what they read or see, and all representations reflect patriarchal power, feminist opposition becomes impossible. The historically accepted vision of pornographic reading has always depended on the maintenance of a clear delineation between those people assumed to read pornographically and those who do not. This delineation has, again, always been part of the structural logic of bourgeois hegemony, which names the masses as the unrestrained body of society, while the role of controlled and controlling intellect belongs to the ruling elite.

Critics of pornography posit its helpless reader as someone *other*. Williams, drawing on the research of Walter Kendrick, points out that according to concerned authorities in mid-nineteenth-century

4 / READING FEMINISM'S PORNOGRAPHY CONFLICT

England, "the person most endangered by obscenity was a young, middle-class woman, whose 'pornography' consisted of romantic novels" that might fill her head with dangerous longings.[35] In the recent debates, the primary version of that highly suggestive person has become a lower-class male, and the dangerous longings that might fill his head after consuming pornography are assumed to be urges to rape, physically hurt, and/or objectify and disdain women.[36] I would add that given contemporary discourses of criminality, this construction of the lower-class male can also be understood to participate in racist stereotypes.[37] Whether the *actual* readers of pornography resemble these demographic profiles has been beside the point in pornography debates.

Most antipornography feminists adopt this model of the pornographic reader as automaton—and as an identifiable *someone else*—because it supports the contention that texts can produce harm, yet maintains a separate, uncontaminated place for (white, genteel, female) critics of the texts' ideology. But this theory of readership makes antipornography feminism ultimately incompatible with postmodernity. For if, as I have argued, in the postmodern context all consciousness is the product of texts, no group of readers can hold itself apart; thus if one adopts the pornographic model of readership as direct cause and effect, no critical space can exist. Antipornography critics defy their own logic by assuming they can be immune to the effects of pornographic texts.

This contradictory theory of pornographic reading—which both denies and retains the concept of critical distance—is evident in the rhetoric of critics who condemn Acker's and Carter's novels. For example, Robert Clark begins his essay on Carter's work by asking "to what extent the fictions of Angela Carter offer their readers a knowledge of patriarchy—and therefore some possibilities of liberating consciousness—and to what extent they fall back into reinscribing patriarchal attitudes."[38] For Clark, agency cannot come from "reinscribing" existing representations; "consciousness" must remove itself to someplace elsewhere if it is to be subversive. "Knowledge of" the conditions of patriarchy clearly depends on distance in this formulation; it is something separate from those conditions, a self-contained object that can be "offer[ed]" to readers on a plate. To "fall back *into*" the conditions under examination would prevent knowledge. In his formulation, rereading society necessitates avoiding the site of pornography, for that is apparently the one location where readers have, by definition, no distance.[39] Clark therefore decries

Carter's suggestion, in her book-length essay on pornography, *The Sadeian Woman*, that pornography can itself be employed to critique the power imbalances in sexual relations; he asserts that "the ideological power of the form [is] infinitely greater than the power of the individual to overcome it." How Clark himself, as an "individual" reader, has managed to "overcome" the "ideological power" of Carter's reproductions of pornography remains an untheorized mystery.[40]

I would agree with Clark that the reader of pornography becomes the model of readership in Carter's novels, as in Acker's. However, I believe their texts' model of readership can also account for the apparently anomalous ability of some readers (such as Clark) to exercise agency within this role. While Clark assumes that the consciousness of the pornographic-automaton reader merely reproduces itself at each new encounter with a text, I think it useful to focus on the ways in which Acker's and Carter's feminist postmodernism shows that that consciousness never stops being produced; each pornographic text, and each new reading occasion, produces it slightly differently. The possibility for reshaping and redirecting desire arises in this slight, contextual difference that turns each act of reading into a retrospective *re*reading of the accumulated texts comprising subjectivity.

I am proposing a different model of the pornographic reader, as something other than a site of simple reproduction. The critical potential of Acker's and Carter's rereadings of classic pornographic scenarios comes not, as Clark suggests it would have to, from "the power of the individual" author to overcome existing textual ideology but from the force of the social (i.e., *non*-individual) needs that readers bring to texts at each reading. These varied needs shape the meaning readers make of a given text; they have themselves been shaped in part by previous encounters with texts.

In the case of pornography, a range of socially acquired needs or desires—for control, for punishment, for disavowal of sexual desire through a fiction of helplessness—will dictate how readers interact with a given pornographic text on a given occasion in order to achieve arousal. Jennifer Wicke proposes that readers of pornography engage in a "transcription of images or words so that they have effectivity within [the reader's] own fantasy universe. . . . This will often entail wholesale elimination of elements of the representation, or changing salient features within it."[41] In addition, this process of what Wicke calls "accommodation" may include the reader's identification at various times with different roles within the pornographic scenario: masculine or feminine, active or passive, giver or taker.[42] In other words, this theory of textual use suggests that through interaction with texts, readers may be able to step out of a binary relation between self and Other, consumer and consumed.

Kobena Mercer proposes a theory of "ambivalence" to explain both the various positions a reader may occupy in relation to a sexual text and the limits on such mobility. Reading his own complex reaction to Robert Mapplethorpe's eroticized portraits of black men, Mercer notes that he, as a gay black, occupies simultaneously the position of desiring spectator—"sharing the same desire to look as the author-agent of the gaze . . . the position that I said was that of the 'white male subject'"—and that of aestheticized object.[43] Yet he also qualifies Wicke's and Williams's sense of free movement, suggesting that his doubled positioning is made possible in part by the fact that both of this text's subject-positions are designed for male bodies. I would seek, in turn, to modify Mercer's emphasis on sex over other categories of identity; for instance, the pleasure some women (straight and lesbian) get from using a dildo suggests to me that one's capacity to relate to the experience of erections and penetration may not be sex-dependent.[44] If viewers can identify with sexual subject-positions across race, as both Mercer and Asian-American critic-artist Richard Fung suggest, might readers not also identify across gender (or sex), especially when compelled by the limited availability of arousing images designed for those physically like them? This, while still recognizing that the need to do so may go "hand in hand with many problems of self-image and sexual identity."[45] Pornographic reading thus becomes the exemplary case of reading *not* because it inscribes woman as man's Other, but because it offers readers the possibility of shifting, contextual, and multiple relations to power—while nevertheless recognizing that the range of variation in these relations is always vexed, never freely fluid.

I want to develop this alternate model of the pornographic reader as postmodern reader step by step, illustrating each stage of my argument by drawing on Acker's or Carter's work. I will draw my examples from Acker's *Don Quixote* and Carter's *The Infernal Desire Machines of Doctor Hoffman* because these novels seem most explicitly concerned with the issues of reading, representation, and sexuality that run throughout each writer's oeuvre.

Premise one: Women have to read (in its broad sense of decoding) existing images of gender in order to have any identity or social location. Contrary to the position taken by antipornography feminists, Acker's and Carter's novels continually emphasize the fact that women can't *help* participating in representation, *especially* sexual representation. In the central section of *Don Quixote*, Acker's female Quixote has to reread male texts because she finds that she—like the antiporn feminists who, in the name of separating themselves from male images, recreate a preexisting discourse of racialized, bourgeois womanhood—has no other language.

The problem Acker's Quixote engages throughout the novel is how a woman can actively love and desire in a culture with a long history of defining women as passive objects, mere receptacles of male desire. For Quixote, the ability to pursue sexual love is the key to female agency, for women have primarily been constructed in sexual terms, as beings whose significance and very essence lies in their (passive) sexual relation to men. Women like Quixote, who violate or seek to transcend that relational definition, have always been punished; the dilemma of female agency is thus: "If a woman insists she can and does love and her living isn't loveless or dead, she dies. So either a woman is dead or she dies."[46]

This patriarchal concept of woman as sexual Other pervades the texts Quixote rereads in the novel's central section, "Other Texts." Her rereading of Frank Wedekind's *femme fatale*, Lulu, whom she overlays with George Bernard Shaw's Eliza Doolittle, emphasizes this entrapment in existing (male) language. Professor Schön "rescues" Lulu from the street, aghast at her class-bound inarticulateness. He tells her, "You do not know who you are because you do not know how to speak properly. . . . Your soul's language is the language of Milton and Shakespeare and the English Empire. Wouldn't you like to be able to speak properly?" Lulu is unable to answer (78). Schön makes clear that acquiring subjecthood means accepting language, which in turn means accepting class hierarchy, the valuation of male representations (Milton and Shakespeare), and the racial hierarchy of Empire; Lulu's only other option is silence. There is "speak[ing] properly" and there is not speaking at all.

If a woman is not to be silent and penniless, however, the entry into language is inherently an entry into sexuality. Schön plans to transform Lulu, by giving her language, into a fit wife for someone elevated (78). In "the language of Milton and Shakespeare," a woman's identity is through her sexuality: as wife, lover, and/or mother. The relation between Acker's Lulu and Schön underlines this construction linguistically: Schön marries Lulu, yet she calls him

"Daddy"—he is the father-creator of an object defined by its relation to him sexually.

This creation, through language, of Lulu as essentially sexual leaves her in an impossible bind. While her being depends on her sexual relation to Schön, he cannot possibly return her desire, for she is an object he constructed, "brought out of nothing" (82), "a piece of shit" (88). So Lulu is doomed to suffer at the hands of a man who does not love her and whom she cannot stop loving. As she puts it, "I can not say 'No' to love to my appetite for love, and yet I must. To survive I must not love" (90). The terms of her existence and her survival contradict one another. Schön's and Lulu's (and Quixote's) world is composed only of patriarchal representations; yet Schön, in his terrified rejection of Lulu, suggests a way women might gain power without exiting representation: "What you call 'love,' if I paid any attention to it, would rip me (and this world) apart" (90). What frightens Schön is the prospect of women gaining access to representation; Lulu threatens to do this by rereading an existing discursive construction, love, from the context of the "wrong" reader. However:

Premise two: The ability to make new meanings from old representations depends on a reader's historically constructed needs. Readerly agency does not derive from women's *essential* or *biological* identity as the "wrong" readers. Such a claim would be quite compatible with antipornography theory's attempt to remove women from implication in male representations and to privilege gender over all other forms of difference. Rather, all readers occupy varying positions of "ambivalence" in relation to texts, depending on the context of reading—a context of needs and desires created in part by previous representations of each reader's identity and by the meaning or value of that identity at the present moment. There is a big difference between essentializing women's ability to misread male representations and basing a theory of subversive reading on any reader's shifting needs and experiences, which also include experiences of race, class, and sexuality, and can recontextualize a given image. Such a theory introduces the possibility of a *range* of specifically female (reading) positions that are not contained by or limited to binary representations of human heterosexuality, and not already fixed by a personal history of living out those representations.

Premise three: Readers' identities and needs—and therefore their interpretations of texts—are not established once and for all but must be continually reiterated in each new context. The mistake would be to assume that if the position from which one reads representations of gendered identity is determined by one's history, and if one's history is itself overwritten by encounters with previous representations, one always reads from an unchanging, designated gender position. However, history never stops happening; it is constantly being (re)written. The meanings that arise when a reader with established needs and images of identity meets a new text can retroactively change that reader's interpretation of previous texts, and therefore, of his or her identity. Agency results from this constant contextuality of reading, not from occupying a fixed, oppositional identity as representation's Other.

I am again drawing here on Judith Butler's formulation of gendered identity. Butler maintains that "what is signified as an identity is not signified at a given point in time after which it is simply there." Rather, establishing one's gender "requires a performance that is *repeated*" and "'agency,' then, is to be located within the possibility of a variation on that repetition."[47] This is true, I would argue, not only of one's gender but also of one's racial identity and one's sexuality. It may be especially true of sexuality, given that the markers of this identity, sexual desire and pleasure, cannot be sustained over time but must be continually produced anew—unlike gender and race, which present the *illusion* of being consistently present. The fact of this visible discontinuity suggests again why pornographic reading may be a useful model for other forms of discursive self-construction. Not only pornographic texts but all texts produce models of desire and identity, and these models cannot stand for long; they must be continually reiterated in order to address new contexts. This reiteration leaves room for intervention.

For example, in Carter's *Hoffman* (one of the novels Clark condemns), Desiderio works for a time in a traveling peep show, a place whose sole purpose is to produce pornographic desire. The waxwork miniatures in the various viewing-machines are classic pornographic images of fragmented female bodies, their body parts framed as food to be consumed or as sites of murderous violence, like the decapitated woman clad only in "the remains of a pair of black stockings and a ripped suspender [garter] belt of shiny black rubber" whose slashed breast hangs open "to reveal two surfaces of meat as bright and false as the plaster sirloins which hang in toy butcher's shops."[48] Carter reproduces these horrific tableaux in pornographic detail, and the language of Desiderio's descriptions emphasizes the painstaking artificiality of each detail—the very *re-*

*produced*ness of sexual desire Clark insists upon. The wax breast "meat" is doubly distanced from real flesh by its comparison to fake (plaster) meat in a fake context, a "*toy* butcher's shop." It is not even the fake meat hanging as advertisement in a real butcher's shop.

Desiderio describes the first image in the peep show sequence—an image titled, appropriately, "I HAVE BEEN HERE BEFORE"—in a range of terms evoking the deliberate production of spectacle:

> The legs of a woman, raised and open as if ready to admit a lover, formed a curvilinear triumphal arch. The feet were decorated with spike-heeled, black leather pumps. This anatomical section, composed of pinkish wax dimpled at the knee, did not admit the possibility of the existence of a torso. A bristling pubic growth rose to form a kind of coat of arms above the circular proscenium it contained at either side but, although the hairs had been inserted one by one in order to achieve the maximal degree of verisimilitude, the overall effect was one of stunning artifice. The dark red and purple crenellations surrounding the vagina acted as a frame for a perfectly round hole through which the viewer glimpsed the moist, luxuriant landscape of the interior. (44)

This vastly hyperbolic description of a sexual region that can "not admit the possibility" of connection to a body associates the pornographic image with society's most elevated institutions: the viewer (who is the imagined lover) enters the woman as a conquering hero entering a "triumphal arch"; he passes under the "coat of arms" that legitimates his nobility, through "red and purple crenellations," the colors and the fortress of royalty, to survey his kingdom within.[49] The vaginal "proscenium" is the site of the elaborate staging of male power.

I read the contrast between the grotesquely pornographic emphasis on detail and Carter's exorbitantly rich language as an "attempt to achieve the maximal degree of verisimilitude" while producing an "overall effect . . . of stunning artifice." In other words, this description calls attention to the fact that desire is neither inherent nor natural; it must be artificially produced, or induced, by means of representation. Carter's language enacts the irony that all the peepshow designers' anxious efforts to attain a realistic effect only serve to highlight the manufacture of desire. This is not to say that, in my reading, this passage achieves ironic or critical distance on the construction of pornography and therefore cannot itself be read, unironically, as pornography; much pornography is couched in equally overblown language that does not appear to create a Brechtian distancing effect, and anyone who has watched a porn film knows it does not depend on an illusion of naturalness in order to do its job. However, *in the context of Carter's novel*, this foregrounding of the effort involved in producing pornographic desire becomes the key to articulating a different, postmodern model of reading. For if desire depends on constant acts of representation, it can take on different shapes in different contexts of reception.

The reappearance, later in the novel, of images from the peep show supports the idea that pornographic texts produce pornographic desire, but also that those texts change as they are read in new contexts. On one level, pornographic images seem to serve as predictors of future erotic encounters. While still working at the peep show, Desiderio participates in an orgy that reminds him of a sequence of images at the show of "a girl trampled by horses" (110). He subsequently has cause to dimly recall that image again, when Albertina is gang-raped by the centaurs (180). However, the recurrence of the pornographic text in the mind of its reader, Desiderio, is *not* a simple matter of reproduction or duplication. While pornographic texts may shape or even cause readers' subsequent experiences of desire, the new, discrete context of each occasion of desire also shapes and changes the meaning of the previously read pornographic text. The new occasion becomes a rereading.

Thus the orgy, in the stables of a traveling circus, has "certainly some resemblances" to the trampling scene from the peep show, including one reveler's rib being broken when a horse kicks her, but it is also "teasingly different" (110). In this event, Desiderio is positioned not as the controlling viewer who draws sexual pleasure from witnessing a woman's helplessness, as in the image, but as himself the helpless one. The circus performer Mamie Buckskin, who is his "virile mistress" at this point—a "fully phallic" lesbian who loves to shoot guns and is attracted by Desiderio's passivity—propels him bodily into the midst of the orgy (109, 108). While female, Mamie is also blonde and from the United States, in contrast to the racially and colonially disempowered Desiderio. She is cast as the trampling animal, "reeking" with lust, "paw[ing] and claw[ing]" at our overwhelmed (but not unwilling) narrator. The consumer of pornography may reenact the image but he takes pleasure, in this new context, from occupying the role of the Other.

The context of Albertina's rape again rereads the initial image, while recasting the meaning of Desiderio's helplessness. This context undoes the eroticization of both his racialized passivity and the initial position of voyeur, for he is pinned down while his lover—an equally brown-skinned woman—is attacked next to him. This time, when he recalls the "teasing image," he thinks of it as "a horrible thing, . . . the most graphic and haunting of memories" (180). Desiderio is not like the centaurs, those pure products of the human imagination, whose blind obedience to existing representations is figured not only by their rigid adherence to their scriptures and by the ritual rape which they undertake "grimly, as though it were their duty" (179) but by the traditional tattoos covering each one's body, their very bodies existing only to repeat conventional representations. Desiderio constantly reinterprets the pornographic representations he has seen, so that each new context of reading becomes a rewriting. By the end of the novel, he can resist acting out his most intense desire—the desire to make love to Albertina—because of the terrible meaning it would take on in context, the context of Hoffman's plan to harness their exceptional "eroto-energy" in order to take over the nation. As a (post)colonial, mixed-race subject, he already knows how supposedly "individual" sexual relationships can serve to further national conquest.

Thus even the reader of pornography—the archetypal automaton who is presumed, as Vladimir Nabokov explains in his afterword to *Lolita*, to want only endless repetition of the same clichéd images— cannot make use of representations except by reading them in light of a specific context, formed in part by previous readings but also itself rewriting those previous texts.[50] In order to be arousing, an image must become, as Desiderio puts it, "teasingly different" from the last, even if it is the same image that has served to tease and tickle in the past; it must be adapted to the present context. Which leads me to *Premise four: Reading is repetition, but no repetition is possible without revision.* (Or, one cannot step into the same river twice.) The only question remaining, then, is how revisions of existing images can be directed toward specific feminist ends.

I will read another scene from *Don Quixote* through this alternate model of readership, in order to suggest that it offers feminism the tools to address the multiple axes of difference among women, which have too often seemed to paralyze feminist organizing. This scene offers an example of characters who become active readers of pornography and use pornographic representations to think their way out of the conventional heterosexual, binary view of female identity. The scene appears toward the end of Acker's novel, and is perhaps its most sexually explicit. It is based on a plagiarism of the Marquis de Sade's *Juliette*, an emblematic text in feminist pornography debates because it presents a heroine whose immense sexual pleasure and political agency are equaled only by her male-identified cruelty toward and disdain for (most) other women and the "lower" classes; antiporn critic Robin Morgan has referred to her feminist opponents as "Sade's new Juliettes."[51]

Quixote's protean sidekick Villebranche narrates this scene. In a slippage that seems to support the classic model of pornographic reading as absorption or assimilation, she begins by telling about a book she has read, whose story quickly dissolves into her own dream. However, readers familiar with Sade's text will immediately notice that it has been changed in this dream version; all the male characters have been eliminated, so that Juliette's S/M initiation in the crypt of the girls' school chapel now takes place only among women and girls.[52]

But one need not have this extraneous knowledge in order to recognize this scene as a rereading rather than a reproduction, for it also rereads an earlier episode in Acker's novel, a complex S/M encounter between Villebranche—represented here as a dominant lesbian who dresses as a Nazi captain—and De Franville, a submissive bisexual man who masquerades as a young girl. Both scenes emphasize pleasure derived from following step-by-step a conventional narrative that must be repeated out loud: where Villebranche told De Franville, "You're going to be whipped ten times," and he responded by eagerly removing his pants, Juliette tells Laure, "I'm going to have to whip you badly, cunt," and Laure responds, "Oh yes, . . . whip me badly."[53] However, a significant change from the Villebranche-De Franville exchange (as from Sade's text) to the later Juliette scene—a change to which I shall return—is that both partners are now female. This new equalizing of power also draws on the earlier texts' depiction of the characters as both white and young.

This scene is useful for creating a different model of pornographic readership because it highlights the tension between repetition and revision. As the sexual action builds, Acker literally repeats each passage of dialogue from two to four times in succession on the page. In my first chapter, I suggested this was a tactic for disrupting the conventional male reader's trajectory of arousal, slowing it perhaps to a more female pace. However, it can also be read as enacting Acker's (and her characters') attempt to break out of the Nabokovian stereotype of sexual pleasure's dependence on the endless repetition of standard pornographic scenarios—to develop a new paradigm of how porn might be read and pleasure made.[54]

The repetitions end when Juliette finally confronts her own reluctance to feel pleasure and to articulate it, tracing that reluctance to her location in the patriarchal scheme of representation as the silent object of male desire. She recognizes, "I'm scared because I have or know no self. There's no *one* who can talk. My physical sensations scare me because they confront me with a self when I have no self: sexual touching makes these sensations so fierce. I'm forced to find a self when I've been trained to be nothing."[55] She finds that speaking self by using existing representations according to her (different) needs. Juliette rereads the ritualistic script of S/M, making up a narrative that she tells the others present about a girl tied to a stool. She prefaces it, "I who've been without speech speak" (172). As in the classic pornographic model, the reader's speech is a repetition of existing pornography; and as in that model, she soon acts out her storytelling with Laure. But while her acting-out is violent and painful—there is no sense here that getting to agency or even pleasure can be easy—it leads to a new speech. Their sex culminates in the teacher, Delbène, interrogating the "wailing" Juliette: "Do women take no responsibility for their own actions and therefore have no speech of their own, no real or meaningful speech?" Juliette recalls her response: "'No,' I managed to reply. 'I'm coming.' Those were my words" (175). Again echoing (and changing) the Villebranche-De Franville exchange, in which De Franville "had no intention of taking responsibility" for his masculinity, this scene ends with a borrowed pornographic scenario transformed into a "speech of [Juliette's] own," speech indicating active female sexual subjecthood.

This pleasure-claiming act of speech—perhaps readable as an ironic echo of the classic feminist moment of "coming to voice"—is significant as a first step toward agency because it demonstrates that the reader implied by dominant representations is never fully identical with real readers. Both the Sadeian text Villebranche reads in order to create this scene and the S/M script Juliette acts out within the scene are directed toward an implied male reader who finds pleasure within patriarchal, heterosexual norms; but Juliette's assertion that she has been able to find in these texts a different—active, female, lesbian—kind of pleasure suggests the multiple identifications through which readers may be able to locate themselves in a fictional scenario. Juliette is able to assume the role of the character with sexual agency because even while she has not been interpellated as male, other interpellations construct her as sexual (by definition, because she is female) and white; and dominant discourse defines "white" as "having power" and "sexual" as "having power over a woman." In other words, her lesbian pleasure is enabled by a paradoxical combination of the existing "legitimate" subject-positions or reader-positions offered by these representations. While Juliette did not create that contradiction among the identities offered her, she is able to exploit it tactically.

Juliette's reading strategy thus provides an answer to Colleen Kennedy's warning that representations cannot be contained. It suggests that representations cannot be contained because *readers* cannot be contained in the location of implied reader; the implied subject-position from which any text makes sense will always be a combination of various identities, with which not all real readers will correspond perfectly. Recognizing this, it is possible to define subject-positions that are resistant (i.e., that are not identical with representation's implied readers) without needing to be oppositional (i.e., removed from representation). The lesbian subject-position suggested here is neither a separatist "outside" space nor immune to co-optation; Sade's original text stands as a warning reminder that so-called lesbian scenes are a standard fixture of pornography meant for men's voyeuristic arousal. But writing a woman into the role of desiring, active partner need not, as Richard Walsh would have it, "succeed only in recreating the abuses of male sexual dominance, albeit with painful self-awareness."[56] Rather it can highlight the possibility, even within the confines of patriarchal representation, of articulating other models of identity by recognizing the ambivalence—"as a structure of feeling in which one's subject-position is called into question"—that representations can induce.[57]

Therefore, the wider implication of my final premise about a postmodern model of readership—that repetition entails revision—is that identity itself is always a matter of both repetition and continual revision. The political meaning of an identity—woman, lesbian, white woman, and so forth—can change because each such identity participates in multiple discourses—such as sexuality, democracy, consumerism—and itself coexists with other identities in the same body. The relative power and prominence of these multiple identifications will shift according to the context.

Thus the active pornographic reader described by these four premises is, I would argue, a far more appropriate model than the automaton not only for the rereadings that compose Acker's and Carter's texts but also for generalizing to the postmodern political world. For feminism, adopting this model of readership and identity would mean that postmodernity's exacerbation of the fragmentation of the identity, "woman," by race, class, sexuality, age, nation, or body type, could itself be put to use as the source of a complex and fluid, contingent set of resistant tactics. This fragmentation, rather than being a problem to be suppressed, would become a reality to be addressed—and, in part and at times, an asset to be used. Inasmuch as white feminists remain focused on sexuality as the epicenter of social construction, we are likely to continue sweeping race and class to one side. I have, rather paradoxically, engaged with the "sex wars" at some length here in an attempt to do away with that focus. Therefore I want to conclude by being very clear about the stakes of the different models of reading I have outlined.

Adopting a postmodern model of multiply positioned readers does not simply mean accepting, relativistically, that I can read Acker and Carter as feminists, while Kennedy, Clark, or Dworkin can read them as pornographers. Likewise, the fact that Dworkin's own antipornography feminism can be read (and suppressed) as porn if the reading circumstances require it may support my position, but that position will only be useful for political struggles inasmuch as it enables readers to recognize the importance of such "reading circumstances." Any "politics of reading must . . . be articulated on an analysis that, describing practices that have long been in effect, makes them politicizable."[58] I hope a theory of reading as active, contextual *use* might redirect feminists' attention to the widely varying conditions (of race and class, nation, family, and so forth) under which different women negotiate with their surroundings and use literature to do so. While there may well yet be more to learn about representation from focusing on pornography, in postmodern culture the -graphies are multiplying faster than a single-issue campaign can begin to address. Geography, ethnography, and biography may offer far more fruitful sites for investigating women's power and powerlessness.

For this reason, I want to emphasize that the model of readership I have proposed to counter the conventional image of the pornographic consumer *can* and *should,* unlike that conventional image, not remain confined to pornography alone but should be generalized to diverse postmodern acts of reading (which means, to all negotiations with the postmodern world). The feminist antipornography theory of representation is not a theory for postmodernity because, in part, it is unable to extend its critique beyond the categories of gender and sexuality. Feminist strategy in postmodernity must be able to work across lines of race, class, sexuality, and even gender, inasmuch as alliances with, for instance, gay men can advance women's interests. I believe feminism can function in multiple, contingent ways without sacrificing its one defining commitment, to the economic and psychic well-being of women. The alternative is to let feminism be whittled down to an issue only concerning white, straight, middle-class women—not, I want to emphasize, that that is the intention of antiporn feminists; but in a society where the market of representations grows increasingly diverse, contributing to an increasing fragmentation of identity groups, the Powers That Be will use that diversity against each of us (e.g., the *Butler* seizures) if we do not use it to our advantage.

Epilogue: Readers, Disciplinarity, and Social Practices

In closing, I want to attempt very briefly to clarify the nature and scope of the claims this study makes, of what I intend my theorizing about feminist postmodernism to do—or more aptly, what I hope readers might do with it. I want to situate these claims in relation to categories of theoretical practice and academic discipline, and also to suggest their connection to some tactics of resistance that have cropped up "out there" in the world of contemporary politics frequently considered distant from academic studies of literature.

One way to approach this issue is by addressing the question of readers, for while I have often talked of readers and how "they" behave, I have not attempted to describe with any specificity who "they" are. What kinds of people (aside from me) read Acker's or Carter's novels?

In fact, I have deliberately avoided the question of who the readers of feminist-postmodernist writing currently are, in the demographic sense, although I don't think it insignificant; on the contrary, it would be fascinating to discover which women and men are drawn to these texts and are in a cultural, economic, and personal position to be able to read them. Nevertheless, I believe readers are subsequent to ways of reading. I mean this in two ways. First, readers will pick up and read a text only if they have some notion of how to make sense of it. I share the assumption Stanley Fish and other reader-response critics have articulated for some years, that "[interpretive] strategies exist prior to the act of reading and therefore determine the shape of what is read rather than, as is usually assumed, the other way around."[1] I would add that such frameworks determine not only "the shape of what is read" in a particular text but also *which* texts are read by particular readers. If a reader's catalog of interpretive strategies does not include one that can render a given text attractive (or even intelligible), she or he will not read it. This dynamic is particularly visible, in my experience, with Kathy Acker's writing; on the few occasions when I have taught her work in undergraduate or graduate courses, some (but not all) students have simply found it unreadable. It is not universally so—I, and other critics, and apparently enough other people that Grove kept publishing Acker's writing, manage to read and even enjoy it—but I have no doubt that the claim is true for those students who make it. They do not possess, or believe they do not possess (which amounts to the same thing)—and perhaps have no interest in possessing—an appropriate interpretive paradigm through which to approach this writing.

Second, ways of reading also precede readers in a less literal, demographic sense; if, as Fish suggests, interpretive strategies shape what readers find in the text, readers will themselves be formed by what they find there. In paraphrasing Fish here, I have deliberately replaced his "determine" with "shape" because the former implies a one-way relation with little flexibility, as though readers came to a text already fully formed and fixed, and found nothing there to change their notion of themselves. Rather, I believe that readers adjust and expand their interpretive strategies with each new encounter with a text, providing that text is sufficiently close to their already existing expectations to seem intelligible. In doing so, they may develop new ways of reading their surroundings and their own place in those surroundings.

I hope this begins to explain why I have chosen to focus on a way of reading—encouraged by, and practiced within, certain texts—which I have called feminist postmodernism. I have done so because I am concerned with the readers this way of reading might produce. My aim is to aid such a production of feminist-postmodernist readers. Therefore, to the extent that I have discussed "real" readers, they have primarily been the professional critics whose interpretive strategies—in relation to Acker's writing, Carter's, or, in the case of Jameson and Harvey, to the more general texts of postmodernity and postmodernism—establish influential normative readings for other readers to follow.

The reading practice I propose as an alternative to these previous rhetorics of interpretation not only questions the assumptions on which canons continue to be constructed, but also participates in a growing questioning of the disciplinary configuration of literary study. In this, the aims of my study can be situated in relation to a theoretical tendency that, in a sense, picks up where Fish's early reader-response work left off. Where he and other critics asserted that meaning should be sought not in the text but in the reader and in the norms of an interpretive community, a more recent strain of reader-oriented criticism uses interdisciplinary research to develop a historical sense of particular interpretive communities as rhetorical contexts of reception and to theorize their control of textual meaning. As embodied in Jane Tompkins's *Sensational Designs* and in the work of Steven Mailloux (among other places), this historically inclined reader-response criticism examines specific occasions of a given text's reception as instances of more generalized political trends and debates, played out, in part, in cultural discourse. Therefore, this criticism sees literary meaning as inextricably involved in larger cultural conversations, which are carried on in sites far more diverse than those conventionally included in the domain of English departments.

As Mailloux points out, this approach to literature—which he terms "rhetorical hermeneutics"—has many affinities with cultural studies, and frequently it becomes a form of such, studying cultural practices at specific historical sites not neutrally, but in order to intervene in current cultural formations and current modes of knowledge.[2] It intervenes both by reconfiguring traditional academic disciplines and by producing new interpretive strategies that challenge, as Tompkins makes explicit, conventional assessments of cultural value. I share these aims; much of my study has sought to demonstrate that literary critics cannot account for literature as a cultural and political phenomenon without developing such historicized ways of reading.

However, I also want to distance my project from Mailloux's and Tompkins's readings of nineteenth-century literature in order to emphasize that while all reading at any historical moment is contextual, this theory of reading has special significance within the context of postmodernity. If readers have always used texts as one site where cultural and political debates can be played out, postmodern readers have no choice, for with the disappearance of spaces outside representation and outside hegemonic discourses, all contestation is representational (and also material). As I have argued that postmodern subjects can only create resistant tactics and resistant identities from already co-opted texts and discourses, paying attention to how a text's meaning is contingent on specific rhetorical contexts becomes the basis of political practice. I want to close, therefore, by proposing several instances of recent feminist struggle that draw on and benefit from such a theory of rhetorical practice *as* political practice. These might function as practical examples of what can be achieved through such a theory.

The first example is provided by Ann Snitow's personal-cum-theoretical history of second-wave feminism, "A Gender Diary." Snitow, responding to Michéle Barrett's critical observation that postmodernism allows only contingent or ephemeral acts of resistance, counters that "[t]he virtue of the ephemeral action is its way of evading ossification of image or meaning."[3] Subsequently, she describes two contexts in which she and feminists with whom she organized found it politic first to reject, then to embrace, a particular image of "Woman": woman-as-mother. In the first instance, Snitow, recalling the pressure her generation of white, suburban women growing up in the 1950s experienced to give up all other interests for motherhood, argues against a feminist propeace rhetoric invoking women's essential identity as nurturing mothers. In the context of the history of women like herself, she suggests that using such a rhetoric would be disempowering, only repeating "an old, impotent, suppliant's gesture."[4] Some years later, however, she agrees fully with her women's group's decision to invoke just such an appeal to biology as a ground of special, female authority in a high-profile publicity campaign. The context now is the surrogacy case of "Baby M" and the legal and popular condemnation of Mary Beth Whitehead as an "unfit" mother of the child she decided not to give up.[5] Snitow's group circulates a petition supporting Whitehead's claim to the right to decide what's best for her child, as a tactic of opposition to the sexist and classist construction of appropriate motherhood in the press and by the court. Media attention to the petition, signed by a number of prominent women, suggests the power such a familiar and recognizable image of femininity can wield, power that serves in this particular context to contest heightened state control of motherhood.

In an article on the Sears Roebuck Company sex discrimination case that went to trial in the early 1980s, Joan W. Scott explores both the necessity that feminists deploy representations of women with sensitivity to their local aims, and also the difficulties facing such a rhetorical practice in a U.S. legal system founded on the idea of universally applicable precedents. The historian who served as an expert witness for the defense (Sears) illustrated the contingency of meaning by invoking a representation of gender embraced by many feminists—that of women's essential difference—in order to argue that the disparity in Sears's sales hiring practice was a result of the "natural" differences between women and more aggressive men.[6] A feminist historian testifying on behalf of the government (EEOC) was unable to discredit this argument by introducing a more subtle reading of historical variations in gendered work patterns.

Scott suggests that the only tactic that might have worked for the feminist historian, in the face of the prevailing gender wisdom of a conservative moment and of the court's demands for one, consistent explanation, would have been to deploy an alternative representation of multiple differences among both women and men. While Scott seems hesitant, and is perhaps right to be so, about the efficacy of such a "'deconstructive' political strategy in the face of powerful tendencies that construct the world in binary terms," this alternate representation is also drawn from the American repertoire of political myths.[7] I would suggest that the image of Americans as a people characterized by multiple differences (not just the one difference of gender) might invoke in this context a long-standing rhetorical tradition of the courts' responsibility to protect varied behaviors and desires and not allow them to become grounds for exclusion from access to "the American Dream." This representation, mythic as it may be, could function deconstructively in this particular situation to counter the equally compelling representation of women's essential difference.

I will offer one final example of a strategic feminist redeployment of representations. In the early 1990s, the direct action group WAC (Women's Action Coalition) modeled its high-profile, "media savvy" interventions in part on the tactics of ACT-UP (which itself owes a certain amount to earlier radical-feminist disruptions of public events).[8] Following its formation in 1992 by a group of New York artists—in direct response to the highly visible *in*visibility of feminism in the Anita Hill-Clarence Thomas hearings and the William Kennedy Smith rape trial—WAC made media waves, "getting mention in *Newsday*, the *New York Times*, the *New York Post*, *Art in America*, *NYQ*, and the *Voice*," plus *Harper's Bazaar*, *New York* magazine, *ARTnews*, and a number of regional newspapers around the US.[9] Much of the coverage takes a rather questionable feminism's-day-has-come-again approach, such as Pheobe Hoban's narrative in *New York* magazine: "Women in the eighties seemed more interested in proving their prowess in the work force than in raising their consciousness. *Feminist* became an embarrassing term, something sophisticated women preferred not to call themselves."[10] Hoban then lists major public events in the eighties' "backlash," from the Supreme Court's *Webster* decision to the emergence of Camille Paglia, and concludes, "[t]he clock, it seemed, had been turned back twenty years."[11]

Coverage such as Hoban's, which ignores the thousands of apparently unsophisticated women who have never stopped fighting for any number of unglamorous issues such as the formation of unions in woman-dominated fields, highlights the limitations of WAC's approach. However, when (albeit for a moment) the *New York Times* is suddenly referring to "radical feminism" as "the future," I believe there are also positive lessons to be learned.[12] Certainly, WAC had an immediate appeal for many women; within a year of its formation, WAC claimed two thousand members in New York and had developed offshoots in twenty U.S. cities, Toronto, London, and Paris.[13]

Among WAC's much-publicized "actions" were protests at both the Democratic and Republican conventions in 1992, the Guggenheim Museum, and outside courtrooms and abortion clinics; however, the one event I will briefly analyze is the 1992 Mothers' Day action at New York City's Grand Central Station. During the morning rush hour, WAC members unfurled a pink banner over the train information board, reading "IT'S MOTHERS' DAY: $30 BILLION OWED MOTHERS IN CHILD SUPPORT." Then they passed out "fake" Mothers' Day cards, according to an account in the *Village Voice*: "A pretty pink background is adorned with free-floating flowers and looks very sweet. Lots of people take the cards. The language inside is Hallmark. Sort of." The poem inside pointed out that of "developed" nations, only the United States fails to provide day-care and pre-natal care.[14]

This tactical deployment of representations echoes both Snitow's recognition of the cultural force connected to images of motherhood and a national ideology of enlightened egalitarianism similar to that which might have been invoked in the Sears prosecution. By speaking up as, implicitly, mothers, the WAC activists claimed perhaps the one context in which hegemonic gender discourses permit women to be "strident"; they also evoked the immense emotional power associated with Mothers' Day, through the pink banner and the "pretty" cards. The contrast between these rhetorical tokens of the mythology of sacred motherhood and the dry, political discourse of economic and social "facts" may have enabled those facts to have an impact they would not wield in a less theatrical setting.

Let me emphasize that I am not proposing WAC, through this brief sketch, as the ideal blueprint for the women's movement in the twenty-first century. Their tactics could only ever be part of a range of practices and concrete areas of action, and would need to coexist alongside groups struggling for gender justice in more pedestrian, less flashy ways and those representing women less affluent, confident, and/or urban than the majority of WAC members. In fact, WAC—in its original incarnation, at least—seems to have fallen prey to what Certeau identifies as the inevitable fate of such a tactical approach: "Whatever it wins, it does not keep"; it is necessarily fleeting, "incapable of stockpiling," and cannot capitalize on its acts of appropriation to build an enduring base.[15] New York WAC apparently disintegrated amid acrimony and apathy after only about eighteen months, while other chapters endured by becoming more similar to traditional grass-roots political groups in their forms of protest (marches with banners, petitions, etc.) and in their organizational structure (incorporating extensive theoretical discussion, in an attempt to formulate a consistent, shared sense of beliefs and long-range goals).[16]

Nevertheless, the brevity of WAC's existence as feminism's media-designated "vanguard" need not be seen as failure, especially if one thinks in terms of Certeau's model. It is simply the nature of such a practice that its effects are hard to pin down—and therein lies its power. Members of the Chicago chapter suggested measuring their accomplishments in practical terms: if even one woman called an abuse hotline, or got a breast exam, or practiced safe sex because of their actions, they had succeeded.[17] Another way to assess WAC's impact would be to focus on the ways in which it expanded the catalog of possible images, both of women and of feminism, bringing together (or "articulating," in Stuart Hall's term) existing models of political action and of femininity in unprecedented combinations. Ultimately, WAC's tactics suggest one—and only one—way in which the practice of rereading existing representations tactically and contextually that I have advocated in this study might extend beyond the pages of little-known novels to energize formerly apolitical women and offer newly attractive images of the identity, "feminist."

Notes

Introduction

1. Jane Tompkins, *Sensational Designs: The Cultural Work of American Fiction, 1790–1860* (New York: Oxford University Press, 1985), xi.

2. See, for example, Lissa Paul's recent article, "Postmodernism Is Over. Something Else is Here. What?" (in *Transcending Boundaries: Writing for a Dual Audience of Children and Adults*, ed. Sandra L. Beckett [New York: Garland, 1999], 239–54). As early as 1991, the first annual Stuttgart Seminar in Cultural Studies was titled "The End of Postmodernism"; however, there still seems to be a question-mark accompanying that phrase for some, as the title of a 1999 conference—"The End of Postmodernism? A Colloquium to Host Richard Rorty"—at the Australian National University suggests.

3. Susan Rubin Suleiman, *Subversive Intent: Gender, Politics, and the Avant-Garde* (Cambridge: Harvard University Press, 1990), 186.

4. Barbara Herrnstein Smith, *Contingencies of Value: Alternative Perspectives for Critical Theory* (Cambridge: Harvard University Press, 1988), 175.

5. Hal Foster, "Postmodernism: A Preface," in *The Anti-Aesthetic: Essays on Postmodern Culture*, ed. Foster (Seattle: Bay, 1983), xii.

6. Craig Owens, "The Discourse of Others: Feminists and Postmodernism," in *The Anti-Aesthetic*, ed. Hal Foster, 61.

7. See especially Judith Butler, *Gender Trouble: Feminism and the Subversion of Identity* (New York: Routledge, 1990) and *Bodies That Matter: On the Discursive Limits of "Sex"* (New York: Routledge, 1993); Donna Haraway, "A Manifesto for Cyborgs: Science, Technology, and Socialist Feminism in the 1980s," in *Feminism/Postmodernism*, ed. Linda J. Nicholson (New York: Routledge, 1990), 190–233, and *Modest_Witness@Second_Millennium.FemaleMan_Meets_OncoMouse: Feminism and Technoscience* (New York: Routledge, 1997); Bell Hooks, "Postmodern Blackness," in *Yearning: Race, Gender, and Cultural Politics* (Boston: South End, 1990), 23–31; Biddy Martin, "Feminism, Criticism, and Foucault," in *Feminism and Foucault: Reflections on Resistance*, ed. Irene Diamond and Lee Quinby (Boston: Northeastern University Press, 1988), 3–19; Gayatri Chakravorty Spivak, *The Post-Colonial Critic: Interviews, Strategies, Dialogues*, ed. Sarah Harasym (New York: Routledge, 1990); Suleiman, *Subversive Intent;* Trinh T. Minh-Ha, *Woman, Native, Other: Writing Postcoloniality and Feminism* (Bloomington and Indianapolis: Indiana University Press, 1989).

8. Dick Hebdige, "Staking out the Posts," in *Hiding in the Light: On Images and Things* (London: Routledge, Comedia, 1988), 185–203.

9. Nancy Fraser and Linda J. Nicholson, "Social Criticism without Philosophy: An Encounter between Feminism and Postmodernism," in *Feminism/Postmodernism*, ed. Nicholson, 34–35.

10. Michel de Certeau, *The Practice of Everyday Life*, trans. Steven Rendall (Berkeley and Los Angeles: University of California Press, 1984), xix.

11. Andreas Huyssen, *After the Great Divide: Modernism, Mass Culture, Postmodernism* (Bloomington: Indiana University Press, 1986), 44–62; Ann L. Ardis, "Reading 'as a Modernist'/De-naturalizing Modernist Reading Protocols: Wyndham Lewis's *Tarr*," in *Rereading Modernism: New Directions in Feminist Criticism*, ed. Lisa Rado (New York: Garland, 1994), 373–90; Nicola Pitchford, "Unlikely Modernism, Unlikely Postmodernism: Stein's *Tender Buttons*," *American Literary History* 11 (1999): 642–67.

12. Paul Gilroy, *"There Ain't No Black in the Union Jack": The Cultural Politics of Race and Nation* (London: Hutchinson, 1987; reprint, with a foreword by Houston A. Baker, Jr., Chicago: University of Chicago Press, 1991), 28 (page citations are to the reprint edition).

13. Linda Hutcheon, *The Politics of Postmodernism* (New York: Routledge, New Accents, 1989).

Chapter 1: A Politicized Postmodernism: Feminist Reading Tactics

1. Suleiman, *Subversive Intent*, 186.

2. Pitchford, "Unlikely Modernism."

3. See the following essays from *Feminism/Postmodernism*, ed. Nicholson: Seyla Benhabib, "Epistemologies of Postmodernism: A Rejoinder to Jean-François Lyotard," 107–30; Christine Di Stefano, "Dilemmas of Difference: Feminism, Modernity, and Postmodernism," 63–82; Nancy Hartsock, "Foucault on Power: A Theory for Women?" 157–75.

4. Hutcheon, *The Politics of Postmodernism*, 142, 152; Hartsock, "Foucault on Power," 160.

5. Jean-François Lyotard, *The Postmodern Condition: A Report on Knowledge*, trans. Geoff Bennington and Brian Massumi (Minneapolis: University of Minnesota Press, 1984); Owens, "The Discourse of Others," 65. For other discussions that likewise choose to emphasize the complementary nature of feminist and postmodernist projects, rather than their incommensurability, see Fraser and Nicholson, "Social Criticism without Philosophy"; Martin, "Feminism, Criticism, and Foucault"; Suleiman, *Subversive Intent*.

6. Owens, "The Discourse of Others," 67.

7. Hartsock, "Foucault on Power," 163; Hooks, "Postmodern Blackness," 28. See also Nancy K. Miller, "The Text's Heroine: A Feminist Critic and Her Fictions," in *Conflicts in Feminism*, ed. Marianne Hirsch and Evelyn Fox Keller (New York: Routledge, 1990), 118. Carol A. Stabile also makes a similar argument ("Feminism and the Ends of Postmodernism," in *Materialist Feminism: A Reader in Class, Difference, and Women's Lives*, ed. Rosemary Hennessy and Chrys Ingraham [New York: Rout-

ledge, 1997], 399) about the suspicious timing of the shift toward postmodernism within feminism.

8. Sara Ahmed, *Differences That Matter: Feminist Theory and Postmodernism* (Cambridge: Cambridge University Press, 1998), 6.

9. The quoted term is Chantal Mouffe's, from "Hegemony and New Political Subjects: Toward a New Concept of Democracy," trans. Stanley Gray, in *Marxism and the Interpretation of Culture*, ed. Cary Nelson and Lawrence Grossberg (Urbana: University of Illinois Press, 1988), 89.

10. Robert Siegle, *Suburban Ambush: Downtown Writing and the Fiction of Insurgency* (Baltimore: Johns Hopkins University Press, 1989), 109.

11. Tania Modleski, *Feminism without Women: Culture and Criticism in a "Postfeminist" Age* (New York: Routledge, 1991), 11.

12. Martin, "Feminism, Criticism, and Foucault," 17.

13. Hooks, "Postmodern Blackness," 28–29.

14. This is how Linda Alcoff paraphrases such positions in "Cultural Feminism versus Post-Structuralism: The Identity Crisis in Feminist Theory," in *Feminist Theory in Practice and Process*, ed. Micheline R. Malson, Jean F. O'Barr, Sarah Westphal-Wihl, and Mary Wyer (Chicago: University of Chicago Press, 1989), 307.

15. Martin, "Feminism, Criticism, and Foucault," 14.

16. Certeau, *Everyday Life*, xii.

17. Ibid., xiv, xiii.

18. Ibid., 89–90.

19. Ibid., 78.

20. Ibid., 78.

21. Ibid., xix.

22. Ibid., xix.

23. Certeau acknowledges (ibid., xviii, xvii) the "overly schematic character" of his "rather too neatly dichotomized" distinction between producers and consumers, and seeks to nuance the framework through his specific investigations and those of his colleagues in a series of planned companion volumes. But *The Practice of Everyday Life*, as it stands in its English-language version, does not complicate the clean division.

24. Ibid., 18, xix.

25. See Alcoff, "Cultural Feminism"; Suleiman, *Subversive Intent*, 205.

26. Laura Kipnis, "Feminism: The Political Conscience of Postmodernism?" in *Universal Abandon? The Politics of Postmodernism*, ed. Andrew Ross (Minneapolis: University of Minnesota Press, 1988), 149–66; Laura Doan, ed., *The Lesbian Postmodern* (New York: Columbia University Press, 1994).

27. Ihab Hassan, *The Dismemberment of Orpheus: Toward a Postmodern Literature*, 2nd ed. (Madison: University of Wisconsin Press, 1982), 260.

28. John Barth, "The Literature of Replenishment: Postmodernist Fiction," in *The Friday Book: Essays and Other Nonfiction* (New York: G. P. Putnam's Sons, 1984), 195.

29. Ibid., 195–96.

30. Brian McHale, "Editorial Laissez-Faire," review of *The Columbia History of the American Novel*, ed. Emory Elliott, *American Book Review*, August-September 1991, 24.

31. Molly Hite, "Postmodern Fiction," in *The Columbia History of the American Novel*, ed. Emory Elliot; assoc. eds. Cathy N. Davidson, Patrick O'Donnell, Valerie Smith, and Christopher P. Wilson (New York: Columbia University Press, 1991), 698;

NOTES TO CHAPTER 1

José David Saldívar, "Postmodern Realism," in *The Columbia History*, ed. Elliot, 521.

32. Acker in fact came from a Jewish family—a feature of her biography that her writing does not emphasize or address (as far as I am aware).

33. Elizabeth Deeds Ermarth, "Postmodernism and the Novel," in *Encyclopedia of the Novel*, ed. Paul Schellinger (Chicago: Fitzroy Dearborn, 1998), 2:1032–35.

34. In the later 1990s, such work did begin to appear, including a number of articles on Toni Morrison as postmodernist and a volume from the SUNY Series in Postmodern Culture edited by John C. Hawley, *Cross-Addressing: Resistance Literature and Cultural Borders* (Albany: State University of New York Press, 1996). Essays in Hawley's collection discuss comparatively the work of a range of writers of color from across the world (along with one or two white women writers *not* from the United States or United Kingdom)—but there is still, here, no significant border-crossing comparison between writers of color and the canonical postmodernists. I hope that the flowering of multicultural postmodernist criticism is not merely another sign that postmodernism is no longer such a fashionable term in mainstream literary criticism—i.e., a case of Others' being allowed to have the cultural leftovers once again.

35. Ihab Hassan, *Paracriticisms: Seven Speculations of the Times* (Urbana: University of Illinois Press, 1975).

36. See also my discussion of Siegle's *Suburban Ambush* in chapter 2.

37. Hooks, "Postmodern Blackness," 27.

38. Fredric Jameson, *Postmodernism, or, The Cultural Logic of Late Capitalism* (Durham, NC: Duke University Press, 1991), 5.

39. See, for example, *The Gender of Modernism: A Critical Anthology*, ed. Bonnie Kime Scott (Bloomington: Indiana University Press, 1990); Sandra M. Gilbert and Susan Gubar, *No Man's Land: The Place of the Woman Writer in the Twentieth Century* (New Haven: Yale University Press, 1988).

40. Suleiman, *Subversive Intent*, 186.

41. See, for example, Joan Kelly-Gadol, "Did Women Have a Renaissance?" in *Becoming Visible: Women in European History*, ed. Renate Bridenthal and Claudia Koonz (Boston: Houghton Mifflin, 1977), 137–64; Paul Lauter, "Race and Gender in the Shaping of the American Literary Canon: A Case Study from the Twenties," in *Feminist Criticism and Social Change: Sex, Class, and Race in Literature and Culture*, ed. Judith Newton and Deborah Rosenfelt (New York: Methuen, 1985), 34–37.

42. Jameson, *Postmodernism*, 44. I owe this observation to a comment by Larry Scanlon.

43. Haraway, "Manifesto."

44. Jameson, *Postmodernism*, x.

45. David Harvey, *The Condition of Postmodernity: An Enquiry into the Origins of Cultural Change* (Cambridge, MA: Blackwell, 1989), 121, 124.

46. Huyssen, *After the Great Divide*, 188–95.

47. Harvey, *The Condition of Postmodernity*, 147.

48. Ibid., 141. As I discuss in chapter 3, both Stuart Hall and Henk Overbeek, in divergence from Harvey, argue that Britain was an exception to the successful establishment of Fordism elsewhere in Western Europe. Stuart Hall, "The Toad in the Garden: Thatcherism among the Theorists," in *Marxism and the Interpretation of Culture*, ed. Cary Nelson and Lawrence Grossberg (Urbana: University of Illinois Press, 1988), 35–73; Henk Overbeek, *Global Capitalism and National Decline: The Thatcher Decade in Perspective* (London: Unwin Hyman, 1990).

49. Harvey, *The Condition of Postmodernity*, 156.

50. Walter Kalaidjian, *American Culture between the Wars: Revisionary Modernism and Postmodern Critique* (New York: Columbia University Press, 1993), 254.

51. Brandon Taylor, *Modernism, Post-Modernism, Realism: A Critical Perspective for Art* (Winchester [UK]: Winchester School of Art Press, 1987), 77; cited in Harvey, *The Condition of Postmodernity*, 290.

52. Harvey, *The Condition of Postmodernity*, 117.

53. Jameson, *Postmodernism*, 6, 10.

54. Elsewhere in his *Postmodernism* book (131–53), Jameson does address the effects of reading pastiche, in a chapter on the *nouveau roman*. His conclusions are still generalized (to all readers) and predominantly pessimistic.

55. Certeau, *Everyday Life*, xxi, 166.

56. Versions of this essay have appeared in a number of locations under slightly different titles: "Postmodernism, or, The Cultural Logic of Late Capitalism," *New Left Review* 146 (1984): 59–92; "Postmodernism and Consumer Society," in *Postmodernism and Its Discontents: Theories, Practices*, ed. E. Ann Kaplan (London: Verso, 1988), 13–29; and as the first chapter, "The Cultural Logic of Late Capitalism," in Jameson, *Postmodernism*, 1–54. A discussion of the Bonaventure does *not* appear in the very first printed version of the essay, "Postmodernism and Consumer Society," in *The Anti-Aesthetic*, ed. Hal Foster, 111–25.

57. Jameson, *Postmodernism*, 38.

58. Ibid., 42.

59. Ibid., 43.

60. Ibid., 44; Adrienne Rich, "Notes toward a Politics of Location," in *Blood, Bread, and Poetry: Selected Prose, 1979–1985* (New York: Norton, 1986), 215, quoted in Thomas Foster, "Meat Puppets or Robopaths?: Cyberpunk and the Question of Embodiment," *Genders* 18 (1993): 28.

61. Mike Davis ("Urban Renaissance and the Spirit of Postmodernism," in *Postmodernism and Its Discontents*, ed. Kaplan, 86) has chastised Jameson for ignoring the hotel's "systematic segregation from the great Hispanic-Asian city outside . . . , not only the misery of the larger city but also its irrepressible vibrancy." In the *Postmodernism* book version, Jameson responds in a scathing footnote (421 n. 19) that does not really answer Davis's charge. What Jameson dismisses as Davis's "useful urban information" has, I believe, ramifications for Jameson's implied subject.

62. Foster, "Meat Puppets or Robopaths?"

63. Certeau, *Everyday Life*, xvii.

64. Jameson, *Postmodernism*, 44; emphasis added.

65. Suleiman, *Subversive Intent*, 192.

66. Jameson, *Postmodernism*, 326.

67. Certeau, *Everyday Life*, 92.

68. Harvey, *The Condition of Postmodernity*, 65 n.

69. Ibid., 48.

70. Iris Marion Young, "The Ideal of Community and the Politics of Difference," in *Feminism/Postmodernism*, ed. Nicholson, 319.

71. Certeau, *Everyday Life*, 96.

72. Davis, "Urban Renaissance," 84.

73. Certeau, *Everyday Life*, 95.

74. Ibid., 102.

75. Minnie Bruce Pratt, "Identity: Skin, Blood, Heart," in *Yours in Struggle: Three Feminist Perspectives on Anti-Semitism and Racism,* by Elly Bulkin, Minnie Bruce Pratt, and Barbara Smith (Ithaca, NY: Firebrand Books, 1988), 16. Subsequent references to this work are cited parenthetically in the text.

76. Certeau, *Everyday Life,* xix.

77. Kathy Acker, *Don Quixote: Which Was a Dream* (New York: Grove, 1986), 9. Subsequent references to this work are cited parenthetically in the text.

Chapter 2: Kathy Acker's Unreasonable Texts

1. Butler, *Gender Trouble,* 143.

2. Daniel Punday offers the important reservation that "[c]ontradictions between and within discourses can be analyzed at some locale, but such locations themselves arise out of the contradictions and clashes within the discourses." "Theories of Materiality and Location: Moving through Kathy Acker's *Empire of the Senseless,*" *Genders* 27 (1998), par. 1, <http://www.genders.org/g27/g27_theories.txt> (24 September 1998).

3. Hall, "The Toad in the Garden," 49.

4. A slightly different version of this point is central to Joe Moran's chapter on Acker in *Star Authors: Literary Celebrity in America* (London: Pluto, 2000), 132–48—on which, more later.

5. Thus the historic association, not irrelevant here, of the monstrous and the female. Both are figured as at once natural—as opposed to cultured—and unnatural; their artificiality provides the necessary contrast to the "unconstructed" norm of masculinity. See Dean MacCannell and Juliet Flower MacCannell, "The Beauty System," in *The Ideology of Conduct: Essays in Literature and the History of Sexuality,* ed. Nancy Armstrong and Leonard Tennenhouse (New York: Methuen, 1987), 206–38.

6. Acker, *Don Quixote,* 71. Subsequent references to this work are cited parenthetically in the text.

7. Punday, "Theories of Materiality and Location," par. 11.

8. Hutcheon, *The Politics of Postmodernism,* 2.

9. Ibid., 10, 12.

10. Ibid., 12.

11. Ibid., 58.

12. Certeau, *Everyday Life,* 170.

13. Kathy Acker, interview by Paul Perilli, *Poets and Writers Magazine* (March/April 1993): 28–33; Acker, "Reading the Body," interview by Larry McCaffery, *Mondo 2000* 4 (1991): 72–77; Acker, "The *On Our Backs* Interview: Kathy Acker," interview by Lisa Palac, *On Our Backs* (May/June 1991): 19–20, 38–39.

14. Roy Hoffman, review of *Blood and Guts in High School,* by Kathy Acker, *New York Times Book Review,* 23 December 1984, 16; Hoffman's comment is also quoted in Naomi Jacobs, "Kathy Acker and the Plagiarized Self," *Review of Contemporary Fiction* 9.3 (1989): 53.

15. Jonathan Gill, "Dedicated to Her Tattoo Artist," *New York Times Book Review,* 16 October 1988, 9; R. H. W. Dillard, "Lesson No. 1: Eat Your Mind," review of *Empire of the Senseless,* by Kathy Acker, *New York Times Book Review,* 16 October 1988, 9–11.

16. The official Library of Congress information inside U.S. editions of Acker's books lists her birth date as 1948. However, various obituaries—including one in the *Guardian* by her British publisher, and those in the London *Times* and the *New York Times*—stated that she was fifty-three when she died in 1997. To complicate matters, Acker's "friend and lover" Charles Shaar Murray subsequently wrote to the *Guardian* insisting that she was in fact born in 1947. Acker's literary executor, Matias Viegener, tells me that her birth certificate gives the date 18 April 1947 (personal communication, November 2000). Gary Pulsifer, "Kathy Acker: Power, Punk, and Porn," *Guardian* (London), 1 December 1997; "Kathy Acker," *Times* (London), 2 December 1997; Rick Lyman, "Kathy Acker, Novelist and Performance Artist, 53," *New York Times*, 3 December 1997, late edition; Charles Shaar Murray, "Piercing Memories of Acker," *Guardian* (London), 3 December 1997.

17. Ellen G. Friedman and Miriam Fuchs, "Works by Kathy Acker," *Review of Contemporary Fiction* 9.3 (1989): 78; Acker, interview by Paul Perilli, 28. However, when a section from *Politics* was later published in Acker's *Hannibal Lecter, My Father* (ed. Sylvère Lotringer [New York: Semiotext(e), 1991]), it was listed as previously unpublished.

18. See Moran, *Star Authors*, 132, 138, and the London *Times* obituary, "Kathy Acker."

19. Martina Sciolino, "Confessions of a Kleptoparasite," *Review of Contemporary Fiction* 9.3 (1989): 63–64. Also quoted by Moran (*Star Authors*, 133).

20. Moran, *Star Authors*, 144.

21. Ibid., 142.

22. Ibid., 142–47.

23. See, for example, Terry Brown, "Longing to Long: Kathy Acker and the Politics of Pain," *LIT: Literature, Interpretation, Theory* 2 (1991): 167–77; Douglas Shields Dix, "Kathy Acker's *Don Quixote*: Nomad Writing," *Review of Contemporary Fiction* 9.3 (1989): 56–62; Ellen G. Friedman, "Where Are the Missing Contents? (Post)Modernism, Gender, and the Canon," *PMLA* 108 (1993): 240–52; Catherine Joan Griggers, "Reinventing the Popular: Inscriptions of the Feminine Subject in Postmodern Genres" (Ph.D. diss., University of Florida, 1989); Kathleen Hulley, "Transgressing Genre: Kathy Acker's Intertext," in *Intertextuality and Contemporary American Fiction*, ed. Patrick O'Donnell and Robert Con Davis (Baltimore: Johns Hopkins University Press, 1989), 171–90; Siegle, *Suburban Ambush*. A notable exception is Punday's article, in which he reaches toward a definition of materiality in Acker's work, especially *Empire of the Senseless*, which sees it neither as a bodily or prelinguistic absolute nor as a concern merely with existing objects and their socioeconomic effects on the self. Rather, materiality is flexible and interactive, "something produced out of one's *relation* to social and linguistic objects" ("Theories of Materiality and Location," par. 9; emphasis added).

24. Griggers, "Reinventing the Popular," 142, 146, 150. Martina Sciolino, who like Griggers recognizes the slipperiness of gender for the "nonsubject" of Acker's work, nevertheless concludes her article ("Kathy Acker and the Postmodern Subject of Feminism," *College English* 52 [1990]: 443) with the more historicizing assertion that "the difference that constitutes identity is contingent—interrelational and contextual."

25. Hulley, "Transgressing Genre," 179, 173.

26. Ahmed, *Differences That Matter*, 143.

27. Siegle, *Suburban Ambush*, 109.

NOTES TO CHAPTER 2

28. Tom Peters, *Liberation Management: Necessary Disorganization for the Nanosecond Nineties* (New York: Knopf, 1992), 677.
29. Ibid., 500.
30. Ibid., xxxii.
31. Harvey, *The Condition of Postmodernity*, 125–27.
32. Antonio Gramsci, "Americanism and Fordism," in *Selections from the Prison Notebooks*, ed. and trans. Quintin Hoare and Geoffrey Nowell Smith (New York: International Publishers, 1971), 309–10.
33. Peters, *Liberation Management*, 299, 300.
34. Kathy Acker, *My Death My Life by Pier Paolo Pasolini* (London: Pan, 1984; reprint in *Literal Madness* [New York: Grove, 1988]), 301 (page citations are to the reprint edition).
35. Harvey, *The Condition of Postmodernity*, 141.
36. Peters, *Liberation Management*, 667.
37. Foster, "Meat Puppets or Robopaths?" 14–15. Certeau (*Everyday Life*, 1) makes a similar argument in terms of class: "this anthill society began with the masses, who were the first to be subjected to the framework of levelling rationalities. The tide rose. Next it reached the managers who were in charge of the apparatus, managers and technicians absorbed into the system they administered; and finally it invaded the liberal professions that thought themselves protected against it, including even men of letters and artists."
38. Foster, "Meat Puppets or Robopaths?" 15.
39. Kathy Acker, "Punk Days in New York," interview, *Fist* 1 (1998): 9.
40. Acker has described *Pasolini* as an attempt to write an Agatha Christie mystery by a "fucked-up" mind. Ellen G. Friedman, "A Conversation with Kathy Acker," *Review of Contemporary Fiction* 9.3 (1989): 20.
41. Acker, *Pasolini*, 187–92, 200–202.
42. Roland Barthes, "The Death of the Author," in *Image, Music, Text*, trans. Stephen Heath (New York: Hill and Wang, 1977), 142–48; Michel Foucault, "What Is an Author?" trans. Donald F. Bouchard and Sherry Simon, in *Language, Counter-Memory, Practice: Selected Essays and Interviews*, ed. Bouchard (Ithaca, NY: Cornell University Press, 1977), 113–38.
43. See, for instance, Catherine Belsey, "Constructing the Subject: Deconstructing the Text," in *Feminist Criticism and Social Change*, ed. Newton and Rosenfelt, 45–64.
44. Enzo Siciliano, *Pasolini: A Biography*, trans. John Shepley (New York: Random House, 1982), 8.
45. Stefano Tami, *The Doomed Detective: The Contribution of the Detective Novel to Postmodern American and Italian Fiction* (Carbondale: Southern Illinois University Press, 1984), 4.
46. Jessica Benjamin, *The Bonds of Love: Psychoanalysis, Feminism, and the Problem of Domination* (New York: Pantheon, 1988), 184. For a discussion of the equally dualistic gendering of rationality in Conan Doyle's Sherlock Holmes stories, see Belsey, "Constructing the Subject," 58–63.
47. Benjamin, *The Bonds of Love*, 57.
48. Ibid., 64. I will explore some of the more hopeful nuances of S/M configurations in chapter 4.
49. Acker, *Pasolini*, 175. Subsequent references to this work are cited parenthetically in the text.

50. See the complex reading of the film in Naomi Greene, *Pier Paolo Pasolini: Cinema as Heresy* (Princeton: Princeton University Press, 1990).
51. Ibid., 211–12.
52. Siciliano, *Pasolini*, 375.
53. Dale M. Bauer, *Feminist Dialogics: A Theory of Failed Community* (Albany: State University of New York Press, 1988), 11.
54. M. M. Bakhtin, *The Dialogic Imagination: Four Essays*, ed. Michael Holquist, trans. Caryl Emerson and Michael Holquist (Austin: University of Texas Press, 1981), 264.
55. Acker, *Pasolini*, 183.
56. Siegle, *Suburban Ambush*, 96.
57. Acker, *Pasolini*, 301.
58. See Alice A. Jardine, *Gynesis: Configurations of Woman and Modernity* (Ithaca: Cornell University Press, 1985).
59. Acker, *Pasolini*, 332.
60. Acker, *Don Quixote*, 9–10.
61. Ellen G. Friedman, "'Now Eat Your Mind': An Introduction to the Works of Kathy Acker," *Review of Contemporary Fiction* 9.3 (1989): 45.
62. Kenneth M. Jensen and Elizabeth P. Faulkner, eds., *Morality and Foreign Policy: Realpolitik Revisited* (Washington, DC: United States Institute of Peace, 1991); Thomas Hill Schaub, *American Fiction in the Cold War* (Madison: University of Wisconsin Press, 1991).
63. Walter Isaacson, *Kissinger: A Biography* (New York: Simon and Schuster, 1992), 160–61.
64. Ibid., 268.
65. Acker, *Don Quixote*, 106.
66. I'd suggest that Reagan suddenly shows up in the Nixon era because Acker is examining the beginnings of a postmodern politics of appearances in the United States, a politics crucial to Reagan's success.
67. On Hobbes and realpolitik, see Isaacson, *Kissinger*, 654; also David Little, "Morality and National Security," in *Morality and Foreign Policy*, ed. Jensen and Faulkner, 18.
68. Acker, *Don Quixote*, 111, 114.
69. Thomas Schaub points out (*American Fiction in the Cold War*, 21) that realpolitik in the 1940s and 1950s was not only allied with rationalism, but also aimed to take into account "that element of irrationalism which was characteristic of [Reinhold] Niebuhr's and [Arthur] Schlesinger's revised understanding of historical process."
70. Acker, *Don Quixote*, 117.
71. See, for example, Trinh, *Woman, Native, Other*.
72. Acker, *Don Quixote*, 193.
73. Interestingly, Enzo Siciliano (*Pasolini*, 367) identifies just such a tactical piracy with the later writings of Pasolini; the approach of his 1973 newspaper columns was "a matter of provoking, by surprise, one controversy or another: now showing support for those who contested the Communist Party from the left, now espousing arguments that might even appear welcome to the right. It was a matter of making the viewpoint unrecognizable in the immediate sense—making it a 'pirate' viewpoint, so that it would be impossible for anyone to claim as his own."
74. Acker quoted in Friedman, "A Conversation," 17.

75. William Gibson, "An Interview with William Gibson," interview by Larry McCaffery, *Mississippi Review* 47/48 (1988): 228, quoted in Foster, "Meat Puppets or Robopaths?" 13.

76. Kathy Acker, *Empire of the Senseless* (New York: Grove, 1988), 3. Subsequent references to this work are cited parenthetically in the text.

77. Thivai, who has a stake in maintaining patriarchal narratives, may exaggerate the mother's powerlessness in his version of events. In the story of Abhor's childhood that comes through Thivai, she telephones her mother when her father first begins to fondle her, but her mother's intervention is wholly ineffectual (12). When Abhor later recounts the same incident directly, her mother successfully prevents the sexual abuse (67).

78. Luce Irigaray, *This Sex Which Is Not One*, trans. Catherine Porter with Carolyn Burke (Ithaca: Cornell University Press, 1985), 74.

79. Acker, *Empire*, 15.

80. Acker, "Punk Days in New York," 11.

81. Acker, *Empire*, 17.

82. Moran, *Star Authors*, 142–43.

83. Acker, *Empire*, 33.

84. Foster, "Meat Puppets or Robopaths?" 25.

85. Acker, *Empire*, 55.

86. Foster, "Meat Puppets or Robopaths?" 15.

87. Haraway, "Manifesto," 193.

88. Foster, "Meat Puppets or Robopaths?" 14.

89. Acker, *Empire*, 26.

90. I would thus differ with Arthur F. Redding's reading ("Bruises, Roses: Masochism and the Writing of Kathy Acker," *Contemporary Literature* 35 [1994]: 295) of the "new way of tattooing" explored in this scene as "emblematic of an omnivorous and violent sexuality."

91. Acker, *Empire*, 140.

92. Both Abhor and Thivai do get tattooed at the end of part 1, but this is only mentioned briefly (86).

93. Frances E. Mascia-Lees and Patricia Sharpe, "The Marked and the Un(re)marked: Tattoo and Gender in Theory and Narrative," in *Tattoo, Torture, Mutilation, and Adornment: The Denaturalization of the Body in Culture and Text*, ed. Mascia-Lees and Sharpe (Albany: State University of New York Press, 1992), 164.

94. Ibid., 152.

95. Punday, "Theories of Materiality and Location," par. 12.

96. See Moran, *Star Authors*, 136–37, for a discussion of how Acker's own heavily tattooed body may have played into her commodification. Acker argues for her tattoos' resistant power in her interview with Andrea Juno (*Angry Women*, ed. Andrea Juno and V. Vale, *Re/Search* 13 [1991]: 177–85), among other places.

97. Acker, *Empire*, 186.

98. Haraway, "Manifesto," 219.

CHAPTER 3: ANGELA CARTER'S WAR OF REAL DREAMS

1. Hall, "The Toad in the Garden," 36.
2. Overbeek, *Global Capitalism*, 86.

3. Ibid., 88–97, 113, 112, 117, 106–10.

4. All this is not to say that the establishment of Fordism is something inherently desirable. However, Hall suggests ("The Toad in the Garden," 37) that "[h]ad this attempt succeeded, it would have created the historical conditions for a long, settled period of reform capitalism under social democratic management."

5. *The War of Dreams* was the title given to the first U.S. edition of *The Infernal Desire Machines of Doctor Hoffman*.

6. Jonathon Green, *Days in the Life: Voices from the English Underground, 1961–1971* (London: Heinemann, 1989), 427.

7. Alan Sinfield, *Literature, Politics, and Culture in Postwar Britain* (Berkeley and Los Angeles: University of California Press, 1989), 248.

8. Asphodel, "1968: Prague Winter, Feminist Spring," in *'68, '78, '88: From Women's Liberation to Feminism*, ed. Amanda Sebestyen (Bridport, Dorset: Prism, 1988), 9; see also (in the same volume) Mary Kay Mullan, "1968: Burntollet Bridge," 15–24; and Green, *Days in the Life*, 401–2;.

9. Hall, "The Toad in the Garden," 37, 41.

10. Aidan Day, *Angela Carter: The Rational Glass* (Manchester: Manchester University Press, 1998), 8–9, 55. See also Robert Clark, "Angela Carter's Desire Machine," *Women's Studies* 14 (1987): 147–61; Alison Lee, *Angela Carter* (New York: Twayne, 1997), 61–62.

11. Chronologies of Carter's career are available in Lee, *Angela Carter*; Ellen G. Friedman and Miriam Fuchs, eds., *Breaking the Sequence: Women's Experimental Fiction* (Princeton: Princeton University Press, 1989), 308; Elaine Jordan, "The Dangers of Angela Carter," in *New Feminist Discourses: Critical Essays on Theories and Texts*, ed. Isobel Armstrong (New York: Routledge, 1992), 131; and especially in Lorna Sage's much-cited *Angela Carter* (Plymouth: Northcote House in association with the British Council, 1994).

12. Walter Kendrick, "The Real Magic of Angela Carter," in *Contemporary British Women Writers: Narrative Strategies*, ed. Robert E. Hosmer, Jr. (New York: St. Martin's, 1993), 70, 69.

13. Clark, "Desire Machine," 158–59.

14. Ibid., 159.

15. In his reading of Carter's vampire tale, "The Lady of the House of Love" ("SLIP PAGE: Angela Carter In/Out/In the Postmodern Nexus," *Ariel* 20.4 [1989]: 96–114), Robert Rawdon Wilson points out the insistence of historical and contextual references locating the story at the moment immediately preceding World War I. Carter's intertexts—among them, vampire stories, the Gothic, and the tale of Sleeping Beauty—become signifiers of a dying aristocracy that is about to consume in its own violent death throes a generation of young men such as the story's English hero.

16. Lee, *Angela Carter*, x.

17. Angela Carter, *Love*, rev. ed. (London: Chatto & Windus, 1987; New York: Penguin, 1988), 12, quoted in Linden Peach, *Angela Carter* (New York: St. Martin's, 1998), 69.

18. Lee, *Angela Carter*, 62.

19. In addition to Robert Clark's reading, which I discuss below, other critics suggest that the Minister and Doctor can be read as superego and id; that Dr Hoffman is a surrealist and that the novel "can be read as a reflection on the opening pages of Breton's first 'Surrealist Manifesto'"; that "we can read the text as a series

of figures for the defeat of the political aspirations of the 1960s"; or that "Dr Hoffman is a manifestation of the principle of 'L'imagination au pouvoir' of the 1968 students' revolt." Beate Neumeier, "Postmodern Gothic: Desire and Reality in Angela Carter's Writing," in *Modern Gothic: A Reader*, ed. Victor Sage and Allan Lloyd Smith (Manchester: Manchester University Press, 1996), 142; Susan Rubin Suleiman, "The Fate of the Surrealist Imagination in the Society of the Spectacle," in *Risking Who One Is: Encounters with Contemporary Art and Literature* (Cambridge: Harvard University Press, 1994), 128; David Punter, "Angela Carter: Supercessions of the Masculine," in *The Hidden Script: Writing and the Unconscious* (Boston: Routledge & Kegan Paul, 1985), 31; Ricarda Schmidt, "The Journey of the Subject in Angela Carter's Fiction," *Textual Practice* 3.1 (1989): 56.

20. *Oz* 26 (1970): 18–19, 31.
21. Clark, "Desire Machine," 155, 154, 155, 155.
22. Ibid., 155.
23. Dilip Hiro, *Black British, White British: A History of Race Relations in Britain*, rev. ed. (London: Grafton, 1991), 200.
24. Ibid., 261.
25. Ibid., 248; Sona Osman, "Full Circle: 1968–1988: Rivers of Blood," in *'68, '78, '88*, ed. Sebestyen, especially 45.
26. Gilroy, *There Ain't No Black*, 85–88.
27. Hiro, *Black British*, 254.
28. Gilroy, *There Ain't No Black*, 47–48.
29. It is worth noting that *Hoffman* was written while Carter was away from Europe, living in Japan—a sojourn that she comments on as her first experience of being racially Other, conscious of her own marginality as a Caucasian as well as a woman. Angela Carter, "Tokyo Pastoral," in *Nothing Sacred: Selected Writings* (London: Virago, 1982), 33, quoted in Suleiman, "Surrealist Imagination," 126; Angela Carter, "Poor Butterfly," in *Nothing Sacred*, 48, quoted in Sarah Gamble, *Angela Carter: Writing from the Front Line* (Edinburgh: Edinburgh University Press, 1997), 16.
30. Marsha Rowe, introduction to "Women's Liberation Movement," in *The "Spare Rib" Reader*, ed. Rowe (Harmondsworth, Middlesex, UK: Penguin, 1982), 541.
31. Anna Coote and Beatrix Campbell, *Sweet Freedom: The Struggle for Women's Liberation*, 2nd ed. (Oxford: Basil Blackwell, 1987), vii; see also Amanda Sebestyen, introduction to *'68, '78, '88*, ed. Sebestyen, x.
32. Coote and Campbell, *Sweet Freedom*, 95.
33. Elaine Jordan, "Enthralment: Angela Carter's Speculative Fictions," in *Plotting Change: Contemporary Women's Fiction*, ed. Linda Anderson (London: Edward Arnold, 1990), 34; Suleiman, "Surrealist Imagination," 129; Lee, *Angela Carter*, 61.
34. Angela Carter, *The Infernal Desire Machines of Doctor Hoffman* (London: Rupert Hart-Davis, 1972; London: Penguin, 1982; reprint as *The War of Dreams*, New York: Harcourt Brace Jovanovich, 1973), 24 (page citations are to the 1982 edition). Subsequent references to this work are cited parenthetically in the text.
35. Clark, "Desire Machine," 154.
36. Carter, *Hoffman*, 96.
37. Roland Barthes, "Myth Today," in *Mythologies*, trans. Annette Lavers (New York: Hill and Wang, 1972), 121–22.
38. Carter, *Hoffman*, 16.
39. Jordan, "Enthralment," 34.
40. Carter, *Hoffman*, 78–79.

41. The Count's valet—who turns out to be Albertina in one of her many disguises—is named Lafleur, after the syphilitic valet in Sade's *Philosophy in the Bedroom*.

42. Barthes, "Myth Today," 120.

43. Richard Rodriguez, "Mixed Blood," *Harper's Magazine*, November 1991, 47. I feel compelled to note, however, the rather bizarre gender dynamics of Rodriguez's rhetoric in this otherwise elegant essay. He highlights the tropes of seduction, marriage, and rape in which the conquest of Mexico has been figured by various groups and he offers alternative, empowering readings of the significance of the female national symbols, La Malinche and the Virgin of Guadalupe. Yet he reproduces the same gendering of conquest (reversing the racial terms) in his argument that it is in fact Indians and mestizos who have absorbed and will increasingly outnumber the white Europeans and Americans: the essay closes with an image—apparently intended as subversive—of a dark-skinned man silently and hungrily watching oblivious, rich white women.

44. Carter, *Hoffman*, 51–52.

45. The coming-together of race and gender differences also has disastrous results at the moment when Desiderio is officially marked for destruction; when the Determination Police arrest him, they erroneously charge him with being the "son of a known prostitute of Indian extraction," thereby eliding his mother's sex with his father's race (62).

46. Sally Robinson, "The Anti-Hero as Oedipus: Gender and the Postmodern Narrative," in *Critical Essays on Angela Carter*, ed. Lindsey Tucker (New York: G. K. Hall & Co., 1998), 160.

47. Day, *Angela Carter*, 791; Peach, *Angela Carter*, 59.

48. Gamble, *Angela Carter*, 110.

49. Robinson, "The Anti-Hero," 164.

50. Carter, *Hoffman*, 13.

51. Lee, *Angela Carter*, 65.

52. Coote and Campbell, *Sweet Freedom*, 111–13; Arthur Marwick, *Culture in Britain since 1945* (Oxford: Basil Blackwell, 1991), 71.

53. Coote and Campbell, *Sweet Freedom*, 42.

54. Sebestyen, introduction, xii; see also Penny Holland, "Still Revolting," in *'68, '78, '88*, ed. Sebestyen, 135.

55. Coote and Campbell, *Sweet Freedom*, 44, 14; see also Green, *Days in the Life*, 401–9.

56. Rowe, introduction to "Women's," 541.

57. Green, *Days in the Life*, 412.

58. Kenneth Hudson, *Men and Women: Feminism and Anti-Feminism Today* (Newton Abbot, UK: David & Charles, 1968), 146.

59. Coote and Campbell, *Sweet Freedom*, 24.

60. Anne Sexton, *Transformations* (Boston: Houghton Mifflin, 1971); Hélène Cixous, "The Laugh of the Medusa," trans. Keith Cohen and Paula Cohen, in *New French Feminisms: An Anthology*, ed. Elaine Marks and Isabelle de Courtivron (New York: Schocken, 1981), 245–64; Mary Daly, *Beyond God the Father: Toward a Philosophy of Women's Liberation* (Boston: Beacon, 1973). On mythopoeic feminist poetry, see Alicia Ostriker, "The Thieves of Language: Women Poets and Revisionist Mythmaking," in *The New Feminist Criticism: Essays on Women, Literature, and Theory*, ed. Elaine Showalter (New York: Pantheon, 1985), 314–38.

61. Anne Severson, "Don't Get Too Near the Big Chakra," in *The "Spare Rib" Reader*, ed. Rowe, 315.

62. Angela Carter, "Notes from the Front Line," in *Critical Essays*, ed. Tucker, 24.
63. Ibid.
64. Angela Carter, *The Passion of New Eve* (London: Victor Gollancz, 1977; London: Virago, 1982), 6. Subsequent references to the 1982 edition will be cited parenthetically in the text.
65. Carter writes (in her introduction to *Expletives Deleted: Selected Writings* [London: Chatto & Windus, 1995], 5): "It seemed to me, when I first started going to the cinema intensively in the late Fifties, that Hollywood had colonised the imagination of the entire world and was turning us all into Americans."
66. John Berger, *Ways of Seeing* (New York: Penguin, 1972), 47.
67. Carter, *New Eve*, 28. Day (*Angela Carter*, 110) also makes the connection between Berger's model and this scene.
68. Suleiman, *Subversive Intent*, 240 n.
69. Carter, *New Eve*, 23.
70. Suleiman, *Subversive Intent*, 138; Punter, "Angela Carter," 39.
71. Carter, *New Eve*, 72.
72. Coote and Campbell, *Sweet Freedom*, 42.
73. National Women's Aid Federation, "'He's Got to Show Her Who's Boss,'" in *The "Spare Rib" Reader*, ed. Rowe, 443.
74. Coote and Campbell, *Sweet Freedom*, 20.
75. Barthes, "Myth Today," 118.
76. Carter, *New Eve*, 66.
77. A few passages are also deleted in the revised version, according to Lorna Sage (*Women in the House of Fiction: Post-War Women Novelists* [Basingstoke, UK: Macmillan, 1992], 172).
78. Lee, *Angela Carter*, 41.
79. Angela Carter, *Love*, rev. ed. (London: Chatto & Windus, 1987; New York: Penguin, 1988), 113. Subsequent references to the 1988 edition will be cited parenthetically in the text.
80. See, for instance, Peach (*Angela Carter*), Lee (*Angela Carter*), and Sage (*Angela Carter*).
81. Gilroy, *There Ain't No Black*; Ernesto Laclau and Chantal Mouffe, *Hegemony and Socialist Strategy: Towards a Radical Democratic Politics* (London: Verso, 1985).
82. Certeau, *Everyday Life*, 172.
83. Lee, *Angela Carter*, 39.
84. Berger, *Ways of Seeing*, 47.
85. Sage, *Women*, 173.
86. Harvey, *The Condition of Postmodernity*, 285, 290.
87. Certeau, *Everyday Life*, 173.
88. Carter, *Love*, 115.
89. Jordan, "Dangers," 44.

Chapter 4: Reading Feminism's Pornography Conflict

1. Sarah Lyall, "Canada's Morals Police: Serious Books at Risk?" *New York Times*, 13 December 1993, late edition; Carl Wilson, "Northern Closure," editorial, *Nation*, 27 December 1993, 788; Leanne Katz, "Secrets of the Flesh: Censors'

Helpers," editorial, *New York Times*, 4 December 1993. Apparently, Dworkin's books *Womanhating* and *Pornography: Men Possessing Women* were released by "embarrassed" customs officials soon after being seized. John F. Baker, "Canada Customs a Continuing Problem for Bookstores and Distributors; Trial Postponed," *Publishers Weekly*, 20 December 1993, 12; see also Katz, "Secrets."

2. Julienne Dickey and Gail Chester, introduction to *Feminism and Censorship: The Current Debate*, ed. Chester and Dickey (Bridport, Dorset, UK: Prism, 1988), 3; and in the same volume, Pratibha Parmar, "Rage and Desire: Confronting Pornography," 119.

3. Michele Landsberg, "Canada: Antipornography Breakthrough in the Law," *Ms.*, May/June 1992, 14; "Lines in the Dirt," *Economist*, 14 March 1992, 31. While MacKinnon defines *pornography* as discrimination against women, the words quoted here are from the Canadian Supreme Court's definition of *obscenity*. That slippage in terminology may be what allows the ruling to extend beyond the more clearly pornographic materials (i.e., mass-cultural "trash") that MacKinnon and her allies intended (Lyall, "Canada's Morals Police") to more "mainstream and serious" books. On the line between obscenity and pornography and antipornography feminists' attempts to hold the two apart, see Lisa Duggan, Nan Hunter, and Carole Vance, "False Promises: Feminist Antipornography Legislation in the US," in *Women against Censorship*, ed. Varda Burstyn (Vancouver, BC: Douglas & McIntyre, 1985), 130–51.

Antipornography feminists cannot be accused of *wanting* such widespread restrictions. The article in *Ms.* magazine by Canadian feminist journalist Michele Landsberg ("Canada"), haling the ruling when it was handed down, hastened to assure readers that "adult erotica, no matter how explicit, will not be considered obscene" (14). Kathleen Mahoney, the attorney who represented LEAF in the case, subsequently argued (Lyall, "Canada's Morals Police") that the seizures were excessive and did not reflect the ruling's spirit.

4. Baker, "Canada Customs," 12; Lyall, "Canada's Morals Police."

5. That lawsuit, filed on behalf of Little Sister's Book and Art Emporium and backed by several national and international civil liberties organizations, reached the Supreme Court in March, 2000, and is still pending as I write. For a brief summary of the case's history, see Little Sister's website: <http://www.lsisters.com/court.html> (10 August 2000).

6. Amanda Sebestyen, "The Mannerist Marketplace," *New Socialist* 47 (1987): 38, quoted in Robin Ann Sheets, "Pornography, Fairy Tales, and Feminism: Angela Carter's 'The Bloody Chamber,'" in *Forbidden History: The State, Society, and the Regulation of Sexuality in Modern Europe*, ed. John C. Fout (Chicago: University of Chicago Press, 1992), 344.

7. The slippage between "pornography," as a genre, and "pornographic," as a presumed function or effect, is part of the problem facing attempts at regulation—see Jennifer Wicke, "Through a Gaze Darkly: Pornography's Academic Market," in *Dirty Looks: Women, Pornography, Power*, ed. Pamela Church Gibson and Roma Gibson (London: BFI, 1993), 66–68. A wide range of representations can be read as pornographic, depending on context. Lynne Segal's essay in the same volume ("Does Pornography Cause Violence? The Search for Evidence," 15) even proposes that representations of such unlikely but potentially suggestive objects as nuts and bolts can be put to pornographic use.

Linda Williams (*Hard Core: Power, Pleasure, and the "Frenzy of the Visible"* [Berkeley and Los Angeles: University of California Press, 1989], 28–30) offers the most convincing definition of porn as a specific genre, varyingly constructed over time. She backs up her general definition—representations of sexual activity "with a primary intent of arousing viewers"—with a history of various films and types of film and their conditions of circulation. That core definition could serve as the basis of similar concrete research into the historical construction of porn in other media, such as written porn.

8. Williams (*Hard Core*, 26) and Carla Freccero ("Notes of a Post-Sex Wars Theorizer," in *Conflicts in Feminism*, ed. Hirsch and Keller, 319 n) attribute the term "sex wars" to B. Ruby Rich. I understand the sex wars to include disagreements over pornography but also over some women's sexual practices that may be unrelated to porn, particularly S/M (sadism and masochism) and lesbian butch/femme practices. While, as Robin Sheets notes ("Pornography, Fairy Tales, and Feminism," 335), these various issues have increasingly been collapsed into, or displaced onto, the question of pornography and sexual representation, I will use the term "pornography debates" more often than "sex wars" in an attempt to question the assumed slippage between texts and bodily actions.

9. See *Women against Censorship*, ed. Burstyn; Caught Looking Collective, ed., *Caught Looking: Feminism, Pornography, and Censorship* (Seattle: Real Comet, 1988); Gibson and Gibson, eds., *Dirty Looks: Women, Pornography, Power*; Laura Kipnis, *Bound and Gagged: Pornography and the Politics of Fantasy in America* (New York: Grove, 1996); Ann Snitow, Christine Stansell, and Sharon Thompson, eds., *Powers of Desire: The Politics of Sexuality* (New York: Monthly Review, 1983); Carole S. Vance, ed., *Pleasure and Danger: Exploring Female Sexuality*, rev. ed. (London: Pandora, 1992).

10. Freccero, "Notes," 319.

11. Haraway, "Manifesto," 198.

12. Barbara Smith, "Toward a Black Feminist Criticism," in *The New Feminist Criticism*, ed. Showalter, 170.

13. Parmar, "Rage and Desire," 123. Chela Sandoval writes, in her 1982 account, "Feminism and Racism: A Report on the 1981 National Women's Studies Association Conference" (in *Making Face, Making Soul, Haciendo Caras: Creative and Critical Perspectives by Women of Color*, ed. Gloria Anzaldúa [San Francisco: Aunt Lute Foundation, 1990], 55): "Ideological differences divided and helped to dissipate the movement from within between the years 1972 and 1980, so that now feminists are confusing straws and tools in a desperate attempt at its revitalization."

14. Laclau and Mouffe, *Hegemony and Socialist Strategy*, 160.

15. Henry A. Giroux, "Consuming Social Change: The 'United Colors of Benetton,'" *Cultural Critique* 26 (1993–94): 20.

16. Ibid., 29, 20, 27.

17. Williams, *Hard Core*.

18. Nora Ephron, "Women," *Esquire*, February 1973, 14, quoted in *Getting into Deep Throat*, Richard Smith (Chicago: Playboy, 1973), 10; also quoted in Andrew Ross, "The Popularity of Pornography," in *No Respect: Intellectuals and Popular Culture* (New York: Routledge, 1989), 172; and in Williams, *Hard Core*, 99.

19. Melissa Benn, "Page 3—and the Campaign against It," in *Feminism and Censorship*, ed. Chester and Dickey, 29. Lynne Segal notes ("Does Pornography Cause Violence?" 11) that in fact, one study did find an increase in violent imagery in *Playboy* and *Penthouse* in the early seventies; however, violent imagery declined after

1977. Segal attributes this decline to "the feminist critique." I would concur, if the porn business's response to "the feminist critique" is read less as an acknowledgment of moral responsibility, and more as a recognition of a market demand—reflecting not only the possibility that women might start objecting to their husbands' and boyfriends' magazine subscriptions, but also that a meaningful number of men might themselves have absorbed enough feminist rhetoric to find their pleasure in violent images impeded.

20. David Lodge, *Changing Places: A Tale of Two Campuses* (London: Secker and Warburg, 1975; Harmondsworth, Middlesex, UK: Penguin, 1978), 112 (page references are to Penguin edition).

21. Laura Kipnis, "(Male) Desire and (Female) Disgust: Reading *Hustler*," in *Cultural Studies*, ed. Lawrence Grossberg, Cary Nelson, and Paula A. Treichler (New York: Routledge, 1992), 382.

22. The porn industry's various treatments of "women's pleasure" are not all equally cynical—and Kipnis's article on *Hustler* highlights the fact that some are much more openly hostile than others. See, in contrast, feminist filmmaker Candida Royalle's description ("Porn in the USA," *Social Text* 37 [1993]: 23–32) of her motivations for making women-oriented "adult" films.

23. Ann Snitow, "Retrenchment versus Transformation: The Politics of the Antipornography Movement," in *Women against Censorship*, ed. Burstyn, 110.

24. Coote and Campbell, *Sweet Freedom*, 157, 42. On the Williams Committee, see Catherine Itzin, "Sex and Censorship: The Political Implications," in *Feminism and Censorship*, ed. Chester and Dickey, 40; Sheets, "Pornography, Fairy Tales, and Feminism," 337.

25. Snitow, "Retrenchment," 112–13; Ross, "Popularity," 187.

26. Snitow, "Retrenchment," 113.

27. Colleen Kennedy, "Simulating Sex and Imagining Mothers," *American Literary History* 4 (1992): 165, 166.

28. Ibid., 181.

29. Ibid., 166.

30. Ibid., 171.

31. Michael Bronski, *Culture Clash* (Boston: South End, 1984), 167, quoted in Ross, "Popularity," 255 n. 38.

32. See Frédérique Delacoste and Priscilla Alexander, eds., *Sex Work: Writings by Women in the Sex Industry* (Pittsburgh: Cleis, 1987).

33. See Jacquelyn Dowd Hall, "'The Mind That Burns in Each Body': Women, Rape, and Racial Violence," in *Powers of Desire*, ed. Snitow, Stansell, and Thompson, 333; in the same collection, Barbara Omolade, "Hearts of Darkness," 352; and Parmar, "Rage and Desire," 124.

34. Hall, "The Mind"; Parmar, "Rage and Desire," 126–27.

35. Williams, *Hard Core*, 12.

36. Ross suggests ("Popularity," 186) that antipornography feminists reproduce "the old defense of the liberal imagination (against the brutish threat of a pervasive mass culture)." I think this is an unfair simplification. Feminism has never exempted "high" culture from its critique of patriarchal ideology; indeed, feminism has contributed to the increasing breakdown of boundaries between cultural spheres. In addition, Ross implies that feminism was able to simply wipe away the conventional gendering of the mass-cultural threat as *female* (see Huyssen, *After the Great Divide*), along with the denigration of femininity that entailed.

I agree, however, that there does seem to be a major shift in gendered models of mass culture, such that the perceived threat to society now represented not only by pornography, but by violence on television, etc., is based on *masculine* behavior. Theorizing this shift is beyond the scope of my project, but I suspect it does not represent the mere flip-flop Ross suggests. The battle lines are drawn differently in postmodernity, I believe; the same conservative ideologues who call for controls on television violence also decry the degeneracy of current "high" culture.

37. Kipnis notes ("Desire and Disgust"), however, that the resistant "underdog" male reader constructed by *Hustler* is also a white, racist male.

38. Clark, "Desire Machine," 147.

39. See also Kennedy, "Simulating Sex," 171.

40. Clark, "Desire Machine," 153. Patricia Duncker makes a similar argument for the need to get outside previous texts in her highly critical article on Carter's collection of rewritten fairy tales, *The Bloody Chamber* ("Re-imagining the Fairy Tales: Angela Carter's Bloody Chambers," *Literature and History* 10.1 [1984]: 6). Duncker maintains that "the infernal trap inherent in the fairy tale, which fits the form to its purpose, to be the carrier of ideology, proves too complex and pervasive to avoid." For Duncker, as for Clark, there is therefore simply no way to represent heterosexual desire without reinscribing male paradigms. The "outside place," the location of true critique, that seems to be occupied in Clark's formulation by the Marxist intellectual, is in Duncker's essay implicitly occupied by the lesbian.

41. Wicke, "Through a Gaze Darkly," 70.

42. Williams, *Hard Core*, 214–17.

43. Kobena Mercer, "Skin Head Sex Thing: Racial Difference and the Homoerotic Imaginary," in *How Do I Look? Queer Film and Video*, ed. Bad Object-Choices (Seattle: Bay, 1991), 180.

44. Susie Bright comments ("A Star is Porn," in *Susie Sexpert's Lesbian Sex World* [Pittsburgh: Cleis, 1990], 137), on the increasing use of dildos by women in heterosexual pairings: "only their lubricant knows who's playing the boy and who's playing the girl."

45. Richard Fung, "Looking for My Penis: The Eroticized Asian in Gay Video Porn," in *How Do I Look?* ed. Bad Object-Choices, 154.

46. Acker, *Don Quixote*, 33.

47. Butler, *Gender Trouble*, 144, 140, 145.

48. Carter, *Hoffman*, 45.

49. Desiderio goes on to describe the scene depicted within the "vagina," which is, in fact, a fantasy kingdom, complete with brilliant birds, exotic fruits and animals, and a mist-shrouded castle in the distance. Later in the novel, this scene turns out to be Hoffman's (the patriarch's) kingdom and castle.

50. Vladimir Nabokov, "Vladimir Nabokov on a Book Entitled *Lolita*," in *Lolita* (New York: Berkley Medallion, 1955), 284.

51. Robin Morgan, *Anatomy of Freedom: Feminism, Physics, and Global Politics* (Garden City, NY: Anchor, 1982), quoted in Sheets, "Pornography, Fairy Tales, and Feminism," 338.

52. Richard Walsh, "The Quest for Love and the Writing of Female Desire in Kathy Acker's *Don Quixote*," *Critique* 32 (1991): 160.

53. Acker, *Don Quixote*, 139, 173.

54. Walsh ("Quest," 157) makes a similar argument that the "trauma [of repetition] leads to sexual enlightenment," but does not connect this enlightenment to representation and readership.

55. Acker, *Don Quixote*, 171.
56. Walsh, "Quest," 161.
57. Mercer, "Skin Head Sex Thing," 187.
58. Certeau, *Everyday Life*, 173.

Epilogue: Readers, Disciplinarity, and Social Practices

1. Stanley E. Fish, "Interpreting the *Variorum*," in *Reader-Response Criticism: From Formalism to Post-Structuralism*, ed. Jane P. Tompkins (Baltimore: Johns Hopkins University Press, 1980), 182.
2. Cary Nelson, Paula A. Treichler, and Lawrence Grossberg, "Cultural Studies: An Introduction," in *Cultural Studies*, ed. Grossberg, Nelson, and Treichler, 5.
3. Ann Snitow, "A Gender Diary," in *Conflicts in Feminism*, ed. Hirsch and Keller, 19.
4. Ibid., 11.
5. Ibid., 36.
6. Joan W. Scott, "Deconstructing Equality-versus-Difference: or, The Uses of Poststructuralist Theory for Feminism," in *Conflicts in Feminism*, ed. Hirsch and Keller, 139.
7. Ibid., 145.
8. Margot Mifflin, "Feminism's New Face," *ARTnews*, November 1992, 123.
9. Karen Houppert, "WAC Attack," *Village Voice*, 9 June 1992, 34.
10. Phoebe Hoban, "Big WAC Attack," *New York*, 3 August 1992, 32.
11. Ibid., 32; for a similar account, see Catherine S. Manegold, "No More Nice Girls: In Angry Droves, Radical Feminists Just Want to Have Impact," *New York Times*, 12 July 1992, late edition.
12. Manegold, "No More Nice Girls."
13. Ibid.; Amruta Slee, "A Guide to Women's Direct-Action Groups," *Harper's Bazaar*, November 1992, 165.
14. Houppert, "WAC Attack," 34.
15. Certeau, *Everyday Life*, xix, xxi.
16. On the disintegration of New York WAC, see Karen Houppert's fascinating analysis, "WAC Attacks Itself: Will the Direct Action Group Self-Destruct?" (*Village Voice*, 20 July 1993, 28–32); after this article appeared, I heard no more about WAC's founding chapter, and could subsequently find no further press coverage. Houston WAC and Chicago WAC, among others, continued direct actions for another year or more; see Cynthia Thomas, "The Beat Generation," *The Houston Chronicle*, 17 January 1993, Two Star edition, *Lexis-Nexis Academic Universe*, <http://web.lexis-nexis.com/universe> (28 July 2000); "WAC Is Watching: Women's Action Coalition on the Streets of Chicago," *Off Our Backs: A Women's Newsjournal* 24.2 (28 February 1994): 6, *GenderWatch*, <http://www.softlineweb.com/softlineweb/genderw.htm> (28 July 2000); however, the latter article also notes Chicago WAC members' plans for more discussion and agreement on the meaning of feminism. Protestors from WAC appeared regularly outside the O. J. Simpson trial in Los Angeles in 1995, but their placards and chants appear to have blended in with the wide variety already present in that "media circus."
17. "WAC Is Watching," 6.

Works Cited

Acker, Kathy. *Don Quixote: Which Was a Dream.* New York: Grove, 1986.

———. *Empire of the Senseless.* New York: Grove, 1988.

———. *Hannibal Lecter, My Father.* Edited by Sylvère Lotringer. New York: Semiotext(e), 1991.

———. *My Death My Life by Pier Paolo Pasolini.* London: Pan, 1984. Reprint in *Literal Madness,* New York: Grove, 1988. 171–393.

———. Interview by Andrea Juno. *Angry Women.* Edited by Andrea Juno and V. Vale. *Re/Search* 13 (1991): 177–85.

———. Interview by Paul Perilli. *Poets & Writers Magazine,* March/April 1993, 28–33.

———. "The *On Our Backs* Interview: Kathy Acker." Interview by Lisa Palac. *On Our Backs,* May/June 1991, 19–20, 38–39.

———. "Punk Days in New York." Interview. *Fist* 1 (1988): 9–12.

———. "Reading the Body." Interview by Larry McCaffery. *Mondo 2000* 4 (1991): 72–77.

Ahmed, Sara. *Differences That Matter: Feminist Theory and Postmodernism.* Cambridge: Cambridge University Press, 1998.

Alcoff, Linda. "Cultural Feminism versus Post-Structuralism: The Identity Crisis in Feminist Theory." In *Feminist Theory in Practice and Process,* edited by Micheline R. Malson, Jean F. O'Barr, Sarah Westphal-Wihl, and Mary Wyer, 295–326. Chicago: University of Chicago Press, 1989.

Ardis, Ann L. "Reading 'as a Modernist'/De-naturalizing Modernist Reading Protocols: Wyndham Lewis's *Tarr.*" In *Rereading Modernism: New Directions in Feminist Criticism.* Edited by Lisa Rado, 373–90. New York: Garland, 1994.

Asphodel. "1968: Prague Winter, Feminist Spring." In *'68, '78, '88: From Women's Liberation to Feminism.* Edited by Amanda Sebestyen, 7–14. Bridport, Dorset, UK: Prism, 1988.

Baker, John F. "Canada Customs a Continuing Problem for Bookstores and Distributors; Trial Postponed." *Publishers Weekly,* 20 December 1993, 12.

Bakhtin, M. M. *The Dialogic Imagination: Four Essays.* Edited by Michael Holquist. Translated by Caryl Emerson and Michael Holquist. Austin: University of Texas Press, 1981.

Barth, John. "The Literature of Replenishment: Postmodernist Fiction." In *The Friday Book: Essays and Other Nonfiction,* 193–206. New York: G. P. Putnam's Sons, 1984.

Barthes, Roland. "The Death of the Author." In *Image, Music, Text,* translated by Stephen Heath, 142–48. New York: Hill and Wang, 1977.

———. "Myth Today." In *Mythologies,* translated by Annette Lavers, 109–59. New York: Hill and Wang, 1972.

Bauer, Dale M. *Feminist Dialogics: A Theory of Failed Community.* Albany: State University of New York Press, 1988.

Belsey, Catherine. "Constructing the Subject: Deconstructing the Text." In *Feminist Criticism and Social Change: Sex, Class, and Race in Literature and Culture,* edited by Judith Newton and Deborah Rosenfelt, 45–64. New York: Methuen, 1985.

Benhabib, Seyla. "Epistemologies of Postmodernism: A Rejoinder to Jean-François Lyotard." In *Feminism/Postmodernism,* edited by Linda J. Nicholson, 107–30. New York: Routledge, 1990.

Benjamin, Jessica. *The Bonds of Love: Psychoanalysis, Feminism, and the Problem of Domination.* New York: Pantheon, 1988.

Benn, Melissa. "Page 3—and the Campaign against It." In *Feminism and Censorship: The Current Debate,* edited by Gail Chester and Julienne Dickey, 26–35. Bridport, Dorset: Prism, 1988.

Berger, John. *Ways of Seeing.* New York: Penguin, 1972.

Bright, Susie. "A Star Is Porn." In *Susie Sexpert's Lesbian Sex World,* 137–40. Pittsburgh: Cleis, 1990.

Brown, Terry. "Longing to Long: Kathy Acker and the Politics of Pain." *LIT: Literature, Interpretation, Theory* 2 (1991): 167–77.

Burstyn, Varda, ed. *Women against Censorship.* Vancouver, BC: Douglas & McIntyre, 1985.

Butler, Judith. *Bodies That Matter: On the Discursive Limits of "Sex."* New York: Routledge, 1993.

———. *Gender Trouble: Feminism and the Subversion of Identity.* New York: Routledge, 1990.

Carter, Angela. *Expletives Deleted: Selected Writings.* London: Chatto & Windus, 1992.

———. *The Infernal Desire Machines of Doctor Hoffman.* London: Rupert Hart-Davis, 1972; London: Penguin, 1982. Reprint as *The War of Dreams,* New York: Harcourt Brace Jovanovich, 1973.

———. *Love.* Rev. ed. London: Chatto & Windus, 1987; New York: Penguin, 1988.

———. "Notes from the Front Line." In *Critical Essays on Angela Carter,* edited by Lindsey Tucker, 24–30. New York: G. K. Hall & Co., 1998. Originally published in *On Gender and Writing,* edited by Michelene Wandor, 69–77. (London: Pandora, 1983).

———. *The Passion of New Eve.* London: Victor Gollancz, 1977; London: Virago, 1982.

Caught Looking Collective, ed. *Caught Looking: Feminism, Pornography, and Censorship.* Seattle: Real Comet, 1988.

Certeau, Michel de. *The Practice of Everyday Life.* Translated by Steven Rendall. Berkeley and Los Angeles: University of California Press, 1984.

WORKS CITED

Chester, Gail, and Julienne Dickey, eds. *Feminism and Censorship: The Current Debate.* Bridport, Dorset, UK: Prism, 1988.

Cixous, Hélène. "The Laugh of the Medusa." Translated by Keith Cohen and Paula Cohen. In *New French Feminisms: An Anthology,* edited by Elaine Marks and Isabelle de Courtivron, 245–64. New York: Schocken, 1981. First published as "Le rire de la méduse," *L'arc* (1975): 39–54.

Clark, Robert. "Angela Carter's Desire Machine." *Women's Studies* 14 (1987): 147–61.

Coote, Anna, and Beatrix Campbell. *Sweet Freedom: The Struggle for Women's Liberation.* 2nd ed. Oxford: Basil Blackwell, 1987.

Daly, Mary. *Beyond God the Father: Toward a Philosophy of Women's Liberation.* Boston: Beacon, 1973.

Davis, Mike. "Urban Renaissance and the Spirit of Postmodernism." In *Postmodernism and Its Discontents: Theories, Practices,* edited by E. Ann Kaplan, 79–87. London: Verso, 1988.

Day, Aidan. *Angela Carter: The Rational Glass.* Manchester: Manchester University Press, 1998.

Delacoste, Frédérique, and Priscilla Alexander, eds. *Sex Work: Writings by Women in the Sex Industry.* Pittsburgh: Cleis, 1987.

Dickey, Julienne, and Gail Chester. Introduction to *Feminism and Censorship: The Current Debate.* Edited by Gail Chester and Julienne Dickey. Bridport, Dorset: Prism, 1988. 1–10.

Dillard, R. H. W. "Lesson No. 1: Eat Your Mind." Review of *Empire of the Senseless,* by Kathy Acker. *New York Times Book Review,* 16 October 1988, 9–11.

Di Stefano, Christine. "Dilemmas of Difference: Feminism, Modernity, and Postmodernism." In *Feminism/Postmodernism,* edited by Linda J. Nicholson, 63–82. New York: Routledge, 1990.

Dix, Douglas Shields. "Kathy Acker's *Don Quixote*: Nomad Writing." *Review of Contemporary Fiction* 9.3 (1989): 56–62.

Doan, Laura, ed. *The Lesbian Postmodern.* New York: Columbia University Press, 1994.

Duggan, Lisa, Nan Hunter, and Carole Vance. "False Promises: Feminist Antipornography Legislation in the US." In *Women against Censorship,* edited by Varda Burstyn, 130–51. Vancouver, BC: Douglas & McIntyre, 1985. Also in Gail Chester and Julienne Dickey, eds., *Feminism and Censorship: The Current Debate.* Bridport, Dorset, UK: Prism, 1988. 62–75.

Duncker, Patricia. "Re-imagining the Fairy Tales: Angela Carter's Bloody Chambers." *Literature and History* 10.1 (1984): 3–14.

Elliot, Emory, ed. *The Columbia History of the American Novel.* Assoc. eds. Cathy N. Davidson, Patrick O'Donnell, Valerie Smith, and Christopher P. Wilson. New York: Columbia University Press, 1991.

Ermarth, Elizabeth Deeds. "Postmodernism and the Novel." In *Encyclopedia of the Novel,* edited by Paul Schellinger, 1032–35. Vol. 2. Chicago: Fitzroy Dearborn, 1998.

Fish, Stanley E. "Interpreting the *Variorum.*" In *Reader-Response Criticism: From Formalism to Post-Structuralism,* edited by Jane P. Tompkins, 164–84. Baltimore: Johns Hopkins University Press, 1980.

Foster, Hal. "Postmodernism: A Preface." In *The Anti-Aesthetic: Essays on Postmodern Culture,* edited by Hal Foster, ix–xvi. Seattle: Bay, 1983.

Foster, Thomas. "Meat Puppets or Robopaths?: Cyberpunk and the Question of Embodiment." *Genders* 18 (1993): 11–31.

Foucault, Michel. "What Is an Author?" Translated by Donald F. Bouchard and Sherry Simon. In *Language, Counter-Memory, Practice: Selected Essays and Interviews,* edited by Donald F. Bouchard, 113–38. Ithaca, NY: Cornell University Press, 1977.

Fraser, Nancy, and Linda J. Nicholson. "Social Criticism without Philosophy: An Encounter between Feminism and Postmodernism." In *Feminism/Postmodernism,* edited by Linda J. Nicholson, 19–38. New York: Routledge, 1990.

Freccero, Carla. "Notes of a Post-Sex Wars Theorizer." In *Conflicts in Feminism.* Edited by Marianne Hirsch and Evelyn Fox Keller, 305–25. New York: Routledge, 1990.

Friedman, Ellen G. "A Conversation with Kathy Acker." *Review of Contemporary Fiction* 9.3 (1989): 12–22.

———. "'Now Eat Your Mind': An Introduction to the Works of Kathy Acker." *Review of Contemporary Fiction* 9.3 (1989): 37–49.

———. "Where Are the Missing Contents? (Post)Modernism, Gender, and the Canon." *PMLA* 108 (1993): 240–52.

Friedman, Ellen G., and Miriam Fuchs. "Works by Kathy Acker." *Review of Contemporary Fiction* 9.3 (1989): 78.

———, eds. *Breaking the Sequence: Women's Experimental Fiction.* Princeton: Princeton University Press, 1989.

Fung, Richard. "Looking for My Penis: The Eroticized Asian in Gay Video Porn." In *How Do I Look? Queer Film and Video,* edited by Bad Object-Choices, 145–68. Seattle: Bay, 1991.

Gibson, Pamela Church, and Roma Gibson, eds. *Dirty Looks: Women, Pornography, Power.* London: BFI, 1993.

Gilbert, Sandra M., and Susan Gubar. *No Man's Land: The Place of the Woman Writer in the Twentieth Century.* New Haven: Yale University Press, 1988.

Gill, Jonathan. "Dedicated to Her Tattoo Artist." *New York Times Book Review,* 16 October 1988, 9.

Gilroy, Paul. *"There Ain't No Black in the Union Jack": The Cultural Politics of Race and Nation.* London: Hutchinson, 1987. Reprint, with a foreword by Houston A. Baker, Jr., Chicago: University of Chicago Press, 1991.

Giroux, Henry A. "Consuming Social Change: The 'United Colors of Benetton.'" *Cultural Critique* 26 (1993–94): 5–32.

Gramsci, Antonio. "Americanism and Fordism." In *Selections from the Prison Notebooks.* Edited and translated by Quintin Hoare and Geoffrey Nowell Smith, 277–318. New York: International Publishers, 1971.

Green, Jonathon. *Days in the Life: Voices from the English Underground, 1961–1971.* London: Heinemann, 1989.

Greene, Naomi. *Pier Paolo Pasolini: Cinema as Heresy.* Princeton: Princeton University Press, 1990.

Griggers, Catherine Joan. "Reinventing the Popular: Inscriptions of the Feminine Subject in Postmodern Genres." Ph.D. diss., University of Florida, 1989.

Hall, Jacquelyn Dowd. "'The Mind That Burns in Each Body': Women, Rape, and Racial Violence." In *Powers of Desire: The Politics of Sexuality*, edited by Ann Snitow, Christine Stansell, and Sharon Thompson, 328–49. New York: Monthly Review, 1983.

Hall, Stuart. "The Toad in the Garden: Thatcherism among the Theorists." In *Marxism and the Interpretation of Culture*, edited by Cary Nelson and Lawrence Grossberg, 35–73. Urbana: University of Illinois Press, 1988.

Haraway, Donna. "A Manifesto for Cyborgs: Science, Technology, and Socialist Feminism in the 1980s." In *Feminism/Postmodernism*, edited by Linda J. Nicholson, 190–233. New York: Routledge, 1990.

———. *Modest_Witness@Second_Millennium.FemaleMan_Meets_OncoMouse: Feminism and Technoscience*. New York: Routledge, 1997.

Hartsock, Nancy. "Foucault on Power: A Theory for Women?" In *Feminism/Postmodernism*, edited by Linda J. Nicholson, 157–75. New York: Routledge, 1990.

Harvey, David. *The Condition of Postmodernity: An Enquiry into the Origins of Cultural Change*. Cambridge, MA: Blackwell, 1989.

Hassan, Ihab. *The Dismemberment of Orpheus: Toward a Postmodern Literature*. 2nd ed. Madison: University of Wisconsin Press, 1982.

———. *Paracriticisms: Seven Speculations of the Times*. Urbana: University of Illinois Press, 1975.

Hebdige, Dick. "Staking out the Posts." In *Hiding in the Light: On Images and Things*, 181–207. London: Routledge, Comedia, 1988.

Hiro, Dilip. *Black British, White British: A History of Race Relations in Britain*. Rev. ed. London: Grafton, 1991.

Hite, Molly. "Postmodern Fiction." In *The Columbia History of the American Novel*, edited by Emory Elliot. 697–725. New York: Columbia University Press, 1991.

Hoban, Phoebe. "Big WAC Attack." *New York*, 3 August 1992, 30–35.

Hoffman, Roy. Review of *Blood and Guts in High School*, by Kathy Acker. *New York Times Book Review*, 23 December 1984, 16.

Holland, Penny. "Still Revolting." In *'68, '78, '88: From Women's Liberation to Feminism*, edited by Amanda Sebestyen, 134–40. Bridport, Dorset, UK: Prism, 1988.

Hooks, Bell. "Postmodern Blackness." In *Yearning: Race, Gender, and Cultural Politics*, 23–31. Boston: South End, 1990.

Houppert, Karen. "WAC Attack." *Village Voice*, 9 June 1992, 33–38.

———. "WAC Attacks Itself: Will the Direct Action Group Self-Destruct?" *Village Voice*, 20 July 1993, 28–32. ProQuest Direct. <http://proquest.umi.com/pqdweb> (28 July 2000).

Hudson, Kenneth. *Men and Women: Feminism and Anti-Feminism Today*. Newton Abbot, UK: David & Charles, 1968.

Hulley, Kathleen. "Transgressing Genre: Kathy Acker's Intertext." In *Intertextuality and Contemporary American Fiction*, edited by Patrick O'Donnell and Robert Con Davis, 171–90. Baltimore: Johns Hopkins University Press, 1989.

Hutcheon, Linda. *The Politics of Postmodernism.* New York: Routledge, New Accents, 1989.

Huyssen, Andreas. *After the Great Divide: Modernism, Mass Culture, Postmodernism.* Bloomington: Indiana University Press, 1986.

Irigaray, Luce. *This Sex Which Is Not One.* Translated by Catherine Porter with Carolyn Burke. Ithaca: Cornell University Press, 1985.

Isaacson, Walter. *Kissinger: A Biography.* New York: Simon and Schuster, 1992.

Itzin, Catherine. "Sex and Censorship: The Political Implications." In *Feminism and Censorship: The Current Debate,* edited by Gail Chester and Julienne Dickey, 36–47. Bridport, Dorset, UK: Prism, 1988.

Jacobs, Naomi. "Kathy Acker and the Plagiarized Self." *Review of Contemporary Fiction* 9.3 (1989): 50–55.

Jameson, Fredric. *Postmodernism, or, The Cultural Logic of Late Capitalism.* Durham, NC: Duke University Press, 1991.

Jardine, Alice A. *Gynesis: Configurations of Woman and Modernity.* Ithaca: Cornell University Press, 1985.

Jensen, Kenneth M., and Elizabeth P. Faulkner, eds. *Morality and Foreign Policy: Realpolitik Revisited.* Washington, DC: United States Institute of Peace, 1991.

Jordan, Elaine. "The Dangers of Angela Carter." In *New Feminist Discourses: Critical Essays on Theories and Texts,* edited by Isobel Armstrong, 119–31. New York: Routledge, 1992.

———. "Enthralment: Angela Carter's Speculative Fictions." In *Plotting Change: Contemporary Women's Fiction,* edited by Linda Anderson, 19–40. London: Edward Arnold, 1990.

Kalaidjian, Walter. *American Culture between the Wars: Revisionary Modernism and Postmodern Critique.* New York: Columbia University Press, 1993.

"Kathy Acker." *Times* (London), 2 December 1997. <http://www.the-times.co.uk/news/pages/tim/1997/12/02/timobiobi03002.html> (10 July 2000).

Katz, Leanne. "Secrets of the Flesh: Censors' Helpers." Editorial. *New York Times,* 4 December 1993.

Kelly-Gadol, Joan. "Did Women Have a Renaissance?" In *Becoming Visible: Women in European History,* edited by Renate Bridenthal and Claudia Koonz, 137–64. Boston: Houghton Mifflin, 1977.

Kendrick, Walter. "The Real Magic of Angela Carter." In *Contemporary British Women Writers: Narrative Strategies,* edited by Robert E. Hosmer, Jr., 66–84. New York: St. Martin's, 1993.

Kennedy, Colleen. "Simulating Sex and Imagining Mothers." *American Literary History* 4 (1992): 165–85.

Kipnis, Laura. *Bound and Gagged: Pornography and the Politics of Fantasy in America.* New York: Grove, 1996.

———. "Feminism: The Political Conscience of Postmodernism?" In *Universal Abandon? The Politics of Postmodernism,* edited by Andrew Ross, 149–66. Minneapolis: University of Minnesota Press, 1988.

———. "(Male) Desire and (Female) Disgust: Reading *Hustler.*" In *Cultural Studies,* edited by Lawrence Grossberg, Cary Nelson, and Paula A. Treichler, 373–91. New York: Routledge, 1992.

Laclau, Ernesto, and Chantal Mouffe. *Hegemony and Socialist Strategy: Towards a Radical Democratic Politics.* London: Verso, 1985.

Landsberg, Michele. "Canada: Antipornography Breakthrough in the Law." *Ms.*, May/June 1992, 14–15.

Lauter, Paul. "Race and Gender in the Shaping of the American Literary Canon: A Case Study from the Twenties." In *Feminist Criticism and Social Change: Sex, Class, and Race in Literature and Culture,* edited by Judith Newton and Deborah Rosenfelt, 19–44. New York: Methuen, 1985.

Lee, Alison. *Angela Carter.* New York: Twayne, 1997.

"Lines in the Dirt." *Economist,* 14 March 1992, 31.

Little, David. "Morality and National Security." In *Morality and Foreign Policy: Realpolitik Revisited,* edited by Kenneth M. Jensen and Elizabeth P. Faulkner, 1–19. Washington, DC: United States Institute of Peace, 1991.

Lodge, David. *Changing Places: A Tale of Two Campuses.* London: Secker and Warburg, 1975; Harmondsworth, Middlesex, UK: Penguin, 1978.

Lyall, Sarah. "Canada's Morals Police: Serious Books at Risk?" *New York Times,* 13 December 1993, late edition.

Lyman, Rick. "Kathy Acker, Novelist and Performance Artist, 53." *New York Times,* 3 December 1997, late edition.

Lyotard, Jean-François. *The Postmodern Condition: A Report on Knowledge.* Translated by Geoff Bennington and Brian Massumi. Minneapolis: University of Minnesota Press, 1984.

MacCannell, Dean, and Juliet Flower MacCannell. "The Beauty System." In *The Ideology of Conduct: Essays in Literature and the History of Sexuality,* edited by Nancy Armstrong and Leonard Tennenhouse, 206–38. New York: Methuen, 1987.

Mailloux, Steven. "Rhetorical Hermeneutics Revisited." *Text and Performance Quarterly* 11 (1991): 233–48.

Manegold, Catherine S. "No More Nice Girls: In Angry Droves, Radical Feminists Just Want to Have Impact." *New York Times,* 12 July 1992, late edition.

Martin, Biddy. "Feminism, Criticism, and Foucault." In *Feminism and Foucault: Reflections on Resistance,* edited by Irene Diamond and Lee Quinby, 3–19. Boston: Northeastern University Press, 1988.

Marwick, Arthur. *Culture in Britain since 1945.* Oxford: Basil Blackwell, 1991.

Mascia-Lees, Frances E., and Patricia Sharpe. "The Marked and the Un(re)marked: Tattoo and Gender in Theory and Narrative." In *Tattoo, Torture, Mutilation, and Adornment: The Denaturalization of the Body in Culture and Text,* edited by Frances E. Mascia-Lees and Patricia Sharpe, 145–69. Albany: State University of New York Press, 1992.

McHale, Brian. "Editorial Laissez-Faire." Review of *The Columbia History of the American Novel,* edited by Emory Elliott. *American Book Review,* August-September 1991, 24–25.

Mercer, Kobena. "Skin Head Sex Thing: Racial Difference and the Homoerotic Imaginary." In *How Do I Look? Queer Film and Video,* edited by Bad Object-Choices, 169–222. Seattle: Bay, 1991.

Mifflin, Margot. "Feminism's New Face." *ARTnews,* November 1992, 120–25.

Miller, Nancy K. "The Text's Heroine: A Feminist Critic and Her Fictions." In *Conflicts in Feminism*, edited by Marianne Hirsch and Evelyn Fox Keller, 112–20. New York: Routledge, 1990.

Modleski, Tania. *Feminism without Women: Culture and Criticism in a "Postfeminist" Age.* New York: Routledge, 1991.

———. *Loving with a Vengeance: Mass-Produced Fantasies for Women.* New York: Methuen, 1984.

Moran, Joe. *Star Authors: Literary Celebrity in America.* London: Pluto, 2000.

Mouffe, Chantal. "Hegemony and New Political Subjects: Toward a New Concept of Democracy." Translated by Stanley Gray. In *Marxism and the Interpretation of Culture*, edited by Cary Nelson and Lawrence Grossberg, 89–104. Urbana: University of Illinois Press, 1988.

Mullan, Mary Kay. "1968: Burntollet Bridge." In *'68, '78, '88: From Women's Liberation to Feminism*, edited by Amanda Sebestyen, 15–24. Bridport, Dorset, UK: Prism, 1988.

Murray, Charles Shaar. "Piercing Memories of Acker." *Guardian* (London), 3 December 1997.

Nabokov, Vladimir. "Vladimir Nabokov on a Book Entitled *Lolita*." In *Lolita*, 282–88. New York: Berkley Medallion, 1955.

National Women's Aid Federation (UK). "'He's Got to Show Her Who's Boss.'" In *The "Spare Rib" Reader*, edited by Marsha Rowe, 442–49. Harmondsworth, Middlesex, UK: Penguin, 1982. Originally published in *Spare Rib* 69 (1978).

Nelson, Cary, Paula A. Treichler, and Lawrence Grossberg. "Cultural Studies: An Introduction." In *Cultural Studies*, edited by Lawrence Grossberg, Cary Nelson, and Paula A. Treichler, 1–22. New York: Routledge, 1992.

Neumeier, Beate. "Postmodern Gothic: Desire and Reality in Angela Carter's Writing." In *Modern Gothic: A Reader*, edited by Victor Sage and Allan Lloyd Smith, 141–51. Manchester: Manchester University Press, 1996.

Omolade, Barbara. "Hearts of Darkness." In *Powers of Desire: The Politics of Sexuality*, edited by Ann Snitow, Christine Stansell, and Sharon Thompson, 350–67. New York: Monthly Review, 1983.

Osman, Sona. "Full Circle: 1968–1988: Rivers of Blood." In *'68, '78, '88: From Women's Liberation to Feminism*, edited by Amanda Sebestyen, 44–48. Bridport, Dorset: Prism, 1988.

Ostriker, Alicia. "The Thieves of Language: Women Poets and Revisionist Mythmaking." In *The New Feminist Criticism: Essays on Women, Literature, and Theory*, edited by Elaine Showalter, 314–38. New York: Pantheon, 1985.

Overbeek, Henk. *Global Capitalism and National Decline: The Thatcher Decade in Perspective.* London: Unwin Hyman, 1990.

Owens, Craig. "The Discourse of Others: Feminists and Postmodernism." In *The Anti-Aesthetic: Essays on Postmodern Culture*, edited by Hal Foster, 57–82. Seattle: Bay, 1983.

Parmar, Pratibha. "Rage and Desire: Confronting Pornography." In *Feminism and Censorship: The Current Debate*, edited by Gail Chester and Julienne Dickey, 119–32. Bridport, Dorset, UK: Prism, 1988.

Paul, Lissa. "Postmodernism Is Over. Something Else Is Here. What?" In *Transcending Boundaries: Writing for a Dual Audience of Children and Adults,* edited by Sandra L. Beckett, 239–54. New York: Garland, 1999.

Peach, Linden. *Angela Carter.* Macmillan Modern Novelists. New York: St. Martin's, 1998.

Peters, Tom. *Liberation Management: Necessary Disorganization for the Nanosecond Nineties.* New York: Knopf, 1992.

Pitchford, Nicola. "Unlikely Modernism, Unlikely Postmodernism: Stein's *Tender Buttons.*" *American Literary History* 11 (1999): 642–67.

Pratt, Minnie Bruce. "Identity: Skin, Blood, Heart." In *Yours in Struggle: Three Feminist Perspectives on Anti-Semitism and Racism,* by Elly Bulkin, Minnie Bruce Pratt, and Barbara Smith, 11–63. Ithaca, NY: Firebrand Books, 1988.

Pulsifer, Gary. "Kathy Acker: Power, Punk, and Porn." *Guardian* (London), 1 December 1997.

Punday, Daniel. "Theories of Materiality and Location: Moving through Kathy Acker's *Empire of the Senseless.*" *Genders* 27 (1998). <http://www.genders.org/g27/g27_theories.txt> (24 September 1998).

Punter, David. "Angela Carter: Supercessions of the Masculine." In *The Hidden Script: Writing and the Unconscious,* 28–42. Boston: Routledge & Kegan Paul, 1985.

———. *The Literature of Terror: A History of Gothic Fictions from 1765 to the Present Day.* New York: Longman, 1980.

Redding, Arthur F. "Bruises, Roses: Masochism and the Writing of Kathy Acker." *Contemporary Literature* 35 (1994): 281–304.

Robinson, Sally. "The Anti-Hero as Oedipus: Gender and the Postmodern Narrative [in *The Infernal Desire Machines of Doctor Hoffman*]." In *Critical Essays on Angela Carter.* Edited by Lindsey Tucker, 159–75. New York: G. K. Hall & Co., 1998.

Rodriguez, Richard. "Mixed Blood." *Harper's Magazine,* November 1991, 47–56.

Ross, Andrew. "The Popularity of Pornography." In *No Respect: Intellectuals and Popular Culture,* 171–208. New York: Routledge, 1989.

Rowe, Marsha. Introduction to *The "Spare Rib" Reader.* Edited by Marsha Rowe. 13–22. Harmondsworth, Middlesex: Penguin, 1982.

———. Introduction to "Women's Liberation Movement." In *The "Spare Rib" Reader,* edited by Marsha Rowe, 541–42. Harmondsworth, Middlesex: Penguin, 1982.

Royalle, Candida. "Porn in the USA." *Social Text* 37 (1993): 23–32.

Sage, Lorna. *Angela Carter.* Writers and Their Work. Plymouth: Northcote House in Association with the British Council, 1994.

———. *Women in the House of Fiction: Post-War Women Novelists.* Basingstoke: Macmillan, 1992.

Saldívar, José David. "Postmodern Realism." In *The Columbia History of the American Novel.* Edited by Emory Elliot, 521–41. New York: Columbia University Press, 1991.

Sandoval, Chela. "Feminism and Racism: A Report on the 1981 National Women's Studies Association Conference." In *Making Face, Making Soul, Haciendo Caras: Creative and Critical Perspectives by Women of Color,* edited by Gloria Anzaldúa, 55–71. San Francisco: Aunt Lute Foundation, 1990.

Schaub, Thomas Hill. *American Fiction in the Cold War.* Madison: University of Wisconsin Press, 1991.

Schmidt, Ricarda. "The Journey of the Subject in Angela Carter's Fiction." *Textual Practice* 3.1 (1989): 56–75.

Sciolino, Martina. "Confessions of a Kleptoparasite." *Review of Contemporary Fiction* 9.3 (1989): 63–67.

———. "Kathy Acker and the Postmodern Subject of Feminism." *College English* 52 (1990): 437–45.

Scott, Bonnie Kime, ed. *The Gender of Modernism: A Critical Anthology.* Bloomington: Indiana University Press, 1990.

Scott, Joan W. "Deconstructing Equality-versus-Difference: Or, The Uses of Poststructuralist Theory for Feminism." In *Conflicts in Feminism,* edited by Marianne Hirsch and Evelyn Fox Keller, 134–48. New York: Routledge, 1990.

Sebestyen, Amanda. Introduction to *'68, '78, '88: From Women's Liberation to Feminism.* Edited by Amanda Sebestyen. Bridport, Dorset, UK: Prism, 1988. ix–xii.

Segal, Lynne. "Does Pornography Cause Violence? The Search for Evidence." In *Dirty Looks: Women, Pornography, Power,* edited by Pamela Church Gibson and Roma Gibson, 5–21. London: BFI, 1993.

Severson, Anne. "Don't Get Too Near the Big Chakra." In *The "Spare Rib" Reader,* edited by Marsha Rowe, 313–17. Harmondsworth, Middlesex, UK: Penguin, 1982.

Sexton, Anne. *Transformations.* Boston: Houghton Mifflin, 1971.

Sheets, Robin Ann. "Pornography, Fairy Tales, and Feminism: Angela Carter's 'The Bloody Chamber.'" In *Forbidden History: The State, Society, and the Regulation of Sexuality in Modern Europe,* edited by John C. Fout, 335–59. Chicago: University of Chicago Press, 1992.

Siciliano, Enzo. *Pasolini: A Biography.* Translated by John Shepley. New York: Random House, 1982.

Siegle, Robert. *Suburban Ambush: Downtown Writing and the Fiction of Insurgency.* Baltimore: Johns Hopkins University Press, 1989.

Sinfield, Alan. *Literature, Politics, and Culture in Postwar Britain.* Berkeley and Los Angeles: University of California Press, 1989.

Slee, Amruta. "A Guide to Women's Direct-Action Groups." *Harper's Bazaar,* November 1992, 165–67.

Smith, Barbara. "Toward a Black Feminist Criticism." In *The New Feminist Criticism: Essays on Women, Literature, and Theory,* edited by Elaine Showalter, 168–85. New York: Pantheon, 1985. Originally published in *Conditions: Two* 1.2 (1977): 25–44.

Smith, Barbara Herrnstein. *Contingencies of Value: Alternative Perspectives for Critical Theory.* Cambridge: Harvard University Press, 1988.

Smith, Richard. *Getting into "Deep Throat."* Chicago: Playboy, 1973.

Snitow, Ann. "A Gender Diary." In *Conflicts in Feminism,* edited by Marianne Hirsch and Evelyn Fox Keller, 9–43. New York: Routledge, 1990.

———. "Retrenchment versus Transformation: The Politics of the Antipornography Movement." In *Women against Censorship,* edited by Varda Burstyn, 107–20. Vancouver, BC: Douglas & McIntyre, 1985.

Snitow, Ann, Christine Stansell, and Sharon Thompson, eds. *Powers of Desire: The Politics of Sexuality.* New York: Monthly Review, 1983.

Spivak, Gayatri Chakravorty. *The Post-Colonial Critic: Interviews, Strategies, Dialogues.* Edited by Sarah Harasym. New York: Routledge, 1990.

Stabile, Carol A. "Feminism and the Ends of Postmodernism." In *Materialist Feminism: A Reader in Class, Difference, and Women's Lives,* edited by Rosemary Hennessy and Chrys Ingraham, 395–408. New York: Routledge, 1997.

Suleiman, Susan Rubin. "The Fate of the Surrealist Imagination in the Society of the Spectacle." In *Risking Who One Is: Encounters with Contemporary Art and Literature,* 125–39. Cambridge: Harvard University Press, 1994.

———. *Subversive Intent: Gender, Politics, and the Avant-Garde.* Cambridge: Harvard University Press, 1990.

Tami, Stefano. *The Doomed Detective: The Contribution of the Detective Novel to Postmodern American and Italian Fiction.* Carbondale: Southern Illinois University Press, 1984.

Thomas, Cynthia. "The Beat Generation." *Houston Chronicle,* 17 January 1993, Two Star edition. *Lexis-Nexis Academic Universe.* <http://web.lexis-nexis.com/universe> (28 July 2000).

Tompkins, Jane. *Sensational Designs: The Cultural Work of American Fiction, 1790–1860.* New York: Oxford University Press, 1985.

Trinh, T. Minh-ha. *Woman, Native, Other: Writing Postcoloniality and Feminism.* Bloomington: Indiana University Press, 1989.

Vance, Carole S., ed. *Pleasure and Danger: Exploring Female Sexuality.* Rev. ed. London: Pandora, 1992.

"WAC Is Watching." *Off Our Backs: A Women's Newsjournal* 24.2 (28 February 1994): 6. *GenderWatch.* <http://www.softlineweb.com/softlineweb/genderw.htm> (28 July 2000).

Walsh, Richard. "The Quest for Love and the Writing of Female Desire in Kathy Acker's *Don Quixote.*" *Critique* 32 (1991): 149–68.

Wicke, Jennifer. "Through a Gaze Darkly: Pornography's Academic Market." In *Dirty Looks: Women, Pornography, Power,* edited by Pamela Church Gibson and Roma Gibson, 62–80. London: BFI, 1993.

Williams, Linda. *Hard Core: Power, Pleasure, and the "Frenzy of the Visible."* Berkeley and Los Angeles: University of California Press, 1989.

Wilson, Carl. "Northern Closure." Editorial. *Nation,* 27 December 1993, 788–89.

Wilson, Robert Rawdon. "SLIP PAGE: Angela Carter In/Out/In the Postmodern Nexus." *Ariel* 20.4 (1989): 96–114.

Young, Iris Marion. "The Ideal of Community and the Politics of Difference." In *Feminism/Postmodernism,* edited by Linda J. Nicholson, 300–23. New York: Routledge, 1990.

Index

Acker, Kathy, 16, 45, 105, 182, 191n. 32, 197n. 96; agency in, 17, 59, 82, 83, 104, 170, 177; the body in, 61, 67, 93–94, 97–102; critical reception of, 15, 65–68, 152–53, 155, 162–63; desire in, 57, 67–68, 84–85, 90, 98, 100, 170–71, 177; essentialism in, 67, 91, 98, 103; family relationships in, 57, 66, 93–95, 97, 100, 197n. 77; gender in, 56–57, 81–82, 85, 89, 91–92, 95, 170; history in, 60, 64–65, 76–78, 82, 86–88; language breakdown in, 79–81, 83, 96; narrative approach of, 17, 56, 57, 59, 61, 73–76, 78–79, 102; oppositional politics in, 56, 60, 68, 72, 83, 93–94, 96–97; plagiarism in, 59, 72–73, 83, 94, 176; and pornography, 18, 57, 68, 151–53, 155, 163, 175–77, 179; race in, 90, 92, 98–99, 101–2; reading in, 58, 63–64, 67, 89, 104, 155, 168, 169, 170, 171, 176–78; and Reagan era, 17, 60. Works: *Don Quixote*, 55–58, 60–63, 83–93, 169, 170–71, 175–78; *Empire of the Senseless*, 93–103; *In Memoriam to Identity*, 105; *My Death My Life by Pier Paolo Pasolini*, 72–83, 84, 85; *Politics*, 66, 194n. 17
Adam, Andrea, 108
aestheticization, 17, 39, 42, 44, 169; in Carter, 105–6, 110–11, 145, 150
agency, 18, 20, 22, 35, 172; in Acker, 17, 59, 82, 83, 104; in Carter, 106, 124–25, 167; and feminism, 59, 154, 155, 165–66; and otherness, 26, 27–28; and reading, 23, 37, 44, 58, 83, 106, 168, 171, 172
Ahmed, Sara, 25, 68
Alcoff, Linda, 190nn. 14 and 25
Alexander, Priscilla, 204n. 32
Ardis, Ann L., 189n. 11
art market, 42, 147
Asphodel, 198n. 8
autonomy theories, 16

Baker, John F., 202nn. 1 and 4
Bakhtin, Mikhail, 78–79, 103
Barrett, Michèle, 184
Barth, John, 33, 35
Barthes, Roland, 73, 121, 124, 138
Baudrillard, Jean, 14, 162
Bauer, Dale M., 196n. 53
Beauvoir, Simone de, 24
Belsey, Catherine, 195nn. 43 and 46
Benhabib, Seyla, 189n. 3
Benjamin, Jessica, 74–75
Benn, Melissa, 159
Berger, John, 135, 146
body, the, 54; in Acker, 61, 67, 93–94, 97–102; and class, 165, 166; in postmodernism, 46–47, 49–52, 58
Bright, Susie, 205n. 44
Britain, 17, 151; counterculture in, 114, 122, 130, 147–48; crisis of 1970s ("War of Dreams") in, 106–7, 109, 117, 130, 149; race and immigration

218

INDEX

in, 115–17, 122, 158; socialism in, 108, 117; Thatcherism and, 109, 117, 149; women's movement in, 117–18, 129–31, 137–38, 149, 157–58, 159, 161
Bronski, Michael, 204 n. 31
Brown, Terry, 194 n. 23
Burstyn, Varda, 203 n. 9
Butler case, 151–52, 164, 180
Butler, Judith, 14, 59, 172

Campbell, Beatrix, 137–38, 199 nn. 31 and 32, 200 nn. 52, 53, 55 and 59, 201 n. 72, 204 n. 24
Canada, 151–52
capitalism, 63; opposition to, 60, 66, 68–69, 157–58. *See also* Fordism: postmodernity; rationalism
Carter, Angela, 16, 45; aestheticism of, 105–6, 110–11, 145, 150; agency in, 106, 124–25, 167; allegory in, 109, 111–12, 113, 114–15, 119–20, 142; and Britain in the 1970s, 17–18, 106; class in, 143–49; critical reception of, 15, 109–12, 149–50, 152–53, 155; desire in, 112, 123–24, 125–27, 128, 135, 138, 140, 173; gender in, 120, 125–27, 132–33, 134–36, 139–40, 145, 146, 148; history in, 105–7, 111–12, 115, 139, 198 n. 15; intertextuality in, 118–19; myth in, 121–22, 124–25, 132–33, 136–37, 138, 140–41, 145; and pornography, 145, 152–53, 155, 168, 173, 179; postcolonial issues in, 115, 121, 123; race in, 113–14, 115, 117, 120–24, 127, 134, 135–36, 137, 141, 146–47, 174–75, 200 n. 45; rape in, 126–27, 174–75; reading in, 113, 127–28, 129, 143–44, 147, 155, 168, 169, 174–75. Works: *The Bloody Chamber*, 110, 205 n. 40; *Expletives Deleted*, 201 n. 65; *The Infernal Desire Machines of Doctor Hoffman*, 112–29, 140, 169, 172–75, 198 n. 5, 199 n. 29; "The Lady of the House of Love," 198 n. 15; *Love*, 110, 112, 142–49; *The Magic Toyshop*, 110, 112; *Nights at the Circus*, 110, 149; "Notes from the Front Line," 201 nn. 62 and 63; *The Passion of New Eve*, 118, 129–42; *The Sadeian Woman*, 110, 168; *Several Perceptions*, 110, 142; *Shadow Dance*, 110, 142; *Wise Children*, 110, 149
Caught Looking Collective, 203 n. 9
Certeau, Michel de, 15, 29–31, 47–48, 187, 193 n. 76, 195 n. 37; on cities, 49, 52–53, 57; on reading, 44, 147, 201 n. 82, 206 n. 58
Chester, Gail, 202 n. 2
Cixous, Hélène, 131
Clark, Robert, 111, 114–15, 116, 120, 167–68, 172, 173, 179, 198 nn. 10 and 19
class, 55, 56; in Carter, 143–49; and embodiment, 165, 166; and feminism, 153–54, 165, 170, 179, 180, 187; and readers, 47–48, 58, 143–46, 167, 171
Columbia History of the American Novel, 34, 35
Coote, Anna, 137–38, 199 nn. 31 and 32, 200 nn. 52, 53, 55 and 59, 201 n. 72, 204 n. 24
cultural studies, 183

Daly, Mary, 131
Davis, Mike, 192 nn. 61 and 72
Day, Aidan, 128, 198 n. 10, 201 n. 67
de Certeau, Michel. *See* Certeau, Michel de
Deep Throat, 159
Delacoste, Frédérique, 204 n. 32
Dickey, Julienne, 202 n. 2
Dillard, R. H. W., 193 n. 15
Di Stefano, Christine, 189 n. 3
Dix, Douglas Shields, 194 n. 23
Duggan, Lisa, 202 n. 3
Duncker, Patricia, 205 n. 40
Dworkin, Andrea, 84, 151, 179, 202 n. 1

Ephron, Nora, 159
Ermarth, Elizabeth Deeds, 34

Faulkner, Elizabeth P., 196 n. 62

INDEX

feminism: and class, 153–54, 165, 170, 179, 180, 187; definition of, 28, 29; lesbians and, 32, 154, 157–58, 180; and the literary canon, 32–33; "mythopoeic," 131–32; and otherness, 23, 24–28, 154; and pornography, 18, 151–57, 159–68, 170, 171, 179–80; and postmodernism, 12–16, 18–19, 20, 22–29, 32, 52, 53, 152, 154–55, 162; and race, 29, 31, 32, 153–54, 158, 161, 164–65, 170, 179, 180; and reading, 50, 155, 175; and reproduction, 137–38, 161, 184, 186; and sexual practices, 153, 157–58; varieties of, 22, 28–29, 32, 131–32, 161; in women's liberation movement, 117–18, 129–32, 156, 159
Firestone, Shulamith, 137–38
Fish, Stanley, 181–83
Fordism, 40–41, 70, 107–8, 191 n. 48, 198 n. 4
Foster, Hal, 14
Foster, Thomas, 47, 71–72, 98–99, 195 n. 37
Foucault, Michel, 73, 159
Fraser, Nancy, 189 nn. 9 and 5
Freccero, Carla, 154, 203 n. 8
Friedman, Ellen G., 86, 194 nn. 17 and 23, 195 n. 40, 198 n. 11
Fuchs, Miriam, 194 n. 17, 198 n. 11
Fung, Richard, 169

Gamble, Sarah, 199 n. 29, 200 n. 48
gender, 104; and desire, 84–85; and language, 56–57, 81–83, 88, 172; and postmodernism, 25, 32–35, 47; and reading, 47–48, 50–51, 58, 163–64, 170, 171–72, 177. *See also* Acker, Kathy: gender in; Carter, Angela: gender in
Gibson, Pamela Church, 203 n. 9
Gibson, Roma, 203 n. 9
Gibson, William, 94, 98
Gilbert, Sandra M., 191 n. 39
Gill, Jonathan, 193 n. 15
Gilroy, Paul, 18, 116, 117, 143, 199 nn. 26 and 28

Giroux, Henry A., 158
Godzilla, 61–63, 86–87
Gramsci, Antonio, 70, 77
Green, Jonathon, 198 n. 6, 200 nn. 55 and 57
Greene, Naomi, 196 nn. 50 and 51
Greer, Germaine, 114
Griggers, Catherine, 67, 194 n. 23
Grossberg, Lawrence, 206 n. 2
Gubar, Susan, 191 n. 39

Hall, Jacquelyn Dowd, 204 nn. 33 and 34
Hall, Stuart, 59, 107, 109, 149, 187, 191 n. 48, 198 n. 4
Haraway, Donna, 14, 39, 99, 102, 157
Hartsock, Nancy, 24, 25, 189 n. 3
Harvey, David, 182, 191 n. 48, 195 nn. 31 and 35, 201 n. 86; and feminism, 50–51; on postmodernity, 37, 40–42, 52, 157, 192 n. 49; on reading, 44, 49–51
Hassan, Ihab, 32, 35
Hawley, John C., 191 n. 34
Hebdige, Dick, 189 n. 8
Herr, Michael, 48
Hiro, Dilip, 199 nn. 23–25 and 27
history: in Acker, 60, 64–65, 76–78, 82, 86–88; in Carter, 105–7, 111–12, 115, 139, 198 n. 15; and textuality, 65, 74, 78. *See also* postmodernity
Hite, Molly, 190 n. 31
Hoban, Phoebe, 185–86
Hoffman, Roy, 193 n. 14
Holland, Penny, 200 n. 54
homosexuality (male): politics of, 77–78, 100–101; pornography and, 152, 164
Hooks, Bell, 14, 25, 27, 36, 151, 152
Houppert, Karen, 206 nn. 9, 14 and 16
Hudson, Kenneth, 200 n. 58
Hulley, Kathleen, 67–68, 194 n. 23
Hunter, Nan, 202 n. 3
Hustler, 160, 165
Hutcheon, Linda, 18, 23–24, 64–65
Huyssen, Andreas, 16, 40, 204 n. 36

Irigaray, Luce, 197 n. 78

INDEX

Isaacson, Walter, 87, 196 n. 67
Itzin, Catherine, 204 n. 24

Jacobs, Naomi, 193 n. 14
Jameson, Fredric, 13, 14, 37–39, 42, 52, 111, 182; on the Bonaventure Hotel, 45–49, 192 n. 61; reading in, 43, 44, 46, 47, 49, 192 n. 54
Jardine, Alice A., 196 n. 58
Jensen, Kenneth M., 196 n. 62
Jewish identity, 34, 55, 191 n. 32
Jordan, Elaine, 118, 150, 198 n. 11

Kalaidjian, Walter, 192 n. 50
Katz, Leanne, 201 n. 1
Kelly–Gadol, Joan, 191 n. 41
Kendrick, Walter, 110–11, 166
Kennedy, Colleen, 162–63, 178, 179, 205 n. 39
Kipnis, Laura, 32, 160, 165, 204 n. 22, 205 n. 37

Laclau, Ernesto, 143, 203 n. 14
Landsberg, Michele, 202 n. 3
Lauter, Paul, 191 n. 41
Lee, Alison, 111, 112, 119, 198 nn. 10 and 11, 199 n. 33, 200 n. 51, 201 nn. 78, 80 and 83
lesbians, 54, 55, 169, 205 n. 40; and feminism, 32, 154, 157–58, 180; and pornography, 152, 178
Little, David, 196 n. 67
Lodge, David, 159
Lyall, Sarah, 201 n. 1, 202 nn. 3 and 4
Lyman, Rick, 194 n. 16
Lyotard, Jean–François, 25, 48

MacCannell, Dean, 193 n. 5
MacCannell, Juliet Flower, 193 n. 5
MacKinnon, Catharine, 151, 163, 202 n. 3
magic realism, 34
Mahoney, Kathleen, 202 n. 3
Mailloux, Steven, 183
Manegold, Catherine S., 206 nn. 11, 12, and 13
Mapplethorpe, Robert, 148, 169

Martin, Biddy, 14, 26, 189 n. 5, 190 n. 15
Marwick, Arthur, 200 n. 52
Marxism, 14, 25, 130, 146, 205 n. 40
Mascia–Lees, Frances E, 100–101
mass culture, 16, 204 n. 36
McHale, Brian, 34
Meese Commission on Pornography, 151
Mercer, Kobena, 169, 206 n. 57
Mifflin, Margot, 206 n. 8
Miller, Nancy K., 189 n. 7
modernism, 16; relation to postmodernism, 33, 37, 38
Modleski, Tania, 26
Moran, Joe, 66–67, 98, 193 n. 4, 194 n. 18, 197 n. 96
Morgan, Robin, 176
Morrison, Toni, 34, 35, 191 n. 34
Mouffe, Chantal, 143, 190 n. 9, 203 n. 14
Mullan, Mary Kay, 198 n. 8
Mulvey, Laura, 130
Murray, Charles Shaar, 194 n. 16
myth, 83, 89, 118, 121–22, 124–25; feminist uses of, 131–32, 185

Nabokov, Vladimir, 175
narrative, 46; in Acker, 17, 56, 57, 59, 61, 73–76, 78–79, 102; fragmentation of, 48–49, 54, 56, 74; *marche*, 48, 57
National Front, 117
National Women's Aid Federation, 201 n. 73
National Women's Studies Association, 158
Nelson, Cary, 206 n. 2
Neumeier, Beate, 199 n. 19
Nicholson, Linda J., 189 nn. 9 and 5
Nixon, Richard, 87
nominalism, 28, 79–81

Omolade, Barbara, 204 n. 33
Osman, Sona, 199 n. 25
Ostriker, Alicia, 200 n. 60
otherness, 30–32, 52, 71–72, 83, 152; in feminist theory, 23, 24–28, 154; in postmodernism, 23, 24–28, 35, 36, 49, 65–67, 164; and race, 24, 36

Overbeek, Henk, 107, 191n. 48
Owens, Craig, 14, 25, 153
Oz, 114, 130

Parmar, Pratibha, 200n. 2, 203n. 13, 204n. 34
Pasolini, Pier Paolo, 73–74, 75, 77–78, 196n. 73
pastiche, 17, 59, 114, 162–63; politics of, 78, 82–83
Paul, Lissa, 188n. 2
Peach, Linden, 112, 128, 201n. 80
periodization, 12, 23, 36–39, 44
Peters, Tom, 69–70
Poe, Edgar Allan, 144–45, 148
pornography, 76, 77, 173–74; and class, 164, 165, 167; definitions of, 151–52, 152–53, 162, 202nn. 3 and 7; and feminism, 18, 151–57, 159–68, 170, 171, 179–80; and gays/lesbians, 152, 160, 164, 178; growth of, 158–60; and postmodernism, 152–55, 158; reading, 57, 155, 166–70, 174–78, 179. *See also* Acker, Kathy: and pornography; Carter, Angela: and pornography
postcolonialism, 14, 15
postmodernism: and agency, 59, 64; and the body, 46–47, 49–52, 58; and cities, 45, 47–49, 52–53, 54–55, 56, 57; and class, 47–48, 195n. 37; definitions of, 21, 35, 40; and ethics, 13–14; and feminism, 12–16, 18–19, 20, 22–29, 32, 52, 53, 152, 154–55, 162; and gender, 25, 32–35, 47; as historical category, 21–22, 36, 37; Jameson on, 42 and 45–46; in literary canon, 32–34, 191n. 34; and "new democratic struggles," 25, 50–51, 158; and otherness, 23, 24–28, 35, 36, 49, 65–67, 164; as outmoded, 12, 35, 188n. 2; and pornography, 152–55, 158; versus poststructuralism, 68, 81; and race, 25, 32–35, 36, 47, 191n. 34; as reading practice, 21, 155; and relativism, 13, 20; and sexuality, 47–48
postmodernity, 20, 21, 29, 69; characteristics of, 39–44, 94; and otherness,
26, 71–72; political opposition in, 43, 52, 55, 56, 60, 69, 72, 155, 156–58, 161; role of representation in, 37, 39, 41–44, 69, 83–84, 86, 87–88, 109, 153, 156, 159, 167
Powell, Enoch, 116
Pratt, Minnie Bruce, 23, 53–55
psychoanalysis, 67, 74, 95
Pulsifer, Gary, 194n. 16
Punday, Daniel, 62, 101, 193n. 2, 194n. 23
Punter, David, 199n. 19, 201n. 70
Pynchon, Thomas, 33, 35, 40

queer theory, 14

race, 54–55; and feminism, 29, 31, 32, 153–54, 158, 161, 164–65, 170, 179, 180; and immigration in Britain, 114, 115–17, 122, 158; and otherness, 24, 36; and postmodernism, 25, 33–35, 36, 47, 191n. 34; and readers, 47–48, 167, 169, 171, 178. *See also* Acker, Kathy: race in; Carter, Angela: race in
rationalism, 61–63, 72, 79, 86; and capitalism, 17, 60, 62, 68–71, 93; and gender, 81–82, 84–85, 104; and irrationality, 69, 81, 84, 88, 103; and narrative, 73, 74, 76; and violence, 74–75. *See also* capitalism; realpolitik
reader–response criticism, 181–83
reading, 12; and agency, 17, 23, 37, 44, 58, 64, 83, 106, 168, 171, 172; and class, 47–48, 58, 143–46, 167, 171; feminist–postmodernist practice of, 53, 58, 60, 155, 168, 178–79, 182; and gender, 47–48, 50–51, 58, 163–64, 170, 171–72, 177; pornography, 57, 155, 166–70, 174–78, 179; postmodern, 21, 43, 155, 166, 169, 174, 178, 183; and race, 47–48, 167, 169, 171, 178; and sexuality, 47–48, 54, 169, 171, 178. *See also* Acker, Kathy: reading in; Carter, Angela: reading in
Reagan era, 16–17, 60, 86
Reagan, Ronald, 42, 84, 196n. 66

INDEX

realpolitik, 83, 87–88. *See also* rationalism
Redding, Arthur F., 197 n. 90
representation: crisis of, 18, 35, 41, 78, 107, 117, 130, 149, 153; role of, in postmodernity, 37, 39, 41–44, 69, 83–84, 86, 87–88, 109, 153, 156, 159; as site of resistance, 16, 19, 23, 57 (*see also* agency)
Rich, Adrienne, 47
Robinson, Sally, 127, 128, 129
Rodriguez, Richard, 125, 200 n. 43
Ross, Andrew, 161, 204 n. 36
Rowe, Marsha, 130, 199 n. 30
Royalle, Candida, 204 n. 22

Sade, Marquis de, 176, 178, 200 n. 41
Sage, Lorna, 198 n. 11, 201 nn. 77, 80 and 85
Saldívar, José David, 191 n. 31
Salo (Pasolini), 76–77
Sandoval, Chela, 203 n. 13
Schaub, Thomas Hill, 196 nn. 62 and 69
Schmidt, Ricarda, 199 n. 19
Sciolino, Martina, 194 nn. 19 and 24
Scott, Bonnie Kime, 191 n. 39
Scott, Joan W., 184–85
Sebestyen, Amanda, 129–30, 199 n. 31, 200 n. 54, 202 n. 6
Segal, Lynne, 202 n. 7, 203 n. 19
Severson, Anne, 131–32
sex industry, 95, 148, 155. *See also* pornography
"sex wars," 153, 179, 203 n. 8. *See also* feminism: and pornography; feminism: and sexual practices
Sexton, Anne, 131
Sharpe, Patricia, 100–101
Sheets, Robin Ann, 202 n. 6, 203 n. 8, 204 n. 24
Siciliano, Enzo, 73, 75, 196 n. 73
Siegle, Robert, 26, 68, 80, 163, 194 n. 23
Sinfield, Alan, 198 n. 7
Slee, Amruta, 206 n. 13

Smith, Barbara, 158
Smith, Barbara Herrnstein, 14
Snitow, Ann, 161, 184, 186, 203 n. 9, 204 nn. 23 and 26
Spare Rib, 130, 131–32
Spivak, Gayatri Chakravorty, 14
Stabile, Carol A., 189 n. 7
Stansell, Christine, 203 n. 9
Stein, Gertrude, 21, 80
Suleiman, Susan Rubin, 12, 14, 38, 49, 119, 135, 189 nn. 1 and 5, 190 n. 25, 199 nn. 19 and 33, 201 n. 70

Tami, Stefano, 195 n. 45
Taylor, Brandon, 192 n. 51
Thatcher, Margaret, 42, 108
Thatcherism. *See* Britain: Thatcherism and
Thomas, Cynthia, 206 n. 16
Thompson, Sharon, 203 n. 9
Tompkins, Jane, 11, 183
Treichler, Paula A., 206 n. 2
Trinh, T. Minh-ha, 14, 196 n. 71

Vance, Carole S., 202 n. 3, 203 n. 9
Viegener, Matias, 194 n. 16
Vietnam war, 38, 108

WAC (Women's Action Coalition), 185–87, 206 n. 16
Walsh, Richard, 178, 205 nn. 52 and 54
Warhol, Andy, 43
Wicke, Jennifer, 168–69, 202 n. 7
Williams Committee on Obscenity and Film Censorship, 161, 204 n. 24
Williams, Linda, 159–60, 166–67, 169, 203 nn. 8, 9, and 17, 205 n. 42
Wilson, Carl, 201 n. 1
Wilson, Robert Rawdon, 198 n. 15
Wittig, Monique, 137
"woman," 26, 27; as political fiction, 13, 23, 28, 29, 157

Young, Iris Marion, 52